LIVELY ARTS
The Damned
DECONSTRUCTED

MARTIN POPOFF

To Edde,
Book time for Bonzo.

LIVELY ARTS
The Damned
DECONSTRUCTED

MARTIN POPOFF

Bedford, England

First published in Great Britain in 2022
by Wymer Publishing
www.wymerpublishing.co.uk
Tel: 01234 326691
Wymer Publishing is a trading name of Wymer (UK) Ltd

ISBN: 978-1-915246-08-0
(also available in eBook)

Proofreading by Agustin Garcia de Paredes
Edited by Jerry Bloom

Typeset by Andy Bishop / 1016 Sarpsborg
Printed by CMP, Dorset, England.

A catalogue record for this book is available from the British Library.

Cover design: Andy Bishop / 1016 Sarpsborg
Front cover image © Pictorial Press Ltd / Alamy Stock Photo

CONTENTS

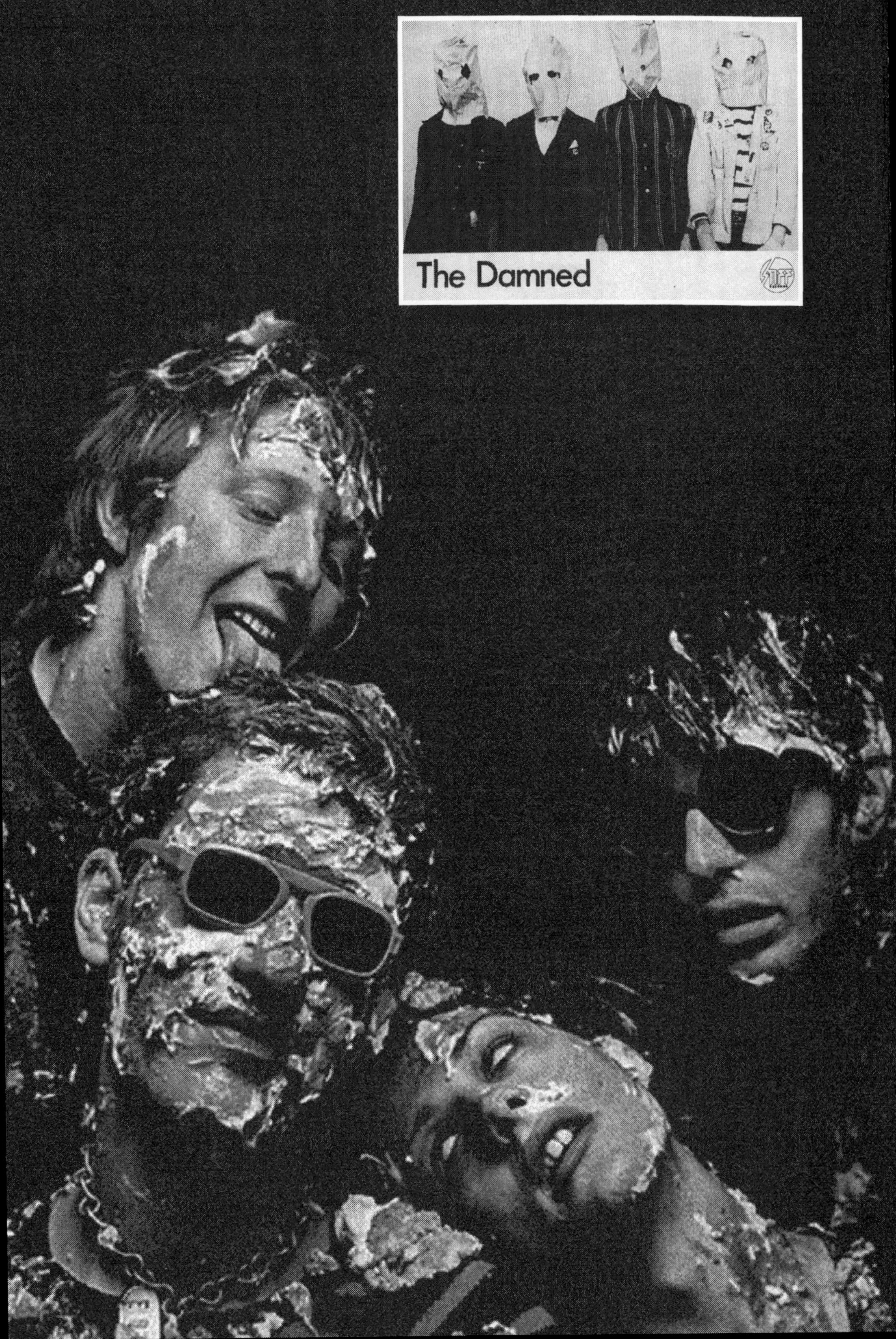
The Damned

Preface

As I've raved at anybody who might listen, there's no band on the planet that I've played over the last twenty years more than The Damned. Not that anybody should care, but it's a question that comes up often, namely, "What have you been listening to lately?" And I'm always a bit embarrassed coming up with an answer, because across all of my books and podcast episodes and video episodes and guesting on other people's video shows—just like anybody else really, the music I've tended to gravitate to has been the music I was into in my late teens. And being old as dirt, that's the late 70s for me.

So yes, not a big new music guy. If I feel I need to defend my cranky staidness further, I point out that there's usually a hundred new albums a year from bands that have been with me since I was a kid anyway, and yes, I'm at least not one of those guys who only likes the early records. I'm definitely not that, but yeah, neither am I listening to anything from bands who are kids right now. Don't care. And let's not even get into all the deep dives I'm periodically executing into vast catalogues from '70s and '80s acts that I had skimmed over back in the day before the internet... hell, before fax machines.

So I'm constantly in that world of heritage acts, talking about those bands on my own shows and in interviews for all my buddies and in the press whenever a book happens or whatever. Fortunately, The Damned come from that era as well, so I've got all the same fond memories about them as I do about two or three dozen other bands in this category, beginning with when mum and dad called me from my room to see a CBC news segment on London's new punk rock craze, spitting included.

But the point is, through their myriad chameleon-like direction shifts, this is a band that keeps on giving, with each era bringing new reasons to go on a Damned vacation. To be sure, there's a new record with new sounds, but inherent in that new batch of propositions, there's always a history lesson that takes me back into the '60s psych and garage bands The Damned guys had heard for the first time in their own teens.

But here's the thing: it's not that The Damned have cranked out records in the '90s and in the new millennium. So, guilty as charged, lots of all that listening I've been doing to them has been revisiting the albums from the '70s and '80s, records that have turned out to be timeless, which is absolutely not the case with many of the classics by other bands that we love.

So yes, I've found reason after reason to keep criss-crossing my way through this accursed catalogue. Unlike most of the bands I've written books about to date, with The Damned I've got all my original vinyl plus the reissues with bonus tracks, and both iPod classics are crammed full with all manner of official albums and dodgy compilations and even dodgier live semi-boot. Accessed whilst driving and jogging around Toronto, with the frequency of visitation doubled in bad weather, be that rain or snow or darkness (which I guess strictly speaking, isn't a weather event). Point being, The Damned are not a summer band.

The other reason I tell you this, is that through all that enjoyment of the band's paranormal panorama of material, the book you are now perusing is the one I've literally considered the last book I have to write before I can say I'm done. Not to say I'll stop here, but yeah, this one was going to have to happen at some point before I quit—it's my white whale. So thank you to Jerry, Gary and Andy at Wymer Publishing for helping making this happen, really, for showing me that someone else wants to take this trip with me.

Now a little bit about the structure of this book. Previous to this, pretty much my two favourite books of the 110 or so that I've written have been *Led Zeppelin: All the Albums All the Songs* and *The Clash: All the Albums All the Songs*, where—you guessed it—I got to write two, three, even four paragraphs on every single song by each band, partitioned as such. I've always had it in mind that that is the same kind of book I would want to do on the Damned, but for a whole different reason. Namely that I wanted to get it straight in my head and then down on paper, my thoughts on all the non-LP Damned songs that have jumbled and tumbled out chaotically over the decades. That remains my favourite goal fulfilled through the writing of this book, namely the treatment of these often-overlooked songs as equals to those on the official albums.

Along with that, it's been great making book-form use of the chats I've had with various Damned members over the years beyond magazine articles and web posts, which are, alas, disposable and disposed of over time.

As well, of course, it's been an absolute punk joy to trawl through the official albums, track by track, and present all sorts of cool trivia about all of those songs, hopefully with the ultimate goal of shoving The Damned firmly into the pantheon of the punk bands that apparently matter the most, which for me would include the likes of The Clash, the Sex Pistols, The Jam, the Ramones and X, I would say, above all others, although I'm very partial to The Saints as well. Oy (Oi!?), here we go again, the endless debate on when to capitalise "the" and when to stick with lower case—I struggle individually to a custom, nuanced decision with each band, based on various factors, and then that struggle is renewed periodically.

But yes, it's sweet justice indeed that myself and the Wymer team (of punk-lovers—you gotta like that! Who knew?!) were able to see this project through to fruition. I've been a fan since the beginning. I got the debut as a new release (UK copy, of course) but I can't really remember the story behind getting it.

What I *do* remember is being in the legendary Strawberry Jam record store in Spokane (first location), our Shangri-La for music. Having grown up in a small British Columbia town called Trail, two-and-a-half hours north of there, and flipping through the new arrivals. There before me was an album cover of geometrics and pastels. As I slowly made out each kooky Barney Bubbles letter, it gradually dawned on me that this was indeed the second Damned album hanging out in Washington State's most inconsequential mid-sized city, minding its own business. That part I remember. The part that will always remain a mystery is this: it was either on this occasion or on the occasion of espying Motörhead's second album *Overkill* in the exact same place on a different pilgrimage, upon which I let out a yelp, followed by a leap, narrowly missing slamming my head into the wooden beam above me. Whichever time it was, everybody in the store stopped what they were doing and turned and glared at this idiot who would dare smash the silent reverie of the previously contemplative collective shopping experience.

And then it was every album as a new release forever after to this very day, accompanied by no particularly poignant memories of each of those confrontations with what Dave and his crew had cooked up for his fearless fans this time.

So there you go. Enough tripping down memory lane. What this book entails will become self-evident soon enough. But just to encapsulate, we begin with a section in which all four of the original Damned members set the scene, in terms of the formation of the band and the motivations thereof, followed by a languish stroll through each and every album, consisting of a dedicated intro, followed by an analysis of each song.

After each album section, we catch up with all the dedicated non-LP singles and B-sides from that era and just after, placed almost completely temporally, as opposed to strictly aligned with where the songs might have occurred on a given expanded CD reissue.

Exempted are a few things too fleeting to be considered songs, live covers and the odd pre-album single version of a song. Again, the point was to ascribe a level of organisation on a catalogue that can get away from you if you're not paying attention.

As one other wee point of process, given how much of a joy it was embarking on the academic and almost monastic process of writing all the entries in the Led Zeppelin and Clash books, in this case I've also resisted the temptation to include any direct band quotes in the song entries other than a few words at a time. Anything I had from the guys that I thought was relevant has been included in the album intros only.

Anyway, I hope at the end of this that you've gained a new appreciation for just how rich and thoughtful The Damned's sprawling catalogue has been through time. Consider this book a sort of detailed roadmap pointing out myriad tourist stops along the way, enjoyed most productively through headphones along with convenient access to fast forward and rewind lest that Monty Mellotron bit needs a quick second assessment.

Martin Popoff

Dawn of the Damned

Maximum chaos quickly, like a smashed atom that instantly results in new chemistry… this describes the formation of each and every one of the three most revered UK punk entities ever, namely the Sex Pistols, the Clash and the forthcoming subjects of our musings here, The Damned.

As history pertains to our hapless heroes, fleeting proofs of concept like London SS, Bastard and an un-named consortium sometimes referred to as Master of the Backside coughed up parts that would gratingly and without lubrication work together to form the first UK punk band with a single and an album, as well as the first to cross the Atlantic and perplex club-goers in America.

"The Pistols had started," explains Damned drummer Chris "Rat Scabies" Millar. "The whole thing came from Bernie Rhodes and Malcolm McLaren. They had decided they wanted three bands to start a new movement, and the Pistols were just about up and running. Bernie was putting a band together called London SS, with Mick Jones, Tony James, Brian James and whoever they could get to play drums. I turned up but they were indecisive. The Buzzcocks didn't arrive until much later and nor did The Clash. The Stranglers were kind of out and playing, and so were The Jam, but even today, I suppose, they're not really regarded as punk bands, more so offshoots from the punk generation with punk attitude."

"I had a band previously called Bastard in and around '73," adds guitarist Brian James (born Brian Robertson), "and in England I couldn't get a gig to save my life. Everybody was into the pub rock thing or glam rock or whatever. We had to move to Belgium to get gigs and play in Belgium and France. I've had spiky hair since a couple years before the punk thing, but I wouldn't say we looked like a punk band—but we didn't look like a bunch of hippies either. And we had attitude. The French were into rock 'n' roll. They knew about Iggy

YOU'VE HEARD THE RECORD, NOW... CENSORED!

THE DAMNED

ON TOUR WITH THE RUTS

THE RUTS NEW SINGLE "BABYLON'S BURNING" OUT 8th JUNE

AND THE LOCAL HEROES (WHOEVER THEY MAY BE)

MAY 31st	MALVERN, WINTER GARDENS
JUNE 1st	NEWPORT (SHROPSHIRE) VILLAGE
4th	EXETER, ROOTS
6th	WHITLEY BAY, THE REX HOTEL
8th	WEST RUNTON, PAVILION
10th	HEMEL HEMPSTEAD, PAVILION
11th	SHEFFIELD, TOP RANK
12th	EDINBURGH, TIFFANY'S
13th	BIRMINGHAM, DIGBETH CIVIC HALL
14th	BLACKBURN, KING GEORGES HALL
15th	STOKE (HANLEY), VICTORIA HALL
16th	LEICESTER, UNIVERSITY (open to public)
17th	BRISTOL, LOCARNO

ADVANCE TICKETS ON SALE NOW – PENSIONERS HALF PRICE

NO REDUCTION WHATSOEVER FOR HOLDERS OF STUDENT CARDS

and MC5 and stuff like that, whereas people in England just didn't. When I'd moved back into London and met up with Mick Jones and Tony James and started trying to get a band together with those guys, it was obvious there was something going on. Then somebody took us down to see this band called the Sex Pistols playing at a party in this big warehouse. And it was just amazing, like, wow, there's more people into the same kind of music as me."

It's a little explored narrative, but Rat sort of echoes James' implication that the punk fuse was lit in France. Clue in point: the copies of *The Stooges, Fun House, High Time* and *Kick Out the Jams* that your intrepid author unearthed in Vancouver, BC and Spokane, WA as a nascent metalheaded punk in the '70s—and still own today—were all French-issue Elektra. Only my *Back in the USA* was American. Hell, I didn't start seeing US copies of these records until I was in my 30s and moved to Toronto. As well, the first time I ever heard The Damned was on a French-issue copy of Vertigo's *New Wave* compilation, bought, again, in Spokane.

"I think the French always had that kind of rock 'n' roll thing," echoes Scabies. "Iggy was popular over there and so was the MC5. I think the French have a kind of natural swing towards organic troublemakers; so too the Belgians. Brian's band Bastard were based in Brussels, and there were a few things happening over there as well. What we had generally were pockets of resistance of people who were already tuned into the Dolls and the MC5 and the Stooges. And then suddenly when '76 arrived, oh yeah, there are other people that can relate and it went public."

With Scabies shut out of London SS, he had joined forces with David "Dave Vanian" Lett, Raymond "Captain Sensible" Burns and future Pretenders leader Chrissie Hynde in the aforementioned provisionally monikered Masters of the Backside.

Once London SS imploded, James collared Scabies to start a band with him. Dave Vanian next auditioned and became the lead singer, but a potential warm body to fill the role of bassist called Sid Vicious didn't turn up for his try-out and Sensible stepped in to complete the shock circuit.

"See, I never played with a guy like Rat before," explains Brian. "I played with jazz people as well as all kinds of rock drummers. But when Rat had come down to audition for what was called London SS, which was a non-gigging band, he exploded. He brought out a kind of

Pete Townshend in me, because of Rat's Keith Moon influence, if you like. His action made me do things on guitar that I didn't really think I could do and had in fact never really occurred to me. And that's why I wanted to take Rat and say, right, let's get our own band together now. And we did, thankfully, with the other guys, and it just inspired me big time. Those riffs I had hanging around from the Bastard days suddenly started to make sense when I played them with Rat—I could now write songs properly from them."

"Rat was a huge inspiration on my songwriting for that first album. I didn't think anyone could get anywhere near Keith Moon. But when you hear Rat, he's like a street version of Keith Moon, loving these sort of percussion cliff-hangers and having fun with it. Really, what Rat does is jazz, although he would never admit it in a million years. But it is. It's totally off-the-wall, feeding off another player, like me and him used to do, like Hendrix and Mitch Mitchell used to do and like Coltrane and Elvin Jones used to do. It's something that happens very rarely between players."

"From there it kind of grew," continues James, recalling the occasion of the band's first show, July 6th 1976. "The audiences started to drift up to the Pistols gigs and when The Damned played our first gig, which was supporting the Pistols at the 100 Club, we found that we were attracting our own kind of fans as well. They opened the Roxy at the end of '76, a club in Central London, and you saw all these people coming out of the sticks with ideas, who wanted to do their own thing. You didn't have to have a master class in music to be able to play this stuff. You just needed to have the balls to get up there, a certain attitude, an ability to reflect people's frustrations."

"Absolutely," agrees Scabies. "It wasn't a contrived invention; it's just the way it was. No one had any money, everybody was unemployed, it was grey, it was miserable. And there was a genuine frustration that we'd been putting up with pompous musicians for years telling us that you weren't worthy to get on stage unless you could perform to a certain proficient standard, which was insulting to the average teen."

"Punk was very diverse at that point in time," muses the man at the mic, Dave Vanian. "It hadn't formulated into a particular sound. Everybody was doing different things, which was what I liked about it, to be honest. And when we started the band, there wasn't a name for this music. The word punk didn't exist over our heads—we were just a band. We just thought of ourselves as similar to the MC5 and the Stooges, that we're gonna do things our way, but also that it was a new era. Sure, the word punk came within six months or something, but people forget that when punk was first coined, it was meant as an insult. It wasn't meant as, "Oh, great, we're a punk band!" It was actually, "Oh, they're just a punk band," meaning they're crap. It wasn't until bands embraced it, when we actually stood up for it and used it as a label as such, that it became what it became. But before that, I remember saying in interviews that The Damned were a garage band, similar to bands in the '60s."

And definitely not a heavy metal band. "No, not as far as I was concerned, nor with Captain either," laughs Dave. "He was more interested in things like Soft Machine and Syd Barrett, although obviously Jimi Hendrix is a huge influence on his playing. Rat was a massive Who fan and Brian was a bit of an enigma, actually. Across most of the time I spent with him, I didn't get to know him well. He was influenced by jazz musicians like Coltrane as well as rock, and he used to like James Williamson and Johnny Thunders a lot. The great thing about Brian's playing is that the second you heard it, you knew it was him. There are only a handful of guitarists that are like that. Brian was a little older, so he knew about '60s garage bands like The Seeds, The Shadows of Knight and Strawberry Alarm Clock, the kinds of things that turned up on the *Nuggets* albums. I knew that stuff too, plus we were interested in the first Richard Hell stuff, with Tom Verlaine. But Brian's influences were a bit more left-field because he was older. When the Ramones hit England, that convinced a lot of people to pick up the guitar and start playing for the first time. Half the audience, if not more than that, at the Ramones' first show were people who became musicians in bands. Those first shows were all friends that would end up being in The Clash and The Adverts."

"Don't ask me anything about heavy metal or I won't be able to stop myself from being rude," chuckles the good Captain, in total agreement with Dave that despite The Damned's "heavy" sound, heavy metal was the enemy. "I hate it, and I hate it because for me, it's the right dressed as the left. Teenage kids that looked at metal thought this is rebellion, which couldn't be further from the truth. Because these metal bands, especially in the past, were saying fuck all. Metal, in part, caused the creation of punk rock in the first place, because of their appalling attitude toward women, the way they treated them like groupies and sluts and whores and the drug abuse— the cocaine overload and the limousines and the feet up on the monitors—that whole rock star attitude was what created punk in the first place. There needed to be an alternative to that rock star bullshit. Appalling. Terrible. Rubbish."

"None of it really had much energy," adds Rat, on the hard rock of the day. "And like Captain says, none of them really had anything to say. None of those bands sounded like they were talking to me when they sang lyrics. It was all about goblins and pixies and their girlfriends and some kind of bullshit about a sculptor, a million miles away from where the real world was for me, which was living on the fucking streets and trying to hustle through and maybe one day I'll be able to join a band."

"And then there was prog," continues Scabies. "Well, nobody could play any of that! When you're 17 and sitting in the bedroom and you've just got a pair of sticks and a drum kit, the last thing you can do is master *Pictures at an Exhibition* or any Yes song. It was try as I might. I couldn't play the drums like the guy on *Blow by Blow*, so I just played as much as I could and tried to be as good as I could, and when I ran into Brian, there was a natural affinity. When punk turned up, it wasn't like a preordained, 'Well, those guys are going to do this.' It was, 'You know what? Hang on, Captain; we don't play like those people and we never will do, but we can do this.' And there were some other guys who'd done it their own way, and does it really matter that it's not mainstream? So what punk did is it kicked everyone up the ass. It was kind of like, 'Listen here guys, you're getting fucking old and lazy and you're not communicating anymore.'"

Ergo, there goes the alternative, irreverently christened The Damned. "Brian named the band," notes Dave. "It was Brian's band, and when I came in, he'd already had the name, The Damned. He picked that because it was the way young kids felt at the time, like they weren't going to get anywhere, disenfranchised—it fit perfectly and in fact it still fits perfectly, unfortunately. It wasn't damned in the biblical sense, but more in the sense of a nowhere generation, like in the beatnik era. I've often wondered if the name of the band was a jinx."

A debut album called *Damned Damned Damned* in the books (more on that in the coming pages), next it was off to the worldwide cradle of punk civilisation, CBGB in Manhattan's Lower East Side.

"They liked us," counters Dave, "although it was a case of, 'What the hell is this?! What are we seeing?!' We drove people out from some of the gigs on that tour. Unfortunately, we got to the West Coast and we were supposed to do some gigs with Television, and Television cancelled us off their gigs. So we got to the West Coast with no shows and no money and we had to hassle around to find a venue that would put us on. We did a couple of shows anyway and it was wild. We never knew why Television cancelled us except that we had heard that they heard rumours of how crazy the shows had been on the East Coast and didn't want any part of it. They were a bit worried."

"I thought it was pretty shit, to be honest," mutters Rat, expectations dashed. "We turned up at CBGB and there were tables and chairs in front of the stage and everybody was eating fucking pizza. It wasn't at all punk. That wasn't what we expected. We were there at the birthplace that they'd been telling us about for so long. This was where punk was from, this was what it was all about and we got there and it actually wasn't. It was a Warholian adventure into polity."

Page 2 SOUNDS November 5, 1977

Jam, Damned hit the road

THE JAM's Paul Weller

THE ALBUM IS

DAMNED DAMNED DAMNED

THE SINGLE IS

NEAT NEAT NEAT

THE BAND PLAY

LIVE LIVE LIVE

ON THE T.REX TOUR

MARCH 10 NEWCASTLE CITY HALL
MARCH 11 MANCHESTER APOLLO
MARCH 12 GLASGOW APOLLO
MARCH 13 VICTORIA HALL STOKE
MARCH 14 COLSTON HALL BRISTOL
MARCH 17 BIRMINGHAM ODEON
MARCH 18 RAINBOW
MARCH 19 PAVILION WEST RUNTON CROMER
MARCH 20 PORTSMOUTH LOCARNO

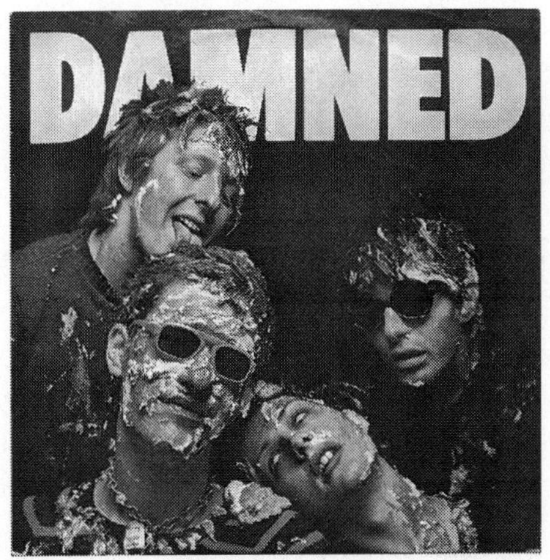

Damned Damned Damned

The recording of The Damned's debut album saw the band crash into Pathway Studios on a high fuelled by cheap speed. A successful dry run had already been executed through the capture of incendiary single "New Rose," backed with "Help," also recorded at Pathway. Plus there had been a series of landmark gigs and even a BBC session, comprising fully of five tracks at BBC's Maida Vale studio for a John Peel sessions.

So the band were primed and ready as they tumbled into the modest North London facility, recording over a sporadic ten-day period anchored in January of '77 utilising a Brenel one-inch eight-track and a Revox two-track, the control booth with custom desk tucked into the corner, the band playing live in the main room.

The end result proved that the debut single's high-strung chaos was deliberate, with Nick Lowe—and quite significantly engineer Barry "Bazza" Farmer—letting the band's songs fly off the gyre, with Rat kicking them in the arse all the way down the alleyway like a Monty Python sketch.

What's remarkable is that across the ensuing story of punk, one would be hard-pressed to find an album more punk than this first punk record ever to come out of the UK. To be sure, the Ramones were both first (*Ramones*) and second (*Leave Home*) with punk albums (proper, from new bands) anywhere in the world, but *Damned Damned Damned*, issued on February 18th 1977, a mere five weeks after *Leaves Home*, set a new frantic standard, in fact single-handedly causing a shift in focus to what was happening in the UK.

"Nick Lowe did a wonderful job of the production," explains Brian James. "He basically captured us live, no frills about it, and Bazza, the engineer, knew this little studio inside out. Nick's strength was that he was one of the guys. He drank with us and messed around with us and he wasn't proud. He'd come from Brinsley Schwartz, a band that had done fairly well, but he had no airs and graces whatsoever."

"And he had a wonderful ear. The very first time we worked with him, we got to the studio and the first thing he said, 'Right, 'round the pub; let's have a couple of pints, come back and bang it down.' His whole thing was bang it down and tart it up in the mix, if it needs it. The great thing he taught me—and I've gone on to produce—is that you've got to get the performance. If you haven't got the performance in the take that you're going to go with, no matter what you try to do later, it's going to be crap. And you've got to have a good engineer who understands you and who gets the right sounds."

"I'd been in studios before in Brussels," continues Brian, "and I was in a studio in London when I was a kid, and it always amazed me how things sounded great in the room you were playing in, and then you walk into the control room and it's like, what happened to all the balls and the guts of it? Once it trickles through those little leads, where did it go? And the engineer or producer is sitting there, 'Well, that's the way it is.' And it's like, 'Huh?' But we walked in with Nick and banged down 'New Rose' or 'Help!' or whatever we were doing that day, then we walked into the little control booth that was like two seconds away and asked Bazza to play it back and it would be like, 'That's exactly what we just heard in the other room—it's amazing!' It was capturing the moment. And Nick did that so well. Plus he was always a pleasure to be around. I think that means a lot as well. He was inspiring in a very kind of low-key way, like just being one of the guys and having fun and inspiring you to have fun and not think too hard about what you're doing—just get on with it."

Adds Captain, "The first album kind of defined the sound of punk in '77, if you like. I thought the *Damned Damned Damned* album was under-produced and perfect for that. The Sex Pistols sounds good to me. I enjoy listening to *Never Mind the Bollocks* but it sounds slick—it's slow and perfectly produced. But for me, punk shouldn't be perfect. It's supposed to have warts and gnarled edges."

This sense of fun verging on anarchy within the record's red-lined grooves spilled onto the album cover as well, with the guys shot mid-pie fight under big yellow "DAMNED" letters. There's no album title on the front or back cover, nor on the legendary black-and-white Stiff labels stuck on the vinyl—to sort that out, you had to squint at the spine. In the live shot on the back cover, the good Captain happened to be facing away from the camera. His solution to prove that yes, the man in the dress was Raymond Burns was to get a photo booth picture of his handsome self stuck on the side of Dave's vocal monitor.

Of course all of this was pointless as far as some punk purchasers were concerned—their copy had Eddie and the Hot Rods on the back, a deliberate error to drum up publicity perpetrated by Dave Robinson and Jake Riviera back at the Stiff offices.

Side 1

Neat Neat Neat
(James) 2:46

Issued simultaneous with the launch of the album as the band's second single, "Neat Neat Neat" was in fact the last selection recorded for the album. The song moves as swiftly as "New Rose" and even includes a similar echo of boogie woogie come chorus time. The brief visit to a happy place is welcome because the rest of the song is ferocious and foreboding, three chords in a minor key, driven by a hooky and hi-fidelity bass line upon which are placed violent James licks, intrusive snare cracks and Dave's laconic vocal, augmented by yelps and snarls come contemplative break time.

Brian left his girlfriend Judy Nylon to provide many of the lyric lines—these are remarks which used to amuse him—with James sort of semi-consciously using the cut-up method pioneered by Brian Eno and David Bowie to come up with the final enigmatic stacking of only casually connected phrases, which, in the hands of Dave Vanian, sound like wise aphorisms.

"Neat Neat Neat" has made incursions into pop culture consciousness, having been used in the *True Crime: New York City* video game, an episode of The Simpsons and an episode of Amazon Prime's *The Boys*, but most notably in hit movie *Baby Driver*, from 2017. It's been covered a few times as well, most notoriously by Elvis Costello, whose quite unappealing live lounge jazz version, first issued as a B-side, can be heard on the expanded reissue of *This Year's Model*.

Fan Club
(James) 3:00

When experienced sequentially, after the single A and B and the first track on the album, "Fan Club" reveals a new level of depth from The Damned, the band slowing things down and Brian going bluesy and yet still angular with his riff, echoing what we'd hear from Television and Richard Hell & the Voidoids on their albums issued in 1977.

Also along those lines is a certain wiry guitar sound, not stomped through distortion pedal and power chords like the Sex Pistols record, but rather direct and more naturally dirty, with Rat's cymbals, through their continual and torrential sizzle, doing to the totality of the experience what a fuzz box would do to the rhythm guitars.

At the lyric end, Brian works us over on a number of levels. The first-person narrative has the budding rock star dealing with the concept of being idolized freshly, for the first time pondering the ritual of the groupie, the letter-writer, gift-giver and the autograph-seeker. But there's the self-doubt, the irony that the fan thinks that Brian—or really Dave, because he ruminates the words so well—has built this great life and yet he's inches away from slashing his wrists. Finally there's a sense of empathy, given that Brian has confessed that he's been there himself, and that indeed so-called rock stars are some of the neediest fans around, idolizing the bands that got them to get into the business in the first place.

At the music end, despite the melancholy and dissonant riffage and subdued atmosphere thereof, Rat still manages to kick up a fuss. Plus there's a break of a dozen seconds or so at the 1:50 mark that verges upon purposeful guitar solo, even if Scabies competes with James for top noisenik.

Then, somehow, there's time still for another verse and round of chorus before the song ominously implodes. Leading up to the final crashed wind-up (in a new key), Dave turns the climactic "I don't know why I'm sad for my fan club" refrain into a question with an upturn on the word club. It's the first and last time he's done it in the song, and coupled with the violent conclusion to the track, one is left to wonder if this story of obsession has taken a murderous turn.

I Fall
(James) 2:08

Slamming action words together in cut-and-paste fashion to create motion, Brian goes for pure attitude here, inspired at the lyric end by the MC5's cock-sure swagger and at the music end by that band's Motown sense of theatricality through punctuated funk structure as applied to the more experimental songs from the third record *High Time*, most notably "Baby Won't Ya," "Future/Now," "Gotta Keep Movin'," "Poison" and "Skunk (Sonically Speaking)."

Captain has called "I Fall" his favourite track on the album, and indeed plumped for it as first single against otherwise unanimous support for "New Rose," loving the challenge of the driving bass line, which has to be articulated, punched and grace-noted just so.

Come chorus time, James breaks into a loopy post-punk riff verging on the comedic, while Rat executes a sort of double-time rhythm. Despite the song's two-minute duration, at the 1:09 mark there's a fully composed 20-second-long break section that is speedy boogie in nature like the "Neat Neat Neat" chorus. This is followed by one of the band's semi-committed guitar solo spots, James wading in with a Chuck Berry duck walk, which makes perfect sense after the

"Bye Bye Johnny" of the break before it. But then things get serious, with Brian exploding with barely contained chaos, which seems to drive Rat mad—truth be told, this is about as violent Rat would ever get toward his drum set, short of hurling it into the crowd after a gig.

Born to Kill
(James) 2:37

"Born to Kill" is an exercise in contrasts, with Brian's cheerful octave-jumping two chord riff being set against a lyric about some sort of killer, evidently one who keeps fairly quiet and casual about it. What's amusing is that Rat kicks off the proceedings with what amounts to a groove. Firstly he counts the song in with high-hat, followed by a single-stroke role on his tightly-tuned snare, before collapsing into the rhythm, hitting the snare hard on two and four for the intro and the first half of the initial verse. But then he changes his mind and goes back to his sort of proto-blast beat default, snare on one and three and possibly, sporadically, all four beats, cymbals creating a near constant din.

Brian says that he was going for a sort of sarcastic Ray Davies biographical vignette for his lyric, but that he requested of Dave that he sing it with a deadpan Lou Reed drawl, having been influenced by Lou, specifically "Sweet Jane."

Indeed Vanian's near spoken beatnik poet delivery of Brian's fragmented musings went well with the Damned front man's elegant Victorian vampire look on stage and importantly in photo shoots. All told, from the words to the singing, "Born to Kill" represents the halfway point along a ruminative descent into madness that begins with "Fan Club" en route to "Feel the Pain."

Stab Yor Back
(Scabies) 1:03

Here's the only Rat Scabies writing credit on a record otherwise penned completely by Brian, save for the one cover version.

"Stab Yor Back" is the shortest song on *Damned Damned Damned* and arguably the heaviest, certainly the most frenetic, hectic and highly strung (redundancies be damned); even if measured by tempo alone, it's essentially tied with the other short shockers on the record. Famously Captain doesn't like the song and would get in rows with his band mates over playing it live, protesting its repetitive brutishly violent lyrics. Indeed, the guys in The Damned would constantly be under threat of violence from rockers and hippies and even Hells Angels in the early days, and one can imagine how shouting "stab your back" over and over again from the stage was sort of asking for it to go off.

The most significant covers of "Stab Yor Back" came in 1991 with Mudhoney's tight but loose rendition, faster but casual with the vocals, and then 2001 with Swedish garage rock critics' darlings The Hellacopters tackling the song soberly and efficiently.

Feel the Pain
(James) 3:37

The one "ballad," so to speak, on *Damned Damned Damned* is more of a funereal dirge, something you might hear in a horror movie. Brian's prime influence was Jonathan Richman's "Hospital," from *The Modern Lovers*, 1972. Only here there's a lot less hope and a lot more decay, with Brian struck by the contrast between the white sterile environment and the idea of being sick.

Dave delivers the lyric gauzy and close at the mic like Alice Cooper on "Desperado," accompanied by a spare Captain on bass, while Brian's single note-picks in a fractured manner through his chording and Rat plays similarly disconnected, with a cowbell for a metronome. Vanian moves over to full croon come the masochistic but still somewhat anthemic chorus ("Feel the pain; it leaves no stain"), at which time Rat gathers the expected head of steam, attacking his cymbals. The song ends with a Who-like churn of a jam which concludes with a section that sounds like "I Fall," the most notable similarity being Captain's bass line.

Speaking of "I Fall," that song, along with "See Her Tonight" and "Feel the Pain" comprised the band's first demo from back in June of '76, recorded at a basement studio in Maida Vale owned by Barry Jones and Matt Dangerfield. "Feel the Pain" stretched to five minutes on the original, with the band playing more conservatively and less dishevelled versus the nightmarish take in its final form. Live at the time, as can be heard on the 100 Club recordings, the song was even more straightened-out, with Rat establishing a bit of a groove and Brian letting his picked single-string notes sustain with distortion.

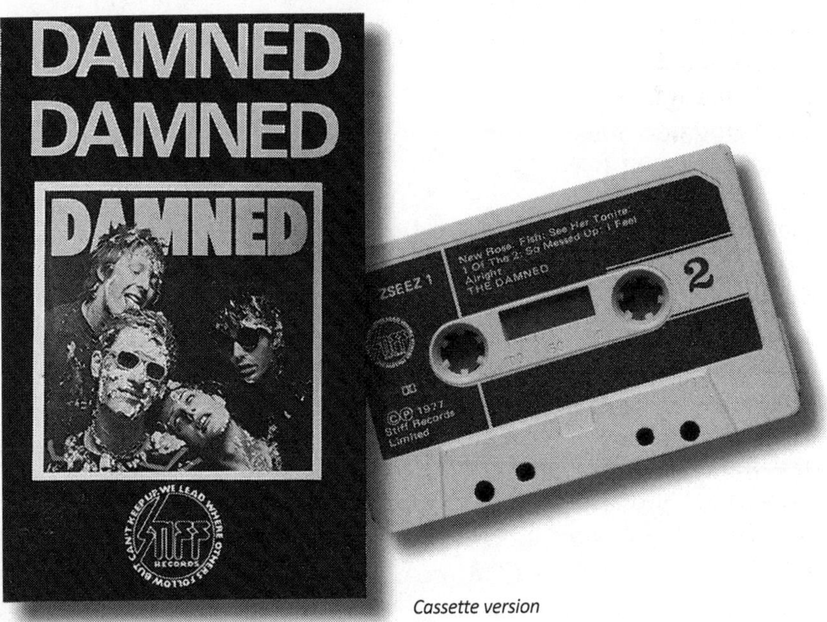

Cassette version

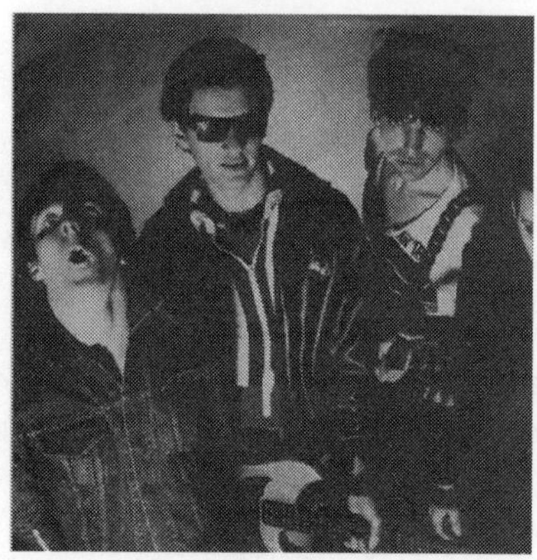

Side 2

New Rose
(James) 2:44

Recorded September 20th 1976 and issued as a single on October 22nd (backed with "Help"), "New Rose" is much celebrated as the very first punk single out of the UK, beating the Pistols' "Anarchy In The U.K." by a month. It's also arguably the most famed Damned song ever, underscored by Guns N' Roses doing a rendition of it on *The Spaghetti Incident?*, the band's platinum-certified covers album from 1993.

The structure of the song goes back to Brian's 1974 Bastard days, beginning life as "Dr. Gong". But it wasn't until James hooked up with Rat Scabies for a run-through of the song in a church in Lisson Grove that the potential of its intensity was revealed. At this point neither Dave nor Captain were in the picture, but Brian knew he had found the perfect replacement for his old skinsman Nobby Goff, who, in James' estimation, wasn't burning with quite the same fire in the belly as this new guy.

In the final Damned configuration, captured and caged in a session lasting four hours and costing £50, the song opens with Dave asking, "Is she really going out with him?," a nod to The Shangri-Las song "Leader of the Pack," followed by Rat's riotous tom-tom attack before Captain serves up a hugely distorted riff.

From there the band transition to what sounds like a speed- and psychosis-induced version of Status Quo's "Down Down"—clearly The Damned are boogie-ing—before we get to the first verse which is all-

carnal punk verging on heavy metal. The energy across the song (in fact fuelled by amphetamine sulphate and cider) is so palpable that any snare whacks from Rat are smothered by continuous waves of crash cymbals along with eager and extended tom rolls and thundering, almost disconnected bass drums.

Holding the fort are Brian's big chords, which are followed by Captain's simple but insistent bass, topped with vocals high in the mix that are both menacing and commanding. But despite the vibrating and opaque wall of sound erected, Brian's lyric is a thoughtful one, with James using the metaphor of a love song to talk about his excitement at engaging with a new cultural and musical scene blooming like a new rose in the cracks of crumbling London.

Fish
(James/Thanx Tony) 1:38

Beginning life as a London SS song called "Portobello Reds," (hence the "Thanx Tony" credit, referring to Tony James), "Fish" is based on the traditional boogie woogie rock structure that some of the London SS material had courted (see The Clash's "1-2 Crush on You").

But that's just the verses. The chorus is typical hepped-up happy punk, with an ascending riff punctuated by Dave yelling "Fish, I said fish!" Despite the song's 1:37 brevity, "Fish" contains Brian's most elaborate patch of guitar soloing on the record, with James shredding away Wayne Kramer-like high up the fret board before coasting with a few chords as he waits for the cue to barrel into the ascending riff 'n' roll that once again announces the chorus.

"Fish" is also distinguished by the heavy amount of distortion Brian plays with, matching the likes of "Born to Kill," "1 of the 2" and "I Feel Alright" for dirtiest songs on the record.

See Her Tonite
(James) 2:29

Brian claims an MC5 influence to this one as well, although in its original form from June '76, played a bit slower than the final, "See Her Tonight" sounds like the soundtrack to the new pogo dance craze.

By the time the guys were ready to lay it down for the album, the song had turned into a high-speed jackhammer of a punky proto-thrasher, distinguished by a pronounced and locked-down four-on-the-floor beat from Rat, meaning bass drum on one, two, three and four. Captain sticks mostly with Rat, but during a section that extrapolates on the chorus, he breaks into a boogie bass line. All the while Brian is strumming remarkably clean guitar lines, "See Her Tonight" representing the largest gulf on the record between heaviness achieved against guitar so subsumed and behaved. For the momentous close, Brian and Captain hammer out two-chord stabs while Rat executes windmill rolls around the kit until everybody decides that they've had quite enough, thanks.

As for the lyrics, Brian claims that there's barely anything to them. However it's easy to equate what's there to the story of "New Rose," this parallel between a female love interest and the exploding punk scene. Indeed if the girl that Dave is so jacked about seeing tonite (sic) isn't a shiny new prototype punk rock chick as the description briefly and enigmatically would suggest, she is punk rock itself.

1 of the 2
(James) 3:10

Reworked from the Bastard days, "1 of the 2" is another bludgeoning rocker adding to the assertion that The Damned were the band most defining of punk as a new kind of music. The Ramones were never this manic and thrashing, and soon-to-arrive records from The Clash and the Sex Pistols would not be so inclined either. The Dead Boys' *Young, Loud and Snotty* and The Saints' *(I'm) Stranded* would prove to be as abrasive in select departments, but still, as each and every one of these bands arrived on the scene in '77 with full-length records, none would bash away with such glee.

Brian's "1 of the 2" lyric would be as frustratingly opaque as any across *Damned Damned Damned*, but if we are to take him at face value, we have to concede that the sound of the words next to each other, and the brief associations made between them one to the next—but not to the next after that—is all he was after, namely awkward spasms of phraseology that sound like something deep coming out of Vanian but might not be. Further proof of this comes from his admission that he finishes the music first, with the lyrics as a sort of panicked afterthought. Still, there's a fair bank concocted for "1 of the 2," which reads a bit like a courtroom drama with the end game being a guilty verdict followed by an execution.

So Messed Up
(James) 1:55

Here's another bludgeoning pile-driver of a rocker, a deep album track as it were, with the type of violence-threatening lyric which wouldn't pass muster today and definitely wouldn't get the good Captain's stamp of approval, especially given how up in arms he is over "Stab Yor Back." Kicked off with a Ramones-like "1, 2, 3, oh, she's so!" the song explodes into wall-to-wall power chords, and that includes Rat, who pretty much plays chords on the drums.

After a black-and-blue beating, the guys sound worn-out by the punk disdain of the thing after a minute-and-a-half, with Dave hurling one last insult, "She ain't even got a brain," before a messy dissolve at the 1:50 mark.

I Feel Alright
(Pop/Alexander/Asheton/Asheton) 4:26

If "Fan Club" and "Feel the Pain" represented additional contours beyond The Damned's punkiest of punk blitzkriegs, so did the inclusion of a cover, even if in the hands of Rat Scabies, The Stooges' "1970"—rechristened "I Feel Alright"—sounded like something Brian wrote and handed to Rat to beat up.

As Brian recalls the story, the band had picked "1970" for a number of reasons, one being that the Pistols had already covered "No Fun," two, that other bands he knew were trying out "I Wanna Be Your Dog," and three, because "1970" was a bit of a deep cut track, not particularly obvious—remember, there's the whole *Raw Power* album up for grabs at this point too, with its title track as well as "Search and Destroy," soon to show up on a 1977 album by the Dictators.

"I Feel Alright" opens with Dave saying, "Hey Keith," which is an homage to Johnny Thunders and his visit to play the UK. That had been the first words out of Thunders' mouth as he took the stage, Keith being his roadie and all-around minder who took care of Thunders' every whim.

After that and a few well-placed screams, Brian kicks off with the song's repetitive if hypnotic riff, sounding like Lemmy playing chords on his bass. It's soon verified that it is in fact Brian and not Captain and effects because here comes Captain with his usual polite, well recorded and not too prominent bass sound, the one Nick's given him throughout the record to keep the proceedings astringent and urgent.

What also keeps the song at the lip of the stage is the fact that Dave is buried deep in the mix, leaving Rat's cymbals and Brian's gnarly guitar to carry us through to the song's conclusion… which is further away than that of any song on the record. Why? Well, the way The Damned do the song, it's practically a medley covering "1970" and "L.A. Blues," the Stooges' homage to white noise also on *Fun House* and in fact the same side of the original vinyl. The only difference here is that there are no horns on The Damned's version, which is essentially a typical Damned wind-up, but the biggest and noisiest on the record because it serves as a blowing-up of the whole album, not any given two-minute song.

DAMNED/DEAD BOYS: London Roundhouse. Friday, November 25 to Sunday 27. Ticket price: £2. Concerts start 7.30 pm. The Damned have definitely lost a lot of momentum. Theirs was easily the weakest debut album of the new wave vanguard and now they've been weakened by the defection of Rat Scabies. The replacement is Jon Moss, formerly with London. Can our heroes avoid the dread chasm of obscurity which beckons beneath them? Supporting them are the Dead Boys, who recently blew CBGB's away.

Singles, B-sides, Bonus Tracks

Help
(Lennon/McCartney) 1:42

The Damned's cover of the Beatles' "Help!" was issued as the B-side to the band's inaugural single, having been recorded at that same session back on September 20th 1976. The Fab Four original (The Damned version is shown sans the exclamation mark in most renderings) was issued as a single back in 1965, serving also as the title track to the film and soundtrack album of the same name.

Producer Nick Lowe had suggested a Beatles cover, and the band had already been doing "Help" live, with Brian telling me that his take on the song was inspired by the Ramones with respect to speed and brevity. Rat doubles up on and inverts Ringo's original beat, putting the snare on one and four, although the snare is so subsumed by cymbals, bass drum and bass guitar that it's hard to tell if he doesn't move it around randomly.

Aside from the obvious up-ratchet in cacophony, noticeable structural adjustments have been made. The Damned replace The Beatles' song-within-a-song intro with some descending chords overtop "Wipe Out" toms from Rat, and from the 1:22 mark to the end, our boys stick in an instrumental passage not included in the original. As well, Dave side-steps John Lennon's original falsetto note at the chorus, opting for a sort of sour melody that makes the listener wonder if he wants help at all.

Singalongscabies
(Scabies) 0:57

Rat didn't have to write another song to wedge in another credit. Instead, he offers up this karaoke instrumental version of "Stab Yor Back," which joins the album version to comprise the B-side to the "Neat Neat Neat" single issued concurrent with the release of *Damned Damned Damned*.

Included are drop-outs to just bass and drums and drop-outs in which Rat carries the beat alone, "Wipe Out"-style. The effect is a bit untidy—concerning the drop-outs, it's five times for the former and three times for the latter, as if Captain didn't get the brief to stop playing when Brian does. Still, most substantially through removing the vocal, the exercise draws attention both to the sturdiness of the song and to the drummer stoking the fire in the engine room—cultivated is the cult of Rat.

Sick of Being Sick
(James) 2:30

By the time The Damned laid down "Sick of Being Sick," the album had come out to effusive local reviews and the band had toured the UK supporting T Rex, with Marc Bolan collaring the band after seeing Captain wearing a T Rex shirt.

They'd been on UK TV as well, plus toured America and then come back and done a BBC session. In other words, there'd been a ton of growth and career advancement, as they emerged from Roundhouse Studios in North London on May 19th 1977 with two new gig-tested songs, "Sick of Being Sick" and "Stretcher Case Baby," coaxed to fruition by '60s production legend Shel Talmy, famous for his work with The Who and The Kinks as well as The Creation, Pentangle, Lee Hazlewood and Manfred Mann.

Rat wasn't happy with the results, lamenting that Talmy, now with better gear than he had when he'd worked with The Who in the '60s, had rounded off the band's sharp edges. Indeed from a production standpoint, "Sick of Being Sick" finds The Damned halfway to where they'd be with Pink Floyd's Nick Mason on *Music for Pleasure*.

As a song however, "Sick of Being Sick" was a cracker, written by Brian, based around a remark made by an American girlfriend of his who was worn-out from having been laid up sick in bed for a week. At the music end, Brian is ornate with more of a note-dense riff than usual along with lead fills at bar's end. Rat is similarly multi-dimensional, using his usual licks but slicker at it, more thoughtful, while Dave has similarly dialled it down, singing more deliberately, utilising less of his conversational style. There's also a two-section break and a false ending, before the band careen back into a few more go-'rounds of the anthemic, crowd-favourite chorus.

The results of the Damned-Talmy collaboration would be issued as a single on July 3rd 1977 with the A-side, "Stretcher Case Baby," eventually seeing reissue on the band's second album, re-recorded with Mason, title truncated to "Stretcher Case."

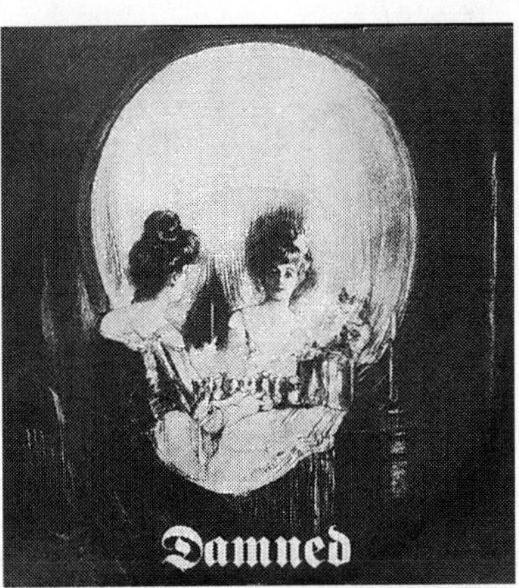

The single was designed as a 5,000-run give-away item, used for an *NME* contest and also a thank you to members of the Damned Disciples fan club. But it was mostly used as a freebie to the crowd at the Marquee shows with the Sex Pistols to celebrate the band's first anniversary since their debut gig at the 100 Club on July 6th, 1976, which also was in support of the Sex Pistols.

When it came time to record *Music for Pleasure*, "Sick of Being Sick" would be left off the docket, becoming the most substantial and considered non-LP composition from the band clear through to April '79 when "Suicide" and "Burglar" arrive and summarily overwhelm anything from the second album, granted a distant memory by that juncture.

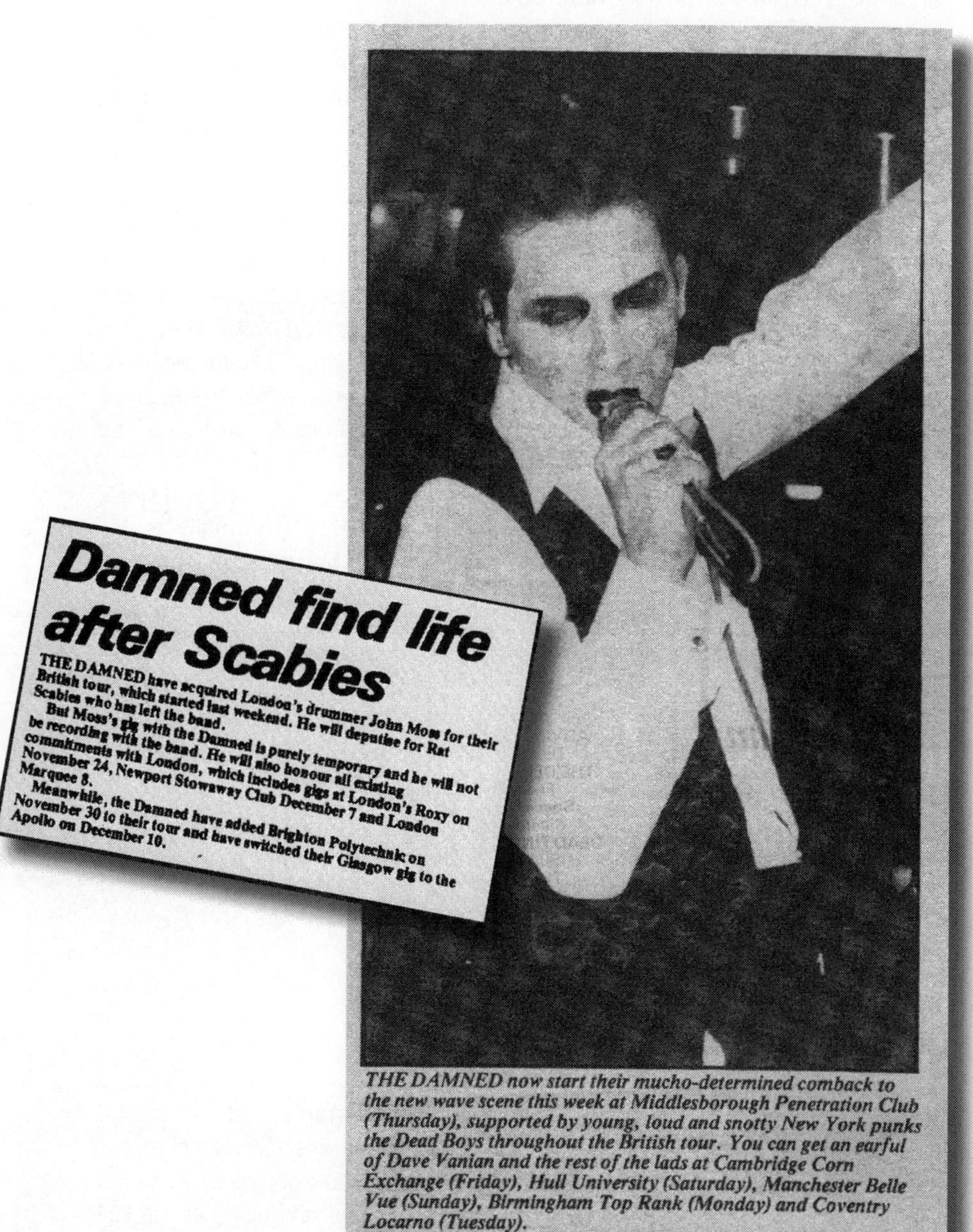

Damned find life after Scabies

THE DAMNED have acquired London's drummer John Moss for their British tour, which started last weekend. He will deputise for Rat Scabies who has left the band.

But Moss's gig with the Damned is purely temporary and he will not be recording with the band. He will also honour all existing commitments with London, which includes gigs at London's Roxy on November 24, Newport Stowaway Club December 7 and London Marquee 8.

Meanwhile, the Damned have added Brighton Polytechnic on November 30 to their tour and have switched their Glasgow gig to the Apollo on December 10.

THE DAMNED now start their mucho-determined comback to the new wave scene this week at Middlesborough Penetration Club (Thursday), supported by young, loud and snotty New York punks the Dead Boys throughout the British tour. You can get an earful of Dave Vanian and the rest of the lads at Cambridge Corn Exchange (Friday), Hull University (Saturday), Manchester Belle Vue (Sunday), Birmingham Top Rank (Monday) and Coventry Locarno (Tuesday).

damnedeadboys
damnedeadboys
damnedeadboys
damnedeadboys
damnedeadboys
damnedeadboys
damnedeadboys
damnedeadboys
damnedeadboys
damnedeadboys
ontour

Nov	17*	Middlesbrough Town Hall	Dec	2	Kings Hall Derby
	18	Cambridge Corn Exchange			Pier Pavilion Hastings
	19	Hull University			Top Rank Southampton
	20	Elizabethan Ballroom Manchester		6	Top Rank Cardiff
	21	Birmingham Top Rank		7	Mountford Hall Liverpool University
	22	Coventry Locarno		8	Huddersfield Polytechnic
	23	Sheffield Top Rank		9	Clouds Edinburgh
	25	Roundhouse London		10	Strathclyde University Glasgow
	26	Roundhouse London		11	City Hall Newcastle
	27	Roundhouse London			
	28	Leicester De Montfort			
	30	Brighton			

* Penetration will replace Dead Boys for this date

a damned certainty

The D

Page 36 SOUNDS - December 10, 1977

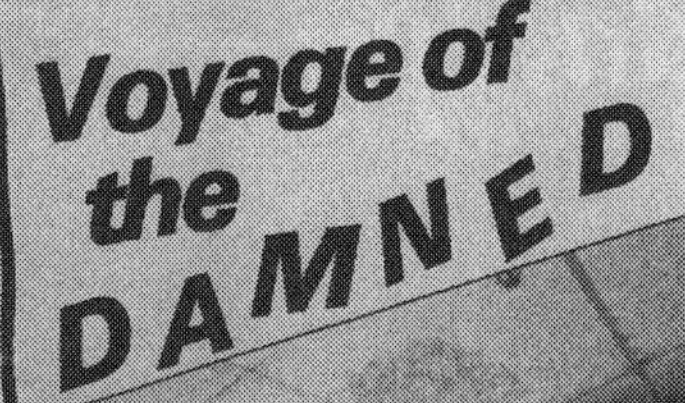

Above: Brian and Erica. Far right: Dave Vanian. Right: Lu. Left: The Captain.

'We're in the dumpers. No-one wants to know us'

Stowaways/excess baggage: PETE SILVERTON (wurdz) and STEVENSON (pixz)

A RAINY Friday afternoon in stiff publicist Glen Coulson's office. Glen ruffles his hair, takes a swig from a can of warm Heineken and expounds the benefits of woolly plaid lumberjacket shirts.

CONTINUED NEXT PAGE

amned

Page 28 SOUNDS December 10, 1977

DEAD BOY Stiv Bators: these Noo Yawkers do it best

DAMNED/DEAD BOYS

From page 27

spits were so patently forced and false. He did it so often that you could say he was the boy who spewed wolf.

My favourite moment was when he spat beer over the crowd and one of the wessed returned the compliment. Naturally, things being as they are — one law for the stage, another for the bear pit — the stage heavies leaped off and sorted out the offender.

When I asked the promoter about this inequality, he came up with the non-sequito of the weekend.

"Well, you see, last night, we had someone flicking paper clips at the stage."

'Sonic Reducer' got the biggest crowd reaction but I was most struck by Stiv's most concerted attempt at outrage. He edged his trousers down to his ankle with his back to the audience and then turned round to display his all . . . but the cheat had tucked his cock and balls between his legs. the resultant curly triangle made him look like a Fellini hermaphrodite. A suitable image of the band. They'll probably be very successful.

AT 9.28 p.m. precisely, the enigmatic Brian James arrives. Erica, who's with him, points me out and he comes over and asks why I called him a poser and a pain in my review of the Damned album. I don't think he believed me when I told him it was because he was a chronic poser and kicked the habit when things started to get rough in the Damned camp.

"What do you mean by poser? And you're one anyway."

I don't think I charmed much either, when, by way of changing the topic of conversation, I told him he moved onstage very like Mick Jones and Tony James, both of whom were with him in the London S.S.

Fortunately, Lu had just found out who I was and, to celebrate the fact, daubed a large J (for journalist) on my cheek.

Leaving Lu to reminisce with B. P. Fallon about the slightly exclusive school they both went to, I asked Captain why their manager wasn't there.

"He ain't interested in us, is he? First of all, Jake went off with Elvis. I have Elvis. He nicked our manager. Now we never see the other one, Robinson. He's always somewhere else."

His spleen sent, Captain settled and quietened down, subdued and even vulnerable.

Then the Damned's security man, a being of few, mostly unintelligible words told us all to clear out of the dressing room so the band could go onstage.

Now, most people seem to have written the Damned off, assured that they can no longer cut the cake. Myself, I see things differently. Sure, they aren't the same rush of primal energy they used to be. But, as I said in my review of the album, they are trying to move on from their mostly vaudevillian origins. (Does my insistence on movement mean that we'll soon be faced with progressive punk? God forbid.)

They have not been content and complacent enough to stay where they were six months ago. And before you say they still haven't moved far enough, remember that the Pistols still haven't caught up, musically speaking, with where they were a year ago with 'Anarchy'.

Live, Rat's leaving meant that Captain Sensible is the Damned. James and Lu might weave around the stage, apparently caught up, trance-like in their own music. But it's Captain, his wigs and tutus that define and extend the inherent cruelness of the Damned loonshow.

Both nights at the Roundhouse he executed a remarkable piece of theatre. A roadie came on and slipped him a piece of paper. Hamming shock he stumbled to the mike and announced: "Quiet a minute . . . quiet . . . I've got something to tell you . . . a famous rock star has died . . . Rod Stewart . . . (and while everyone was deciding whether it was a joke or not) . . . this one's for him . . . 'Stretcher Case'."

Tasteless maybe but my sense of humour has always inclined to the macabre.

Captain is a continuous visual attraction. Whether he's kicking roadies off stage, losing his wig, getting his foot caught up in his own lead or strangling Lu with the same lead, he's a constant balance for Vanian's deficiencies as a front-man.

And they sound more like banshees than the Banshees will. Incessant, piercing sheets of sound from Lu and Brian trying to play louder than each other and slightly-more-subtle-than-Rat kit smashing from John Moss.

Not that they're aren't problems. It was clear that the Damned still aren't quite back on the right track. They couldn't seem to quite shake a certain mechanicism about their playing on the Saturday night. On the Friday, that was avoided because Lol Coxhill graced the proceedings with his presence. Standing immobile by the left-hand PA stack for most of the set, looking like an omniscient, vicious bodyguard for something we couldn't see, he added his wailing soprano to the last few numbers, creating a sound that's probably feel much happier the other side of the Styx.

Given time and space, I'm sure they'll manage to weld the mixture of old and new material into some kind of chaotic cohesion. Above all, they no longer seem happy to remain the three Stooges of rock 'n' roll.

After the show, they seemed quite pleased with the show, only annoyed that the promoter Curd had refused to allow them to go back for a second encore (whether it was warranted is another question).

Lu showed me how the abstract shapes on their new album cover — surely the best of the year — were in fact cunning little drawings of the Damned.

"There's Brian, notice the slitted eyes."

A voice boomed out.

"What's wrong with Lu? Why won't I have him in the group? He's ugly, that's what. I'll only accept him in this group as a skapegoat."

The Captain didn't calm down till everyone had left the dressing room. He asked me if I was coming again the next night.

"Nah. Sorry, I'm gonna see Graham Parker."

"I hate that c—. He's another one that's nicked our manager."

November 12, 1977 SOUNDS Page 19

uneasy listeni

the damned
music for pleasure
seez 5
album out now

Music for Pleasure

Pretty incredible watching from afar how quickly the UK music weekly press could move on from a band, or as the rockers themselves would put it, turn on a band.

This most definitely happened with The Damned, who were at the receiving end of universally negative reviews for their second album, *Music for Pleasure*, issued November 18th 1977, a blurry nine months since the fire-starter debut.

Was this a case of a band believing its own press, in this instance, their bad press? Because, also very quickly, the guys themselves began disparaging the record, placing the blame on producer Nick Mason, on deteriorating band relations, on general burn-out, on adding a second guitarist (Lu Edmonds) and probably with most validity, on the pressure to produce another album so soon.

Not that it matters but count the author as one lone voice (well, there's Henry Rollins too) who prefers *Music for Pleasure* over the debut, appreciating since the day I first heard it the improvement in musicality and the variety across tracks, while still retaining most of the structural heaviness, if not the heaviness of delivery.

In this (stretcher) case, making up for the seething anger of the debut's execution—and still directly in this realm of heaviness—was the more distorted and power-chorded recording to the guitars, along with the greater incorporation of bass guitar into the overall sound picture. While Rat's snare is still tuned impossibly tight, his toms take on greater authority here versus the almost apocalyptic trashiness to their sound across the blighted landscape of *Damned Damned Damned*.

"Number one, we didn't want to repeat the first album, like the Ramones had done," explains Brian. "It wasn't in our style to do that. We had no time to write stuff. We were pushed into doing it. We had been touring the first album, *Damned Damned Damned*, and then finally Jake and Dave (the Stiff Records bosses) turned around to us and said, 'We need a new album. When can you be ready to go in the studio?' And it was like 'What?!' I mean, I had had a couple songs written and some riffs together and I said that I'd go play some stuff and write some lyrics. But I said, 'Look, I need help here.' I'd written the first album, but I said to Lett (Dave Vanian) and Captain, 'We need a new album—do you have any ideas?' It's not the way I like to work, to be absolutely honest with you. Working under that kind of pressure."

"But once we started to formulate ideas, there was no way it was going to be like the first album. In a way, it was like we were drawing on all of our whole inspirations this time, like getting Lol Coxhill in to blow sax on the song, 'You Know,' things like that. It gave us an excuse to experiment and say look, punk rock isn't all about going 'bang, bang, bang, bang, bang.' It's doing what you want to do and giving it some attitude, which is not always 'bang, bang, bang' either. Just follow your heart and do your thing. And that was obvious by the first wave of punk bands: every band was really different. It wasn't all rock 'n' roll like the Pistols and The Clash. Everybody had their own personalities."

Subconsciously, one has to wonder if some of the bile directed at the record came from the choice of Nick Mason as producer. After all, was there a loftier and more distant rock corporation in the world at the time than Pink Floyd? And across the conceptual lyrics and sleepy execution of their quiet songs, were Floyd not the very least punk of prog bands? To my mind, Mason becomes a scapegoat, because I'm missing where there's any problem with the sounds he gets on this record.

As the legend goes, Nick was the consolation prize when first choice Syd Barrett proved unrealistic. "Originally the second album was supposed to be produced by Syd Barrett, but Syd was too out-to-lunch," explains Dave. "Our publisher was Pink Floyd's publisher and we were told we could get him and he was interested in doing it, but unfortunately his mental health was too unstable. And we ended up having Nick Mason, the drummer from Pink Floyd, which is a big difference (laughs). And I don't think we really got the album that we were thinking of. Plus Brian was a little bit burnt-out then. He wasn't quite sure what was happening, and soon after, he actually split the band up."

"Well, I don't know," adds Rat, sort of downplaying the accepted narrative that Nick was a surprise switcheroo. "Everybody sort of said, 'Let's get Syd to do it' because they were all Syd Barrett fans. But Syd at that point wasn't really capable of doing anything like that. Eventually everybody knew we were going with Nick Mason. When he turned up at the studio, it wasn't that we suddenly arrived and Nick Mason was there instead of Syd Barrett. But it's a funny story."

"As Dave said, we had the same publisher as Pink Floyd," adds Brian, "and Jake said he could get us the Floyd studio really cheap and all this and 'Who do you want to produce it?' And it's like, 'Well, any chance of getting hold of Syd Barrett?' Because he was one of our favourite guitar players as well. But he was in no condition to do anything. And then he said, basically, just before we went in, 'Well, Nick Mason is up for it.' And it's like, 'Oh, okay, let's give it a shot.'"

But, perhaps predictably, this was a case of two solitudes separated by a wide gulf. "It went from one extreme to the other, really," says Scabies. "On the one hand, there's Nick Lowe with bits of lolly sticks, you know, ice sticks, taped onto the soundboard, a bottle of cider and a cigarette burning while he's mixing 'Neat Neat Neat.' When we mixed the snare drum in, we didn't want it too far up. And then on the other hand there was Nick Mason in a luxury air-conditioned huge studio, Britannia Row, with more flashing red lights than I'd ever seen in my life before. It was all a bit strange, kind of two extremes. I think we got Pink Floyd's sound. You can hear everything that's going on. And if I do have a criticism, that's it. I think Nick's view on producing us was that he wanted to get the actual musical elements that make The Damned work. And I think what the guys in The Damned miss on it is their personalities."

"But Nick was really cool (laughs) and a really nice guy, and great to work with. We were at that difficult second album stage and really, the band was in quite a bit of turmoil at that point. I was halfway through leaving the group and everything and we were burnt-out so poor Nick was into a bit of a loser from the start, really."

"He didn't understand it at all," reflects Brian, offering a harsher assessment. "But we were being pushed all the time to get the second album recorded and there really wasn't that much time for discussing producers. We went in and Nick, really, was more interested in talking about his collection of Ferraris than doing rock 'n' roll. He couldn't believe that we could put a track down and turn around and say, 'Yeah, that'll do.' He's like, 'What?!' He was used to spending like months on a drum sound, let alone getting in and out. We just wanted to get on with it. It was strange. Plus his studio was so big, it was just ridiculous. You could fit Pathway Studios into the gentleman's toilet. It was just crazy; it wasn't our place at all."

Then there was the album cover, an iconic Barney Bubbles production, which nonetheless perplexed prospective buyers. For the piece, Barney channelled Russian futurist Wassily Kandinsky, specifically "Composition VIII," unwittingly revealing the band as fractured, disintegrating, soon to fly off in disparate angled directions. Not only is it hard to read any of the text on the tin, but the vibe was incongruently artsy against what The Damned represented. This continued onto the back where, really, only Rat is recognisable as himself—Captain looks like Brezhnev!—given the house of mirrors manipulation of these shadowy head shots.

"Barney was hanging out at Stiff Records at the time," recalls Rat, "so he was around. He was such a brilliant artist and such a nice guy. I remember he was just on the phone with Jake Riviera and Jake said, 'That's good.' Actually, the cover is everybody's favourite thing about the album. That type of thing wasn't done on a computer back in those days. It was done on a board with overlays and stuff."

Adds Brian, "To my mind, there aren't too many geniuses you come across in life, and Barney was one. He was an amazing artist and a very, very sweet guy. I heard after he died, after he had committed suicide, that he had a really depressive side but I never saw that. I used to go 'round his place for dinners and he was always very up and jolly. But I used to think, 'Wow, Barney, how the hell did you think of that?!' He knocked me out, man. That was a sad, sad loss."

"I wouldn't say we've disowned any of our records," says Dave in closing, "but we didn't like *Music for Pleasure* very much; it was a fractured album."

"It's too flat," adds Brian, "too cleaned-up, uninspired—it doesn't work for me. Still, I think we'd come up with some fairly good songs. I went for ages and ages not listening to it, and it's only a couple of years ago that I listened to it again and I was pleasantly surprised. People get different things out of it, with some now saying the album was ahead of its time and all this. But I would love to get my hands on the original tapes so I could remix it, to see whether I could do a bit of a job on it."

"I think Nick did what he could," sighs Rat. "Nick did the best job that he was able to do. Everybody was expecting the producer to come in and make the record for us and find the magic solution to what The Damned should be doing next. Nick didn't do that but that wasn't his job; that wasn't what he was supposed to do. Everyone says, 'Oh, the record should've been more psychedelic,' but everyone was there at the time and nobody was really saying anything other than, 'Okay, that sounds good to me. Let's get on with it.' But it's the album nobody ever talks about. In retrospect, listening to it—and listening to our peers that even got around to making a second album—it actually came out good. There was a different side to The Damned that was coming through that wasn't just a three-minute blast of punk mayhem. We were starting to develop, even if we didn't really know which way to go."

****

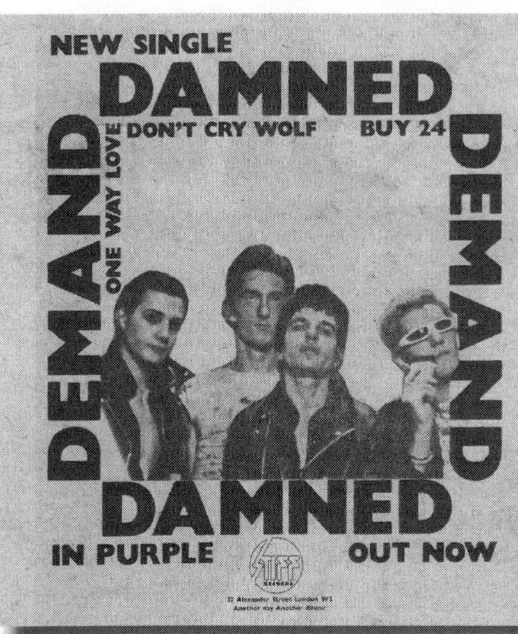

THE DAMNED: 'Problem Child' (Stiff Buy 18). Great chunky Who-type staccato riffing introduces a rather obvious 'you will identify with this won't you (please)?' line in lyrics. Actually it's the first time I've been able to make out most of the lyrics on a Damned song on first playing but I see this as consistent with the trend towards cleaner productions of new wave material.

Will it be a gigantic smasheroo though? It's certainly catchy enough to get plenty of airplay but it'll also be competing with the Clash and the Pistols to name but 15. My guess is that, despite the fact that we haven't heard much from them in a while, they've still got enough charisma to make us save up our pennies.

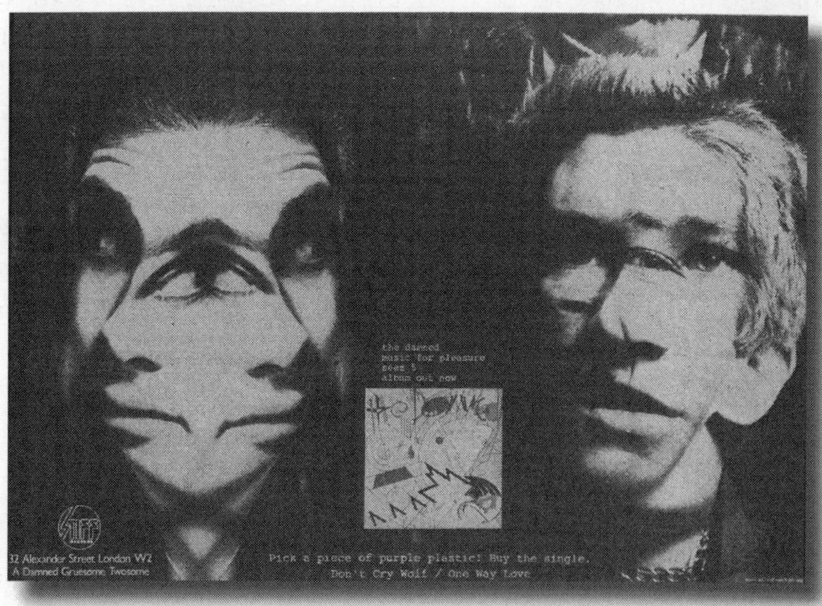

Side 1

Problem Child
(Scabies/James) 2:12

Problem child or a disciplined Damned? Take your pick, because this exquisite and expertly placed opener offers both. After a chug of guitars and a sober roll around the kit from Rat, Dave starts singing and Rat plays nothing but marching snare while Brian and new guitarist Lu Edmonds palm-mute an A chord and nothing else.

Soon chaos is restored as the song explodes into a full-throated chorus with everybody thundering along like the old days. But then we're back to the crouching verse, this time in E, with Dave elevating the proceedings with a sophisticated vocal melody to go with what is a textbook display of dynamics, like AC/DC from *Dirty Deeds* and *High Voltage*, through to the likes of "For Those About to Rock" and "Thunderstruck."

Brian says that the influence on this one was early Who, but then he'd handed the job of lyrics over to Rat, who obliged with a chorus and two verses, one of which was evidently good enough to use twice. The subject is juvenile delinquency, with our miscreant James Dean wannabe going out at night, drinking, stealing cars and then coming home at 3AM and playing his records, presumably waking mum and dad.

Again along the dynamics tip, the lyrics are deftly placed to be heard as zingers after musical punctuation marks, right down to the descending "Your daddy's gonna tan your hide" line of the chorus. This sets up the next machine-like verse until the very last go 'round where the song ends large on a shouting of the word "hide," a final abrupt halt in a song rife with exclamation points.

"Problem Child" was issued as an advance picture sleeve single on September 28th 1977, backed with "You Take My Money." The song failed to chart, suffering the same fate as the badly reviewed album at large, a considerable disappointment, given that *Damned Damned Damned* managed an impressive No.36 showing earlier in the year.

Don't Cry Wolf
(James) 3:13

Further indicative of the band's increasing musicality, "Don't Cry Wolf," written in totality by Brian, opens with James and Scabies sounding downright funky, with Rat utilising the bell of his ride against rhythmic licks from Brian. Once the Captain joins in, the guys have switched to the dependable "Louie Louie" chords that we'd soon learn comprise the chorus space. For a verse we're in familiar Damned terrain, Rat doubling up the beat over an ominous ascending chord sequence.

As concerns the lyric, Brian lays out almost too plainly the punk manifesto—at one point telegraphing "Smash It Up"—set against a chorus sentiment that doesn't quite connect with the rote rebellion of the verse exhortations. Also come chorus time, Dave's vocals are multi-tracked with a vague attempt at harmonies. Elsewhere on this uncharacteristically long song, there's a proper break section as well as a reoccurrence of the opening lick, this time with handclaps, before another go 'round of the second verse, followed by the chorus done regular and then with modulation.

If anything is to be gained from Brian's uncharacteristically *Hallmark* card suggestions on how to be a punk, it's his pointing out that "there ain't no uniform." Indeed, this is one of the things that the critics noted about The Damned, namely that this most definitive and mainlined of punk experiences live and on record (even now as relative sophisticates), dressed as if they were blowing up any notion of punk fashion.

"Don't Cry Wolf" was issued as the second single from *Music for Pleasure* on December 11th '77, shortly after the album had hit the shops, backed with "One Way Love," although both songs were designated "D"-sides. The pink vinyl single was issued in a generic Stiff cut-out sleeve, exposing yellow labels.

One Way Love
(James) 4:23

Given my overall acceptance of *Music for Pleasure* as a square-enough Damned joint, I'll admit that Captain Sensible's slide guitar work on "One Way Love" sent me for a loop, more than the Lol Coxhill saxophone guest slot or the Nick Mason production, both of which count as positives in my books.

But these criss-crossing slide licks... they do nothing but distract, on top of a typical enough Damned song, itchy and urgent like Buzzcocks, heavy contrast of construct between verse and chorus. What time is it? Are we now post-punk or are we back at pub rock? Only ex-hippie Raymond Burns knows. Otherwise, the song has a lot going for it: anthemic chorus, Rat going nuts and captured in pleasant high fidelity, capable and confident energy, a revisit to the band's speedy boogie rock roots, as well as a modulation to a closing section that is a completely new musical theme, a break as it were, but stuck at the end. In essence, interest is kept up despite the song's almost four-minute duration, due to the sturdiness of the proposals delivered efficiently albeit repetitiously.

Brian's lyric is an exposition on the title, the documenting of a doomed one-way relationship, with the best line being, "She ain't worried who's been shooting her" which can have two meanings. Again however, the band rely on repeating a verse, with the tacit suggestion that no one could be bothered to write another.

Politics
(James) 2:25

Deep track, album track, anchor and salt-of-the-earth track... first off, at the music end, "Politics" is a storming rocker in the *Damned Damned Damned* tradition, all fiery anger, hard punk switchbacks and halting double-time Rat rhythms. But then the band go off into a groovy riff rock zone, uptempo versus reverse tempo, for a musical break between exhortations.

But it's those exhortations that make "Politics" remarkable, albeit succinctly. Indeed, there's not much of a bank of lyrics, but what Brian says he makes count. James was taking direct aim at The Clash for their holier-than-thou political stance, noting in interviews that he remembers Mick Jones from his London SS days, and lovely as he was, social change was the last thing on his mind. Furthermore, he mentions that back in school he had no fascist friends, that race wasn't an issue he thought about, and that it was all about rocking out, although the ill-advised and incongruent word "dance" is used instead.

The lines "fascist manager's dreams" and "My politics don't sell clothes" reference the likes of Bernie Rhodes and Malcolm McLaren (The Damned had already cycled through all manner of managers by this point), while the mention of anarchy has one considering the Pistols, and the line "Riots don't sell my soul" has one pondering The Clash and their call to arms, "White Riot."

Stretcher Case
(Scabies/James) 2:32

Here's a song from the recent (accelerated) past brought forward, the single proposal from July 3rd '77 re-recorded in the semi-sober Nick Mason style, stuck on the new record for the perplexed re-consideration of the base. There's a sense of "So Messed Up" to this menacing track, of man-meets-woman not working out as planned, the story of a newly minted pop star being confronted with a love interest who is a king can short of a six-pack.

At the music end, this is The Damned pushing into 1978, offering propulsive punk at the chorus, but getting melancholy, atmospheric and innovatively rhythmic during the verses, telegraphing the idea of post-punk. Of course, breaking all the rules and in effect time travelling, they would regress on the next album, digging in their heels as it were, before readily contributing to a productive post-punk world starting with *The Black Album* and beyond. But songs like "Stretcher Case" exist in that nether zone, nascent and suggestive, as much Magazine as it is Buzzcocks.

Idiot Box
(Sensible/Scabies) 5:39

If slide guitar wasn't enough to discombobulate punks with torn clothes, before we leave side two of the original vinyl, The Damned reveal their inner Rolling Stones, settling into a tasty roots rock groove after teasing with a sly beat inversion, the first salvo out of an amusing intro that sounds like the band feeling out a song for the first time, jamming. But then it all falls into place, Brian and Lu playing off each other like Keith Richards and Ron Wood, stitching together what sounds like a classic road song.

Which makes sense, because "Idiot Box" is squarely about The Damned's trip across America after the New York gigs to play a few shows with Television in San Francisco and LA, only to be spurned, ostensibly because Tom Verlaine and Co. were scared to follow this band with a recently realised reputation as un-herdable cats.

So Captain put pen to paper and called out every one of them by name—Ficca, Smith, Lloyd and Verlaine—marbling in television references (hence the title), and in very few words managing to make the band look like they think they are TV stars of some sort. For example the band's fans have to wait in the rain to "see that screen Verlaine" and a "haggard" Fred Smith is classed as an insider, working "for the box."

The best bit is when Captain relates that when they got to the West Coast, all they got is "a *Marquee Moon*," referencing simultaneously Television's butt cheeks and their debut album, which had come out just after The Damned's album and was immediately lauded as high art.

But "Idiot Box" offers its own spot of snobby rock in the guise of a flamenco part, which seems to parody Tom Verlaine's origami guitar lines. This meanders on for a full minute near the end of the song's five-minute expanse, after which the band perform an indulgent thirty-second noise rock wind-up, the two parts together reflecting what a lot of punks thought of Television: that they were intellectual and boring. These dual closing tangents represent high contrast to the exquisite verse and jam groove that you just don't want to stop, as does the chorus, which fortunately is good music, typical black-and-blue Damned punk woven nicely into the totality of this outré track.

Addressing a song both ironic and absurd, Brian James—supposedly some sort of dictator in The Damned—cites "Idiot Box" as his favourite song on the album. Not only is it one of the few he didn't write, but it's hugely diametrically opposed to anything he's given the band so far, or that anyone else has dared propose for that matter.

Again though, that bluesy James lick is a hook for miles, and one wonders if The Damned might have had a smash hit with this song, given the rapidly evolving appetite in the UK at the time for all things post-punk, beyond punk, anything and everything but punk (unless you're The Adverts, who weren't allowed to change).

Side 2

You Take My Money
(James) 1:59

As much as fans were shocked with the non-punk music on The Damned's second album, at least at this end with me an' my buds, there was also some almost subconscious dismay with this idea of toned-down parts, as exemplified by the verses of both side-starters. "Problem Child" has Dave singing over a mechanical riff an' Rat playing just snare, while "You Take My Money" features the same checked-out guitar, while Rat double-fists the high-hat and softly pumps his bass drum—that's it. In both cases, it's a set-up for more noise, noise, noise come chorus time, so there's method to the madness. This doesn't happen anywhere else on the record, but opening tracks on album sides get outsized attention, not to mention the fact that the similarity in structure is underscored by the former being a single A-side, with the latter picked as the single's B. To boot, the song is predicated upon two chords which modulate to another two chords, which begins to wear on the brain after a while. Fortunately there's a break but it's... one chord, after which it's back to the chorus, a repeated verse, more chorus then out.

There's not much to the lyric either, with Brian complaining about women who are all happy when you're a rock star but then are gone once you're broke—or in The Damned's case, are gone once they find out you are broke and always have been broke, rock star or not.

Alone
(James) 4:15

The Damned covered The Stooges on the first record, and "Alone" sounds very much like Brian writing his own "1970," Rat playing like he did on "I Feel Alright" ("1970" renamed) and how Scott Asheton played on the original. Then there's Brian's manic and screechy soloing, which sounds like brother Ron "Rock Action" Asheton across those first two Stooges albums. Let's not stop there—the opening salvo sounds like James Williamson circa *Raw Power*, "Penetration" coming to mind, after which Dave snarls like Iggy and we collapse into the tribal din of "Alone" which never lets up.

The title of the song represents how Brian was feeling in The Damned at this point, with respect to doing all the writing and with respect to wanting to evolve away from the blitzkrieg punk expected from the band's rabid base. Stressed and stretched creatively, James went back to an old Bastard song called "Comfort," speeding it up, Damned-ifying it to the point where it was good enough to replace "Sick of Being Sick," which had been considered for re-recording and inclusion.

There are only two portions of the song that sound like a break: the first time they perform the verse muted, quietly, and then for the closing wind-up it's ascending chords. Elsewhere, the chorus is barely discernable as such, given how it's welded to the endless hypnotic verse riff, with the end effect being a song that just steamrolls for three-and-a-half minutes, long by early Damned standards.

Lyrically you could call "Alone" a bridge between "Born to Kill" from the first album and "These Hands" from the third, a sort of Jack the Ripper story that looks so right coming from the sartorial but sleep-deprived Dave Vanian, Esquire.

Your Eyes
(Vanian/James) 3:30

There's something charmingly under-written about "Your Eyes." In effect, the song consists of a pre-chorus and a chorus and no verses, and all of it predicated on a sort of '60s-rooted garage rock/doo-wop chord sequence from the "Louie Louie" family, coloured at the edges by Brian playing little locomotive train song licks like Johnny Thunders.

We've talked about reasons not to be cheerful about *Music for Pleasure*—the production, the slide on "One Way Love," the light writing on "Idiot Box," the toned-down verses of "Problem Child" and "You Take My Money—well, add "Your Eyes" to the list of songs that are a long way from punk. But there's more: at nearly three minutes, a song this spare sounds like it could use an edit, editing being something the band were ruthless at on the first record. And that's a pattern here, with "Don't Cry Wolf," "You Take My Money" and "Alone" also arguably overstaying their welcomes (although a ten-minute "Idiot Box" would have been fine by me).

"Your Eyes" is famed for being the first song for which Dave bothered to get in there and write some lyrics, which pleased Brian to no end, having come up with his quixotic and vague and accidentally often poetic phraseology across the catalogue so far almost by default, grudgingly.

And Vanian does a nice job, painting a film noire picture of his nascent, fragile Goth self sitting in a bar, cigarette in hand, staring into his drink and seeing those eyes that use and confuse him. Dave's vocals are sparingly double-tracked and he acts them well an' thespian, which also pleased James, who thought that he did a good impression of Alice Cooper, one of Dave's favourite singers, although personally I'm not hearing a lot of Alice in this one.

Creep (You Can't Fool Me)
(James) 2:14

It's down to "Politics" and the freshly written "Creep" to provide connectivity to the thrashy punk of the debut, and again, count this fan as perfectly happy how these wall-of-sound constructs emerged on record at the hands of producer Nick Mason (and, it must be said, engineers Nick Griffiths and Brian Humphries, given how the guys variously gripe that Mason was more into cars and motorcycles during the sessions than he was making a record).

The guys also keep this one short, chucking in a modulation but not bothering with a break section. What's amusing is Rat's decision-making, masquerading as indecision. When he hits the first verse, he plays a fast conventional beat with the snare on two and four, but then switches to "hurry-up mode," double-time snare on one and three for parts two, three and four of the verse. Come chorus time, he does the same thing, and then he sticks with this pattern throughout the song for both verses and choruses—that is until the very end, where the guys break out all guns blazing with Rat in hurry-up mode throughout all runs at the closing chorus.

Lyrically, "Creep" bookends "You Take My Money," with Brian grousing about hangers-on and yes-men, fakers who fawn over rock stars for personal gain, with the over-riding message being that Brian can spot them a mile away.

You Know
(James) 5:02

Music for Pleasure ends with the album's longest song, a dark, hypnotic and heavy rocker that again echoes the Stooges' (and MC5's) tendency to land on a riff and hammer it into the memory banks. There is however a "break" section as it were, which is more of a brief instrumental linkage featuring one of the most complex chord sequences of the Brian era.

Also referencing the Stooges and MC5 (and Hawkwind) is the inclusion of freeform sax work to the proceedings. The band had run into the legendary and prolific Lol Coxhill at a rest stop on the motorway one day and instantly took a liking to this funny old hippie, inviting him to play on the album.

Coxhill can be heard tucking in at the two-minute mark of "You Know" and then staying for the duration, in fact taking over at the end, strangling cats like Nik Turner. The erstwhile Krautrock jam to close the record mirrors what "L.A. Blues" did for *Fun House* seven years earlier, essentially drawing parallels between punk and jazz as complimentary forms of renegade music, arguably both hard on the ears and less arguably, not likely to earn the practitioners much money.

The motivation behind Brian's lyric are bigger (as stated in interviews) than we get within the typically spare, inscrutable and repetitive sentiments snarled by Dave Vanian. Brian had been reflecting upon the band's trip to America, which he considered something of a police state and a place that was inward-looking because it didn't have much of a history. He had also been disappointed at the New York punk scene he had previously romanticised, finding it arty and fake, full of posers and careerism. This last bit indeed comes through in the few remarks we get, through lines like "pretty as a mirror," "ugly as your smile" "plastic cards," "you can't relate" (presumably to the real poverty and social unrest of punk London) and most point-blank, "you can't create."

THE
DAMNED
new Single
I Just Cant Be Happy today
Ballroom Blitz
+ Turkey Song
Chiswick
CHIS 120
Blitz on Ballroom Bass by Lemmy

THE DAMNED
MACHINE GUN
Etiquette
ALBUM IN THE SHOPS NOW!!
New Single-Out Now!
I Just Cant Be Happy Today
Ballroom Blitz
+ Turkey Song
CHIS 120

Page 62 — New Musical Express 24th November, 1979
THE DAMNED
ON TOUR
November
22 LEICESTER DE MONTFORT HALL
23 CAMBRIGE CORN EXCHANGE
24 PETERBOROUGH WIRRINA STADIUM
25 CARDIFF TOP RANK
26 SHEFFIELD TOP RANK
28 BRIGHTON TOP RANK
30 LONDON RAINBOW
December
4 GLASGOW APPOLLO
5 BRADFORD ST GEORGES HALL
7 COVENTRY NEW THEATRE
9 WOLVERHAMPTON CIVIC HALL
10 MANCHESTER APPOLLO
11 BRISTOL COLSTON HALL
15 HULL CITY HALL
MACHINE GUN Etiquette
NEW ALBUM IN THE SHOPS NOW!!
I Just Cant Be Happy Today
Turkey Song

Machine Gun Etiquette

Post-*Music for Pleasure*, The Damned had actually disintegrated to a shambles. Drugs and drink were rampant, as was infighting and on-tour destruction, causing big bills and a deepening sense of debacle. First to go was Rat—even before the last album had come out—replaced briefly by Dave Berk from Johnny Moped. Captain Sensible himself had been part of that band, going back to 1974 when they were known as Johnny Moped and the Five Arrogant Superstars, and the two had got along great.

Berk would return to Johnny Moped and be replaced by Jon Moss, who would perform on the first bank of UK dates promoting *Music for Pleasure*, support being Cleveland's finest, the Dead Boys, the closest thing to The Damned that America had on offer.

But the new album was selling poorly, at 20,000 copies, half of what the debut had done, and everybody was losing hope. Even Dave Robinson and Jake Riviera were breaking up back at the Stiff offices, leaving The Damned with split loyalties re: both management and label affiliation.

With no label, new management and Moss recovered from a bad car accident, the band played a few shows and then busted up, with Brian pulling the plug after a gig on February the 14th that resulted in £2,500 in damages.

Recalls Brian, "When Rat left The Damned, in '77 and we had to get another drummer in, there was no one that inspired me like Rat had done, playing those songs. All of a sudden the energy level just dropped. Jon Moss was a good drummer and he went on to do other things but it just wasn't the same, which is like a large part of the reason I split the band up in early '78."

Eventually, after everybody spent time stumbling through various band situations, Captain and Rat found themselves writing songs together at Captain's parents' house, where he had been living with his Dutch girlfriend Cursty. "The band had broken up," explains Rat, "but me and Captain were still living quite close to each other, so we decided we were going to work together again and put a band together. When it came to singers, we couldn't really find anybody and we realised that it wasn't working. Then we thought, well, if we get Dave, we could put The Damned back together again. The whole thing with Brian, he's a great writer, but he's not really good with other people's material. And by this time we had started writing our own songs and Captain wanted to be the lead guitar player. Obviously it wouldn't have worked out between him and Brian, which is kind of how it was. So we went back to being The Damned and the rest is history."

The guys indeed brought Dave back into the fold and reformed first as The Doomed, thinking that Brian owned the name The Damned, although they liked the idea of starting as something fresh as well. Captain moved over to guitar and Lemmy from Motörhead sat in on bass for a legendary London show on September 5th 1978, after which he was replaced properly by Henry Badowski, who soon found himself bullied out of the band, primarily at the hands of a violent Rat Scabies.

Alasdair Mackie "Algy" Ward, a hellion equal to anyone in The Damned, was soon collared and the line-up that would make the next album was now complete. "He was a really good bass player," notes Rat, "In the world of bass players, there weren't many that were as fast and furious as he was, and he was good at it. He used to play in a band called The Saints. He also came from where Captain lived, which was Croydon, and so when we needed a bass player, Captain said, 'Listen, we want somebody who can really play good. So let's get this guy.'"

Signing with Chiswick, the band went into an eight-track studio in Croydon to write and demo tracks for the next record. Riding high off of the success of the first bit of product for the label, namely the "Love Song" single, the guys at Chiswick were generous with the booking, allowing the band to really develop the material in advance of the recording sessions proper, which began on May 21st at Sound Suite in Camden. More sessions followed at Workhouse Studios in Old Kent Road, London before being interrupted by tour dates. It wasn't until July 16th that the band returned to Sound Suite to continue working on the album, followed by final overdubs and mixing at Wessex in early August, where the Clash were recording *London Calling*.

The end result, *Machine Gun Etiquette*, issued November 2nd 1979, consistently tops polls as the greatest Damned album of all time. "That's true," agrees Dave. "We continued with Captain on guitar, because previously he was playing bass. Everybody thought that would be the death of the band, but then we came out with *Machine Gun Etiquette* and we became even bigger." And the title? Captain says we can thank Damned biographer Carol Clerk for that one, Clerk writing in a live review that the band "played their set with the etiquette of a machine gun."

With all the combustible energy of the debut, the songs nonetheless, underneath the mayhem, are sophisticated and varied. Everybody within the band—as well as Brian James looking in from the outside—were surprised at the newfound ability of the guys with respect to songwriting. Everybody pitched in and a record of gleeful, violent dimension ensued, the entertainment factor raised further from the amusing production appointments sprinkled track to track like punk pixie dust.

"There wasn't one," laughs Rat, asked about the production philosophy applied to the record. "It was whoever could shout loudest got turned up; it was a bit like that. You know, Roger Armstrong really did his best to try to hold the album together and keep us all in line, but everybody chipped in. You would comment, have your say, blah blah blah, and generally get ignored. And then the engineer would get on with it. But there was a lot of stuff I didn't see. Captain would be in there for hours overdubbing and tracking and comping and mixing guitars. But I really like the album. I think in some ways we were testing the waters, because we suddenly decided we weren't going to do another bunch of three-minute punk songs. We were going to do slower things with a bit more notes and minor chords and other unusual things. It was what we were listening to at that point, so that put us in a different direction."

"It was the aggression and the attitude," says Algy, asked what drew him to punk and The Damned. "I saw the Ramones in May '77 and that changed my life. That's what did it for me. Which might not have come out of a Yes or an Emerson, Lake & Palmer. Plus with that lot, it was the cost of getting to—and into—the gig (laughs)."

And even though he's soon be leading NWOBHMers Tank, like every good punk, he was anti-heavy metal. "Yes, when all that fucking load of bullshit was going about, I was in The Damned. Iron Maiden and Saxon and everything else... I had nothing to do with all that shit. You have to remember, I was in The Damned from '78 until January 1st 1980, and that's when Maiden and Tygers of Pan Tang and all that God-awful bullshit was going on. I wasn't interested in all that shit."

"But being in The Damned was worse than The Saints," continues Algy. "At that time, fame and fortune and glory were involved—and powders were rampant. As for the music, I was involved more with arranging than anything else. Captain wrote God knows how many songs, you know, just reams of the stuff. They didn't want me in the first place. Scabies had wanted Paul Gray, but he was on contract with Eddie and the Hot Rods. But it was fine; I wasn't a frustrated writer there at all. I was just doing the job. I had a lot of ideas of my own, but with them I just had to learn how to do Captain's ideas and get the songs down."

For his part, Captain tells the bizarre story about panicking over the idea of having to write so many songs and playing a bunch of his favourite TV ads backwards to look for chord sequences! Whatever the method, it worked out.

"Yeah, I think so," reflects Sensible. "*Machine Gun Etiquette* was more my album. *Damned Damned Damned* was more Brian's album. I like both of them, but there are a lot more melodies going on, on *Machine Gun Etiquette*. Don't tell anyone, but I'm a big Abba fan (laughs). I really like The Carpenters and things like that too. But then again I really like loud aggressive guitar music. There's a lot of Pete Townshend too, melodically, definitely. You can't knock The Who;

they broke down all the walls for me. Amazing. What a band. All those great melodies, all those feedback guitar solos and thrashing drums—yeah, fantastic. So this is where I'm coming from: if you marry the two sides—the melody and the amplifiers turned up as far as they can go, sort of to blitzkrieg level—you get The Damned."

****

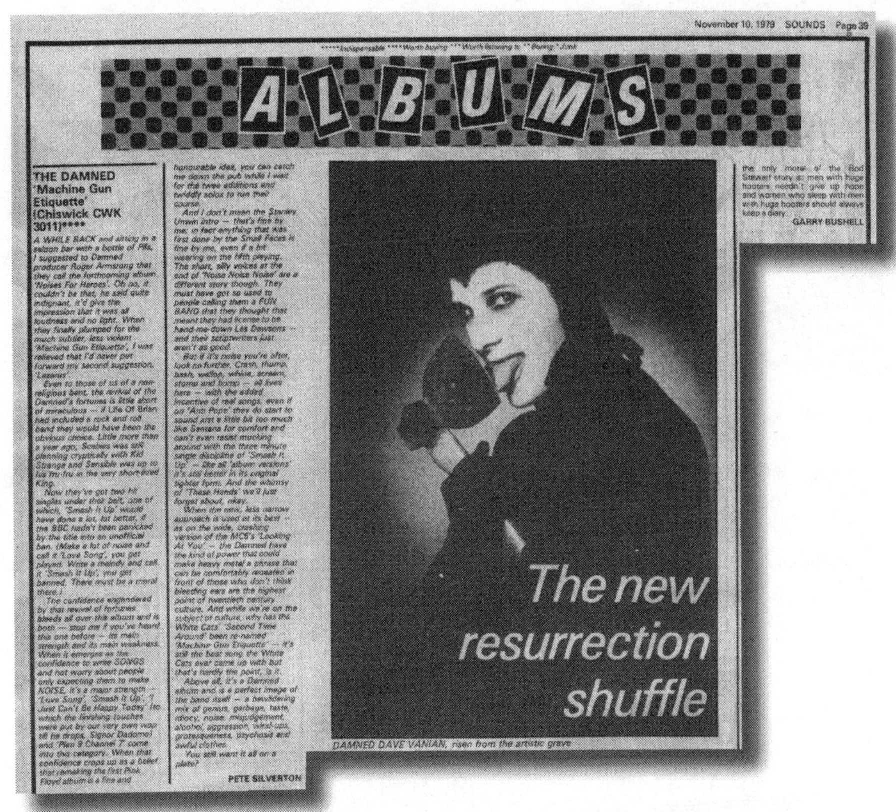

November 10, 1979 SOUNDS Page 39

*****Indispensable ****Worth buying ***Worth listening to **Boring *Junk

ALBUMS

the only moral of the Rod Stewart story is: men with huge hooters needn't give up hope and women who sleep with men with huge hooters should always keep a diary.

GARRY BUSHELL

THE DAMNED
'Machine Gun Etiquette'
(Chiswick CWK 3011)****

A WHILE BACK and sitting in a saloon bar with a bottle of Pils, I suggested to Damned producer Roger Armstrong that they call the forthcoming album 'Noises For Heroes'. Oh no, it couldn't be that, he said quite indignant, it'd give the impression that it was all loudness and no light. When they finally plumped for the much subtler, less violent 'Machine Gun Etiquette', I was relieved that I'd never put forward my second suggestion, 'Lazarus'.

Even to those of us of a non-religious bent, the revival of the Damned's fortunes is little short of miraculous — if Life Of Brian had included a rock and roll band they would have been the obvious choice. Little more than a year ago, Scabies was still planning cryptically with Kid Strange and Sensible was up to his fru-fru in the very short-lived King.

Now they've got two hit singles under their belt, one of which, 'Smash It Up' would have done a lot, lot better, if the BBC hadn't been panicked by the title into an unofficial ban. (Make a lot of noise and call it 'Love Song', you get played. Write a melody and call it 'Smash It Up', you get banned. There must be a moral there.)

The confidence engendered by that reversal of fortunes bleeds all over the album and is both — stop me if you've heard this one before — its main strength and its main weakness. When it emerges as the confidence to write SONGS and not worry about people only expecting them to make NOISE, it's a major strength — 'Love Song', 'Smash It Up', 'I Just Can't Be Happy Today' (to which the finishing touches were put by our very own wop till he drops, Signor Dadomo) and 'Plan 9 Channel 7' come into this category. When that confidence crops up as a belief that remaking the first Pink Floyd album is a fine and honourable idea, you can catch me down the pub while I wait for the twee additions and twiddly solos to run their course.

And I don't mean the Stanley Unwin intro — that's fine by me, in fact anything that was first done by the Small Faces is fine by me, even if a bit wearing on the fifth playing. The short, silly voices at the end of 'Noise Noise Noise' are a different story though. They must have got so used to people calling them a FUN BAND that they thought that meant they had license to be hand-me-down Les Dawsons — and their scriptwriters just aren't as good.

But if it's noise you're after, look no further. Crash, thump, bash, wallop, whine, scream, stomp and bomp — all lives here — with the added incentive of real songs, even if on 'Anti Pope' they do start to sound just a little bit too much like Santana for comfort and can't even resist mucking around with the three minute single discipline of 'Smash It Up' — like all 'album versions' it's still better in its original tighter form. And the whimsy of 'These Hands' we'll just forget about, okay.

When the new, less narrow approach is used at its best — as on the wide, crashing version of the MC5's 'Looking At You' — the Damned have the kind of power that could make heavy metal a phrase that can be comfortably repeated in front of those who don't think bleeding ears are the highest point of twentieth century culture. And while we're on the subject of culture, why has the White Cats' 'Second Time Around' been re-named 'Machine Gun Etiquette' — it's still the best song the White Cats ever came up with but that's hardly the point, is it.

Above all, it's a Damned album and is a perfect image of the band itself — a bewildering mix of genius, garbage, taste, idiocy, noise, misjudgement, alcohol, aggression, wind-ups, grotesqueness, psychosis and awful clothes.

You still want it all on a plate?

PETE SILVERTON

The new resurrection shuffle

DAMNED DAVE VANIAN, risen from the artistic grave

REPENT!
DAVE
THE DAMNED are back!
LOVE SONG · SUICIDE · NOISE NOISE NOISE
Available in 4 full-colour pic bags!
April 20th
Chiswick
CHIS 112
EMI

Side 1

Love Song
(Scabies/Sensible/Vanian/Ward) 2:21

This most improbable of punk hits late for dinner in 1979 began its recorded life as part of the *Dodgy Demo*, recorded at RMS Recording in December of '78 in order to have something with which to chase a record deal. New, it had a white sticker with black ink affixed to a plain white label. Used, by necessity, there had to be a hole punched through the sticker. During the sessions, recorded were future album tracks "Liar," "Melody Lee" and "Love Song" along with "Let There Be Rats," "Burglar" and storming non-LP gem "Don't Trouble Trouble," never to be released in any form.

"Love Song" and "Burglar" would be picked as the cream of the crop for the self-issued single, which was given away, autographed, at the final show of 1978—December 23rd at the Electric Ballroom, plus at the Croydon show into January, with the rest of the 1000-run being sold mail order. That version is arguably the tightest and most conservative that exists (note those vocal harmonies in the chorus), whilst the B-side take of "Burglar" is hilarious in its quaintness versus the roustabout classic that would become widely available.

Later in the month, December 20th, the band recorded the song once again for a John Peel session, Bob Sergeant producing. But things really heat up with the Chiswick single version, produced by Eddie and the Hot Rods manager Ed Hollis, now deceased. "Love Song" would be issued as the band's first spot of product for Chiswick on April 10th 1979, backed with "Noise, Noise, Noise" and "Suicide." There would be four different sleeves produced for the single, one each featuring a member of the band on the front, a ploy that boosted sales.

Which brings us to *Machine Gun Etiquette*. Moving over to the album proper, this quintessential of English punk albums opens suitably-nay-perfectly with a "Ladies and gentlemen, 'ow do?" from the fictional Albert Tatlock of *Coronation Street* fame, played by John Howarth—the recording is from a 1971 album by Howarth in fact called *'ow do*.

Producer of the album to arrive in a month's time, Roger Armstrong, was not happy with Dave's vocal and had decided to re-record him, at Chalk Farm.

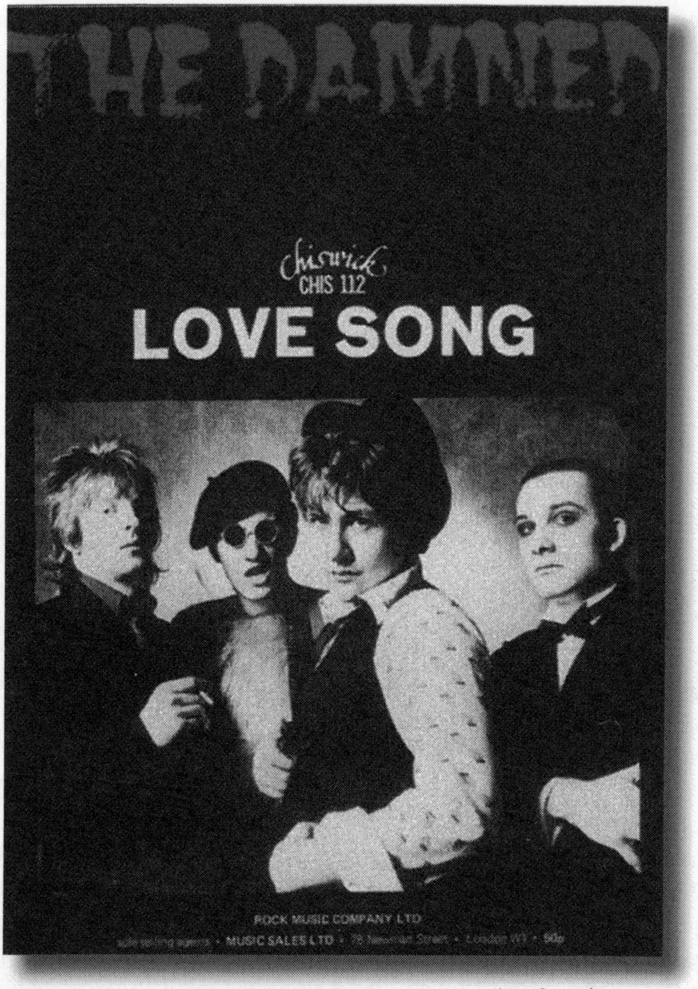

Love Song sheet music

Love Song drinks coaster

As well, restored for the album version from the original recording session (which had been cut for the single release), was the languid opening jam. We get Dave's anguished screams over said textured jam, followed by a "Hey man, what's happening?" and a fierce Algy Ward bass line, clacky, hard to record, says Roger, because Algy insisted on playing loud.

Rat's tight and almost clipped snare carried forward from the last album takes us into what is a carouser of a punk anthem, out of place in late 1979 but welcome by a thirsty old school clinging to the UK Subs' recent *Another Kind of Blues* album representing the last vestige of punk proper as everyone else goes artsy.

"Love Song" is just that, written by Captain Sensible at the music end as well as lyrically at the chorus. Stuck for words, he turned the show over to Rat, who couched the concept in the language of Captain's erstwhile hobby, namely rail systems around the world. Indeed once after interviewing Raymond in person one afternoon many years ago, the author was then peppered with questions about Toronto's subway grid, which Captain had indicated he would be riding and studying until show time.

"Love Song" went to No.20 on the charts which meant, according to the band's contract with Chiswick, that they could now make an album, which—thank God for punk—The Damned did.

Why was this song so instantly beloved at the time? First there's the title, "Love Song" and then there's the sublime sentiment that "It makes me glad to say it's been a lovely day and it's okay."

Q: What could be more punk than that?

A: The next song on the album.

Machine Gun Etiquette (Scabies/Sensible/Vanian/Ward) 1:48

Next on the docket is more unexpected flamethrower rock, unexpected after *Music for Pleasure* and a hiatus for the period, now that music had moved on from 1976 and 1977. "Machine Gun Etiquette" was essentially done like dinner already with Rat's last band, the White Cats, who had recorded a well-appointed John Peel session version of the song in April '79, calling it "Second Time Around," a title that half stuck (it was also known as "Rock and Roll Part 3"). As a composition, it's pretty much cast in stone at that juncture, played a little slower perhaps, and also including an annoying crowd participation bit.

But put in the hands of this most unruly and intractable of Damned line-ups, the song takes on another life. Is it my imagination or is The Damned now more off-the-handle and white-of-knuckle than they were on the debut a lifetime ago? As well, is anybody hearing Cheap Trick's "Elo Kiddies" in this bass line over tribal pounding?

Lyrically the song is a bunch of spewed venom, although hardly a bunch, closer to a fortune cookie's worth. Dave's vocal is double-tracked, with the second vocal processed through a speaker stuck in the bathroom at Wessex. But

It's come to our

ATTENTION

that this amazing piece of

MUSIC

would make a great gift for

LOVERS

everywhere.

THE DAMNED

New Single

I Just Can't Be Happy today

+ Ballroom Blitz

Turkey Song

chiswick

CHIS 120

it's a refreshingly punk singing arrangement with the operative being "second time around," as if The Damned are promising to busy themselves bringing back original punk at least two years after it was declared dead (by The Clash signing to CBS, of course).

Speaking of The Clash, it sounds like the hatchet was buried deep enough to have Paul Simonon and Joe Strummer in from the other studio to provide handclaps. Algy confirms that some of the guitars on the song are courtesy of his usually bass-playing self, although there are so many layers of Captain across the record it's hard to keep count. The racket reaches a fever pitch at the one-minute mark, augmented by Rat revving the engine of his motorbike, which he would park right in the studio. As he did his part, says Roger Armstrong, he peeled out of the place not to be seen for hours.

At 1:49, "Machine Gun Etiquette" is the shortest song on the album, amusing in itself for a title track. But really, this dustbin din of a anarcho-punk conflagration serves as exhibit No.1 that The Damned are back, no apologies, and most pointedly, no particular cognisance of the environment into which the band has thrown one of their management-enraging hotel Molotovs.

I Just Can't Be Happy Today (Scabies/Sensible/Vanian/Ward/Dadomo) 3:42

Priming us for the carousel pop of "Smash It Up," "I Just Can't Be Happy Today" similarly lives upon a stark and stabbing pop keyboard line, effective but daring any hardened punk to pull out his own shiv. But the chorus is dark—dark of lyric and of ascending doom chord sequence—as is the story of dystopian oppression, full-on dictatorship really, with religion even barbarously put down.

Aiding in the writing of the lyrics was *Sounds* rock journo Giovani Dadomo, cajoled in to bail the band out, and the collaboration is a good one, maintaining The Damned characteristic of very few words proffered but with Dadomo making them count.

As for the music, well, "I Just Can't Be Happy Today" is gothic and ponderous enough to overcome its pop appointments, presaging the marriage of punk and psychedelic rock we'd hear writ large on the ensuing Paul Gray albums and later with Monty Oxymoron.

Of note, the guys had decided to use the backing tracks from the eight-track writing and demo sessions conducted at RMS in Croydon. Any variance from the newer productions surrounding it is virtually undetectable—all told, this is a record with a gauzy, throbbing bottom end (that's the Captain on bass on this one though), with Rat's drums recorded wet and somewhat buried in the mix for maximum claustrophobic effect.

Dave has told the story about 10cc leaving behind their Mellotron, with the guys discovering the vocal tapes (the Mellotron worked with tapes) for their groundbreaking vocal showcase "I'm Not in Love" on the machine. Vanian said this became the inspiration for the vocal arrangement on "I Just Can't Be Happy Today." Exhibiting further willingness to stretch out and embrace more of their '70s rock roots, there's a break section comprised of three parts. First there's Dave with bullhorn warning of all hell breaking loose. Second, all hell breaks loose. Third, there's a sense of hope, as a happy slow-motion keyboard solo meanders through the song's mid-riff.

This is a lift from Captain's short-lived King band and their track "My Baby Don't Care," which was recorded as part of a John Peel session on July 20th 1978. King had three ex-Damned members in it, Captain, Dave Berk and Henry Badowski, and on bass was Kym Bradshaw, the guy Algy Ward replaced in The Saints.

"I Just Can't Be Happy Today" was issued as a single concurrent with the launch of the album, backed with "Ballroom Blitz" and "Turkey Song." It reached No.46 on the charts, and along with "Smash It Up" was part of the infamous *Old Grey Whistle Test* session where Captain struggles with his keyboards, Dave reads a book, Algy invents NWOBHM fashion and, well before the song's natural conclusion, Rat smashes it up.

The single issue of the song is 45 seconds shorter than the LP version. There are two changes, actually. After "Smash It Up" got some stick from the BBC and in the press about the violent lyrics, Chiswick's radio programmer Clive Banks got producer Roger Armstrong to tone down the somewhat blasphemous—and actually quite creepy—break at the one-minute mark, Dave singing an entirely new set of lyrics. Roger also clips out a bit of the following instrumental section before things go back to normal.

Melody Lee
(Scabies/Sensible/Vanian/Ward) 2:07

If the December 20th 1978 Peel session is to be taken seriously (along with the original studio recordings from May 16th '79), "Melody Lee" began life with an unrelated chugging heavy metal intro from Captain, rather than the elegant grand piano piece we hear on the album, played on the Bechstein in the studio and taking up nearly a quarter of the final version. The rest of the song arrived pretty much as trundled through for John Peel, albeit a shade slower and quite a bit groovier.

For lyrics, Captain's claim that he lifted them directly from the speech bubbles from a *Bunty's* comic book series about a dancer character called Melody Lee are exaggerated. However the song serves as a touching albeit very brief summary of the "Melody Lee – A Dancer She'll Be" storyline that ran at the time, from the 37 issues spanning October '77 through to June '78.

Captain's melancholy melody fits perfectly the tale of this orphan girl yearning to fulfil her dream, but despite the song's two-minute duration, there are other flashy features, including a breakout heavy metal riff (not the replaced intro lick), an octave-jumping bass line from Algy, and then at 1:16, a glorious triplet-based hard rock sequence with scraping guitars. After this, as if there's no time to lose, Dave yells "Go!" and the band accelerate, raving mad, while Captain executes a shreddy axe attack that lasts all of nine seconds, inside of which he manages to evoke the legacies of both Chuck Berry and Brian James.

After a fancy wind-up to end the song, where Rat rolls around his toms dramatically like a prog rock percussion god, Dave can be heard yelling an accusatory "I saw ya!" This is a nod to The Who's "Happy Jack," where Pete Townshend can be heard saying that after the song's done, directed at Keith who had tried to sneak in on a vocal session he'd been banned from because of his tendency to make everyone laugh and blow the take.

Anti-Pope
(Scabies/Sensible/Vanian/Ward/Burns) 3:19

Captain Sensible's band King only lasted the summer of '78, but the situation coughed up this essentially fully formed future Damned classic, making the official song credit spurious (note: the extra Burns there is Captain's brother Phil), or at least generous, presumably Captain sharing a song he wrote completely (or that he mostly wrote) with his new band mates. I say new, but what's new is old again—in fact The Damned can claim another punk first, namely first punk band in recorded history to reform!

Here's one where the lyric far exceeds the ambitions of the music, which is a little one-dimensional, based on a repetitive riff and rhythm pattern a little too close to the MC5's "Looking at You," covered later on the album. But there are lots of words and they all pack a punch, Captain turning in a thoughtful critique of religion, couched in sophisticated phrasings, mouthfuls of words deftly placed, causing the type of linguistic gymnastics lead singers dread. Proving the lasting power of Captain's screed, American indie rockers Spoon lifted a couple lines from the song for a track called "Jonathan Fisk" on their 2002 album, *Kill the Moonlight*.

Breaking up the straight-line critical mass of "Anti-Pope" is a long, not entirely successful psychedelic jam (including bass solo by Captain), again recalling MC5 but also "Whole Lotta Love." There's added percussion—picture Ian Gillan and his accursed congas—with Sensible, Ward and the session's engineer Mike Shipley tucking into a box of percussion goodies brought in by The Clash who had been using them on *London Calling*, which was also being worked on at Wessex.

Other than the shakers and stuff, the guys stick to their pudding, which wasn't the case on an earlier proposed version, where instead we heard a cacophony of Fripp-loopy Krautrock strings performed by Aleksander Koklowski, now a renowned avant garde musician who has pioneered the use of old Gramophones and other innovative hybrid techniques using antique technology into his classical music works. Soon we're back into another verse and it's a new one rather than a repeat, again, distinguishing this song with respect to its scope, about the day Captain became anti-Pope.

These Hands
(Scabies/Sensible/Vanian/Ward) 2:02

Chalk this spot of soundtrack-like Victorian psycho-killer music up to the man who looks the part, Dave coming in with lyrics and the skeleton of a music idea, which he then hummed and sang to Captain, who transferred Vanian's brief onto musical instruments. The heavily produced track is set to three-over-four waltz time, and features at the start the previously discussed Aleks Koklowski on violin.

The line "These are the hands of a demented circus clown" is a Marty Feldman reference, but also refers to an ongoing band joke about musicians protecting their maestro hands. At the conclusion of what is exactly that, "demented circus clown" music (seemingly stuck like an old record player), Dave laughs politely but then becomes increasingly unhinged, before one of his multiple personalities' yells, "Stop laughing!" Heard next are the hurried high-heeled footsteps of a woman (Dave's very proto-Goth wife Laurie, recorded outside in the Wessex parking lot) followed by her gasping in fright and Dave, close of mic, once more laughing.

As with "I Just Can't Be Happy Today," the band were pleased enough with the version of "These Hands" recorded on eight-track during the RMS writing and demo sessions, bumping the backing tracks to 24-track later and adding overdubs and final mix.

DAMNED DOGS

THE DAMNED and SLAUGHTER AND THE DOGS will be playing a joint British tour next month. Dates are now being finalised but the two bands will share equal billing and will be supported by Victim.

Slaughter And The Dogs, who will have a new single called 'You're Ready Now' (the old Frankie Valli number), also have dates of their own this month at West Runton Pavilion October 12, Liverpool Erics 13, Manchester Factory 19, Nottingham Sandpipers 25, Sheffield Limit 26.

Side 2

Plan 9 Channel 7
(Scabies/Sensible/Vanian/Ward) 5:08

Somewhat of a thing with this band, "Plan 9 Channel 7" (provisionally titled "Creatures Theme") uses a few choice words, and then those words are repeated to prompt a second pondering, as a sort of bold brushstroke on a canvas that would need so many more dabs of colour to reveal the full portrait. The song is inspired by a friendship that might have been more, between James Dean and Maila "Vampira" Nurmi, the original female Goth icon, host of a horror series called *The Vampire Show*, in California (aired on Channel 7) but also star of Ed Wood cult classic, *Plan 9 from Outer Space*. Think Morticia Addams from *The Addams Family*, Cruella de Vil from *One Hundred and One Dalmatians* and Elvira, Mistress of the Dark and you get the drift. You could add Dave's wife Laurie to that list as well, underscored by the fact that the lyrics were mostly hers.

As the story goes, Vampira was spurned by Dean, who soon after died in a car crash, with rumours going 'round that Dean's "Black Madonna" had predicted and then caused his death through the application of a curse at her very own black magic altar, with a voodoo doll of Dean to make doubly and devilishly sure. Most of what The Damned say on the subject concerns Vampira's reflections on the doomed relationship after Dean's death, but the best line is from before that, namely "Two hearts that beat as one, and eyes that hardly ever saw the sun."

At the music end, "Plan 9 Channel 7" was instigated by Dave on a three-string guitar given to him by Rat—he's also said it had two strings, and that it was broken. The song feels part of a trilogy with "Love Song" and "I Just Can't Be Happy Today," the three sounding like the work of world-weary old souls, each dour of melody yet uptempo, a little post-punk like *Eternally Yours* (Algy's album with The Saints), if not exactly Magazine, The Cure or Joy Division.

As for features of the track, Captain gets to indulge his new predilection for keyboard drones while Dave performs in a sort of round with himself, later yelping in falsetto. To close out the song, Captain builds upon all the licks that have come before, embarking on a long bluesy guitar solo excursion, somewhat buried in a mix dominated by wallowing, non-articulated bass from Algy and drums from Rat that are drenched in reverb.

The totality of the experience is a song considered the masterwerk of the album, given its mournful yet thoughtful melody lines, the gravitas of the storyline and its sustain drama over a full five minutes, which is an eternity for The Damned—to be sure, there are a couple other songs that long on *Machine Gun Etiquette* but both dish a lot of typical Damned nonsense to fill the docket.

Noise, Noise, Noise
(Scabies/Sensible/Vanian/Ward/Scabies) 3:09

Like "Love Song," "Noise, Noise, Noise" also exists in an earlier version, produced by Ed Hollis, given its presence along with "Suicide" as a "Love Song" B-side. Comparatively, Dave's vocals on the album version are less aggressive and raw, plus, with top end clipped from them, more integrated into the thick sound soup that pervades and unifies the songs on the album.

"Noise, Noise, Noise" began life as a song written by Rat and his girlfriend Jennet Ward (credited on the original vinyl as the second Scabies) called "Boiler Song." Lyrics and music support each other in a symbiotic relationship like that of the penners: the protagonist in the song is yer basic goofball punk who takes every opportunity he can to play music loud, at home with mum and dad at 7AM, at the pub at 1PM and then at 8PM during his gig at the church hall. Dogs, cats, drunken fools and vicars try get in the way, but noise is for heroes.

In fact Rat had been known to philosophise about the value of noise as it pertains to Damned records, "getting the noises just right" as it were, whether that be the right amount of grime smudged into the production or hitting enough drums as part of the desire to be heard above and beyond everybody else in the band, who Scabies saw good-naturedly as competitors on any given song.

The soundtrack to this day in the life is a happy racket of swooping, bar-straddling drum rolls, exaggerated punctuating wind-ups and holler-along gang vocals, courtesy of Joe Strummer, Paul Simonon and ex-Damned plunker of the fat strings Henry Badowski. There's a brief break, ended by maniacal laughter, plus a suitably headache-inducing guitar solo, but then not much else that justifies taking this thing to over three minutes, save perhaps for the admirable structure lyrically and the comedic "Isn't it nice in here?" closing bit.

Looking at You
(Kramer/Smith/Tyner/Davis/Thompson) 5:07

The Damned's decision to cover MC5's "Looking at You" goes back at least as far as the BBC session the guys conducted on December 20th, 1978. The arrangement that day included keyboards, which was a first for the band, with keys becoming pervasive moving forward.

"Looking at You" fits the script for a cover, given the appreciation for MC5 amongst the band members, the idea that MC5 are an important proto-punk band and that the other proto-punk band, The Stooges, got taken care of on the first album. As well, it's got the tempo and it's squarely punk-worthy across its octave-jumping two-chord structure and it's from the MC5 album (the middle one) that seems most akin to The Damned's garage rock way of thinking at this time. The guys even got to tell Wayne Kramer that they were doing the song. On the interim US tour, after checking into their hotel in New York City, the band trundled off to the Hurrah at 36 West 62nd and lo and behold, the ex-con MC5 guitarist was playing a solo set. Kramer was pleased to hear about the cover but told the guys to make sure he got his royalty cheque for it.

The original version of the song from 1970's *Back in the USA* feels long at three minutes. On the current rendition, recorded on May 25th at the Workhouse, The Damned stretch it to fully five minutes with a ton of guitar soloing marbled throughout, plus a brain-numbing quiet section and then finally a noisy squall of a collapse held tenuously by retro keyboard drones.

At five minutes, it gets boring fast to be sure, but it's not a complete snooze of a song, given how the counterintuitive and conversational vocal melody and attendant phrasing pick up the slack from the chord structure, first with Rob Tyner and now with Dave, who does an energetic and thespian job with this actually quite touching lyric about love at first sight.

Liar
(Scabies/Sensible/Vanian/Ward) 2:43

The most cheerfully punk proposition across the album, "Liar" is mostly Algy Ward's whopper, with the future Tank leader playing the bass and the rhythm guitars and even peeling off the guitar solo. There's heavier pure punk on the album ("Machine Gun Etiquette") and more thoughtful chord changes upon fast punk ("Love Song"), but arguably, "Liar" is the most accessibly melodic without leaning pop, making it feel somewhat heavy metal as it were.

And it helps that the lyric is an amusing one, with Dave unapologetically laying out his rogue credentials, warning the listener not to trust anything he says. Despite the action swiftly splashing the sides like sloshing water in a leaky rowboat, the guys manage a break section of completely different music, announced by a solo Rat doing his best Sandy Nelson impression. This leads into Algy's guitar break, punctuated by Dave doing some falsetto yelping. Then we're into another verse (with a Hitler name-check), followed by another round at the blazing chorus where The Damned invent Oi! with big "liar, liar!" gang vocals that overtake the musical chaos, both put into a fade, but the music first.

October 13, 1979 SOUNDS Page 29
THE DAMNED
Smash it up
OUT THIS FRIDAY
B-SIDE BURGLAR
EMI
CHISWICK RECORDS - CHIS 116

Smash It Up
(Scabies/Sensible/Vanian/Ward) 5:11

I've been known to go on and on why people weren't more up in arms about The Cult *Electric* or the *Sabbath Bloody Sabbath* album cover. Well, back in 1980, me an' my buddies were also scratching our heads why more people weren't complaining about Judas Priest's "Living After Midnight" and a few months earlier, The Damned's "Smash It Up."

Shamelessly silly and pop, "Smash It Up" was actually just liked a lot, getting to No.35 on the UK charts (backed with "Burglar") before the BBC boycotted it because of the lyrics. Which were more nihilistic than anarchic, given how softened they sounded on top of the US new wave of the musical back track. What's more, the song quickly became the big deal at any given live show, with the message being sent that if we gave you a bunch of seriously well-crafted songs of levity earlier in the night, don't think we meant it, because we're just a bunch of goofballs.

If you've noticed, I've taken a stand and just called this damn thing "Smash It Up." The back cover of the original vinyl says there's a "Smash It Up (Part 1)" and a "Smash It Up." The actual record label just says, "Smash It Up." Consistently, the single issue of the song has "Smash It Up" emblazoned on the cover and indeed delivers the 2:53 known as such. In later years, the formal title has been somewhat standardised as "Smash It Up (Parts 1 & 2)" or some messy variation thereof.

Sonically, on *Machine Gun Etiquette*, there are indeed two sections, with the first being an elegant and sophisticated piece of instrumental kicked off by Rat and finished by Captain in tribute to Marc Bolan, killed in a car crash September 16th 1977. Captain recalls sitting in his back garden at home, with his dad poking his head out the back door to deliver the news. The entire band went to the funeral.

As for the song proper, the music was composed by Captain and his brother Phil at home, with some punk friends of theirs (Roger, Peter and Gent from the Croydon Punks Ltd.), coming up with the "smash it up" chorus bit. Captain claims a Groundhogs influence on the song, both in terms of the angst-ridden lyrics and the interesting chord fingerings and changes. Rat plays an uptight four-on-the-floor over which the band get silly to an incessant Farfisa organ-type key line (all the bass on this song is by Captain—Algy simply wasn't around, nor did he like the song).

The lyrics ain't much, nor are the vocal melodies and the music is even less compelling, with the only points of interest being the dropped beat and some guitar licks from Captain. Even the break at 3:16 seems ill-fitting, of no consequence, announced by an uninspired tom roll from Rat (contrast with "Liar").

There are a few failed attempts at making the song sound epic by modulating up. The brief "Glastonbury hippies" bit was a lift from the Small Faces "I Feel Much Better," and once the band comes out of this thin and noisy bit, there are two chords played on The Clash's grand piano stuck in here—and only here—to try thicken the sound.

They aren't mixed in too loudly, so one supposes the effect is achieved, without causing distraction. After another round of the song's hyper, itchy uptempo verse structure and chorus, the guys let the air out of the balloon with a deflating and also grating "Auld Lang Syne" section where apparently "everybody's smashing things down" even if it sounds like everything's already been smashed.

The best part of the song—to these ears anyway, and I know, "Smash It Up" is one of the band's most loved songs, unfathomably—is the closing repeated line "Nibbled to death by an okapi." Rat says that he used to come up with trivia to keep the band amused, and they'd have to figure out if he was lying or not. One such nugget involved the sort of modified zebra known as the okapi, and the guys loved the word so much, they vowed to use it. Whether this was synchronistic or the true story, producer Roger Armstrong says that Algy's brother, who roadied for the band, had been in the studio taping *The Hitchhiker's Guide to the Galaxy* off the radio right when Roger had walked in and heard that line. Then there's Captain's furry suit, which was referred to by the band as his okapi suit.

In fact the band had offered the label fully four different smashed-up parts to this song, but only two made the record. The whole thing can be heard on the CD single version of "Smash It Up," issued in 2004, with the first previously unreleased section being a mid-tempo slice of instrumental pop, a bit surf and bluesy, like the Shadows, notes Captain.

For the last bit, we get a change of key and a tough four-on-the-floor beat from Rat, with Captain playing more of the clean and twangy surf lines heard on the other bit. Again, all of the unused material, like "Smash It Up (Part 1)," is instrumental. Missing on the official intro is any of the loungy soloing, put aside for tuneful yet suitably mournful chords, both individually plucked by string and politely strummed.

THE DAMNED
ON TOUR
November
22 LEICESTER DE MONTFORT HALL
23 CAMBRIDGE CORN EXCHANGE
24 PETERBOROUGH WIRRINA STADIUM
25 CARDIFF TOP RANK
26 SHEFFIELD TOP RANK
28 BRIGHTON TOP RANK
30 LONDON RAINBOW
December
4 GLASGOW APPOLLO
5 BRADFORD ST GEORGES HALL
7 COVENTRY NEW THEATRE
9 WOLVERHAMPTON CIVIC HALL
10 MANCHESTER APPOLLO
11 BRISTOL COLSTON HALL
15 HULL CITY HALL
I Just Can't Be Happy Today
+
Ballroom Blitz Turkey Song
Chiswick
CHIS 120
Smash it up
Rainbow OUTLAW CONCERTS PRESENT
THE DAMNED
+VICTIMS
FRIDAY 30th NOVEMBER 7·30pm
TICKETS £3·00, £2·50, £2·00
FROM BOX OFFICE, LONDON THEATRE BOOKINGS,
PREMIER BOX OFFICE, TICKET MACHINE.

November 10, 1979 SOUNDS Page 23
DAMNED CHEAP
363 Oxford Street, London W.1. (next to Bond Street tube)
Bedford
Birmingham
Bradford
Brighton
Bristol
Coventry
Derby
Edinburgh
Enfield
Exeter
Glasgow
Gloucester
Gravesend
Holloway
Hull
Kingston
Leeds
Leicester
Lewisham
Liverpool
Luton
Manchester
Newcastle
Nottingham
Notting Hill Gate
Plymouth
Portsmouth
Southampton
Stockton
Stratford
Sunderland
Sutton
Swansea
Wolverhampton
NOW OPEN IN NORWICH at Top Shop/ Top Man.
THE DAMNED
Machine Gun Etiquette
the HMV shop
'Machine Gun Etiquette' the new album from The Damned, released this week, is
£1·50 off
list price at all HMV Shops, now.
And at the HMV Shop every week:
The HMV Shop Top Albums up to £2.00 off list price.
The HMV Shop Top Cassettes at 70p off list price.
The HMV Shop Top Singles only 90p.
New Release: Marianne Faithfull's album 'Broken English' is out now.
And it's £1.50 off list price at the HMV shop now.
We sell what others fear to sell!

Singles, B-sides, Bonus Tracks

Suicide (Scabies/Sensible/Vanian/Ward) 3:15

I swear, half the reason I wanted to write this book was to celebrate all the Damned B-sides which, by nature, tend to get lost in the cracks. Fortunately with this band, the reissues were done right and there have always been compilations, so these songs are not particularly lost. But yes, folks always exaggerate when championing some band's B-sides as better than most of the songs on the album, but with The Damned, that's occasionally, periodically through time, true.

Witness the Brian James-styled "Suicide," issued along with album track "Noise, Noise, Noise" as the B-side to "Love Song," stuck out by Chiswick on April 10th 1979, fully seven months before we got *Machine Gun Etiquette*. Busted open by four flammed snare cracks from Rat, the song marauds into view, after which Dave takes over, high and exacting in the mix, plotting out his impending self-imposed doom. We then get a nicely integrated pre-chorus after which the band then lurch to a stop. Rat is left alone to count in the chorus by knocking his sticks together and then we're into what sounds like Dave and his death throes.

When he promises that "I'm going to kill myself because of you," we're sent back to the Iggy Pop croon of songs like "Born to Kill," with Iggy conjured again at the improvisational yelping during the quiet guitar solo break. Three times the charm, with the "L.A. Blues" triumphing in the end as our depressed protagonist makes good on his promise over a closing twenty seconds of terror, the last portion set on repeat like a stuck record.

Burglar (Vanian/Ward/Scabies/Sensible) 3:33

"Burglar," recorded in May and July '79, first showed up at the back door of the "Love Song" *Dodgy Demo*, where most of the bits and pieces had already been put into place, although not to the breathless vaudeville standard we get here on the backside of the "Smash It Up" single.

We got to hear this top-shelf B-side on October 5th 1979, a month before *Machine Gun Etiquette* came out, at which time we found out it wouldn't be on the album. Sacrilege I say, because to these ears, "Burglar" is up there with "Love Song," "Plan 9 Channel 7" and "Liar," and actually a conceptual partner in crime to "Liar," with the same sort of gleeful bad-to-the-funny-bone lyrics.

Besides bashing the song to death with a sack full of oranges (and toms instead of high-hat), Rat sings this one, sounding like a loveable rogue as he peels of comedic lines about the lengths he'll go to enrich himself. And just in case there's any doubts, there a part recorded backward, which right way around says, "Yes, I'm a real villain."

At the music end, the song begins with siren sounds and an unruly punk burp and into the mosh pit we go. This one's practically Oi!, but then there's the melodic guitar lines that reminds one of U2 or The Cult, rougher by a mile, but still sort of textural and sublime and very post-punk over the racket. Back comes the Oi! (or at least Sham 69) with the pubby "Burglary is the life for me!" refrain and jars clink after a job well done.

Fully the last minute finds our protagonist back at work, the action picking up until all best laid plans fall apart. There's the voice of God, the sirens are back and then Rat, presumably in his iconic powder-blue suit, is handcuffed as he confesses. All of a sudden we hear the pinched-nose voice of a judge (Is he trying to avoid the smell?) sentencing Rat to six months and ordering him gone from his sight. At the close it's just sirens and a dog barking and finally just the dog, as if Rat is sitting in jail mulling over his last few seconds of freedom before getting nicked.

Ballroom Blitz
(Chinn/Chapman) 3:27

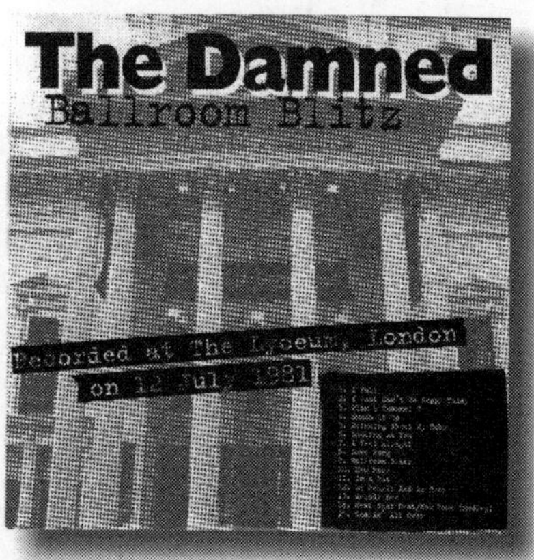

This cover of Sweet's smash 1973 hit "Ballroom Blitz" was supposed to constitute The Damned's contribution to a split single with Motörhead under the title *Motördamn*, with Lemmy, Fast Eddie and Philthy Phil bringing "Over the Top," one of their own. Taking place on one day, May 14th '79 at the Workhouse, both bands were supposed to play ensemble on both tracks. "Over the Top" got run through once before the sessions became a shambles, with everybody drunk and Eddie and Phil getting it on with some girl on the pool table, between trips to the grocery store for more booze.

The guys managed to get "Ballroom Blitz" done, mainly because Lemmy insisted on carrying it through, on top of the fact that Dave swanned in late and was the only sober party, so that key piece went without a hitch.

But it's not to plan, being essentially The Damned minus Algy plus Lemmy, who plays the bass, including a perfunctory bass solo, plus apparently some backing vocals—if he or anybody does any backing vocals, they are mixed so far back as to be essentially inaudible. Dave sings fine, but he's chosen to duck the notes, making for more of a spoken vocal melody, while Captain does a fine job of the manic Steve Priest vocal parts.

One nice touch is Rat's sort of combination drum figure. As the story was told to me by Andy Scott, the Sweet guys ran into The Damned in a line-up somewhere. Rat went up to Mick Tucker and played "Ballroom Blitz" for him on his thighs. Mick goes, "That's not how you play it," to which Rat replied, "That's how I do it, mate." In fact, Rat mixes it up—punks it up in fact—rarely playing it like Mick but not repeating himself much either. But it's Lemmy that dominates the mix, with Roger Armstrong recording him much the way he did Algy on the album, tough of tone with just a touch of fry.

The Motörhead song didn't come out until a low-key archival vinyl compilation in 1988, but The Damned made use of it, sticking it on the back of the "I Just Can't Be Happy Today" single along with "Turkey Song."

Turkey Song
(Vanian/Ward/Sensible) 1:32

Used as an unlisted B-side to "I Just Can't Be Happy Today" along with "Ballroom Blitz," "Turkey Song" is a brief bit of children's music, really, namely a children's lyric on top of the type of bluegrass/country music one can picture as a back track to a children's song.

The entire thing is about a turkey in the house and a rhino in the room, both of which need to be shooed outside. Captain provides the lead vocal, double tracked and harmonised, plus he plays mandolin and near-constant electric guitar soloing in a country western style. Singing this low, he sounds like Dave.

At the rhythm end is a suitable country music octave-jumping bass part and Rat doing a four/four on bass drum accompanied by tap-tap-taps on the rim of one of his drums. The mandolin was always around at Wessex when the band were recording, resulting one day in a folk rendition of "New Rose" with Joe Strummer singing. Captain was always looking for a way to get mandolin onto the album, but Roger wouldn't allow it.

White Rabbit
(Slick) 5:13

The plan was for The Damned's cover of Jefferson Airplane's "White Rabbit" to be their next single. Algy was sacked at the end of 1979, but the demoing of "White Rabbit" began as early as January of 1980 at RMS without a bassist, along with what would become both its B-sides. Once Paul Gray was on board as the band's new bassist, sessions were booked at Wessex in April to get the song done properly. Once mixing was taken care of, May 6th at Maison Rouge, Chiswick got as far as a test pressing (dated May 15th 1980) before the band decided they didn't like the version, with Dave in particular not happy with his vocals, having to sing the song in a key unnaturally high for him, particularly once the multiple modulations kicked in.

As for his backing track, the guys had radically overhauled the song, eschewing the military beat of the original for a busy and groovy drums-and-bass workout, not much guitar anywhere, Gray high in the mix (mixed exactly like Algy, really), driving, diving, driving. At the close however, Captain rips off an articulated lead, weirdly placed but welcome all the same.

Chiswick issued the single on June 2nd 1980 against the band's wishes, most popularly in France through an arrangement with EMI, but also in Germany on Metronome. Of course it got imported and talked about back home, with the band playing down the song in the press.

Come 1983, with The Damned no longer on the label, the single was reissued domestically on the associated Big Beat imprint, with the band's previous three-year anniversary slogan updated to read "Five Years of Anarchy, Chaos & Destruction." The 12" included "Curtain Call" as the B-side, and for the 7", the original "Rabid (Over You)" and "Seagulls."

Seagulls
(Scabies/Sensible/Vanian) 2:36

"Seagulls," recorded at Wessex in February 1980, points to the prog and psych future of The Damned as it would exist in the Paul Gray era, given that essentially this is a Gray showcase, with a little bit of supporting Captain guitar. Although during the disconnected outro I hear a little soft bass drum—it's not even an outro; rather it's a new instrumental and not even that, more like some noisy noodling. But the first two minutes is like "Smash It Up (Part 1)" without drums, something one could imagine as a Roger Waters-dominated respite stuck in an *Animals* song rendered live.

Rabid (Over You)
(Scabies/Sensible/Vanian/Andy Le Vien) 3:41

An odd one here, an expanse of relentless itchy agitprop Hawkwind-cum-XTC set to a new wave disco beat with new distorted synths we've not yet heard on a Damned joint, courtesy of Anthony More.

The lyrics overflow, with more words—most of them enigmatic and poetic—than we've ever seen in a Damned song, hyperactive, everywhere at once as a verbalisation of how fast Rat is operating his high-hat. This accounts for the Andy Le Vien credit, Andy being the engineer at the original RMS demo sessions with Captain and Rat. Andy says he had a bunch of lyrics he had written handy in an old notebook, but also acknowledges that an old Soft Cell roadie by the name of Tony Robinson also contributed.

Captain had plumped for "Rabid (Over You)," recorded during the same sessions as "Seagulls," to be the band's next single. But there's zero accessible about it, the band sounding as if they start the track and then give up and all swan-dive into the crowd. There's something vaguely Boomtown Rats about the energy of "Rabid (Over You)" but the production is crammed into the middle frequencies and too much is attempted all at once.

Heavy-duty chord changes race by, the centre cannot hold and all the while Rat pounds out an impossibly fast four-on-the-floor—if you've gathered already, I'm not a fan of four-on-the-floor. Kudos to the band though: this is the tightest and most sober we've heard them up to this point. Not that it makes for good music though, rather more of an academic exercise, or letter of intent.

Page 72 — New Musical Express 22nd November, 1980
THE DAMNED
The Black Album
TWO FOR THE PRICE OF ONE
Double album set for ordinary list price of £5
THE TOUR
NOVEMBER
19 LEICESTER Polytechnic
20 NEWCASTLE Mayfair
21 WAKEFIELD Unity Hall
22 WESTRUNTON Pavillion
23 SHEFFIELD Top Rank
24 SOUTHAMPTON Gaumont
25 CARDIFF Top Rank
26 ST AUSTELL New Cornish Riviera
28 HUDDERSFIELD Cleopatras'
29 DERBY Ajanta
30 BRISTOL Locarno
DECEMBER
1 LIVERPOOL Bradies
2 BIRMINGHAM Odeon
3 LONDON Hammersmith Odeon
4 MANCHESTER Apollo
5 EDINBURGH Odeon
7 GLASGOW Apollo
8 DURHAM University
9 BLACKBURN King Georges
THE TOUR

© Larry Schorr

© Larry Schorr

© Larry Schorr

© Larry Schorr

© Larry Schorr

THE DAMNED
The Black Album
TWO FOR THE PRICE OF ONE
Double album set for £5, or less!
Psssst! We all know There ain't no sanity clause
–the 3 track single out now
THE TOUR
NOVEMBER
19 LEICESTER Polytechnic
20 NEWCASTLE Mayfair
21 WAKEFIELD Unity Hall
22 WESTRUNTON Pavillion
23 SHEFFIELD Top Rank
24 SOUTHAMPTON Gaumont
25 CARDIFF Top Rank
26 ST AUSTELL New Cornish Riviera
28 HUDDERSFIELD Cleopatras'
29 DERBY Ajanta
30 BRISTOL Locarno
DECEMBER
1 LIVERPOOL Bradies
2 BIRMINGHAM Odeon
3 LONDON Hammersmith Odeon
4 MANCHESTER Apollo
5 EDINBURGH Odeon
7 GLASGOW Apollo
8 DURHAM University
9 BLACKBURN King Georges
THE TOUR

The Black Album

Hard to believe there's only a year's gap between The Damned's third record and their fourth, because *The Black Album* represents (ironically) a huge expansion of the band's colour palette. The confidence to wander further might, in part, have come from the jettisoning of the band's hard-drinking bassist.

"Algy decided that he was going to be a metal boy and that's what he did," laughs Rat. "He loved the thing of making this fucking huge high-speed and high-energy racket, and to have the bass really grinding. It wouldn't be fair to say that he saw it coming. I think it was just something that was there and he wanted to do it. And I think he had enough of being spat at by the punks. Thinking back, I remember a drunk guy. He was really cool when he was together and organised, but it didn't take long for him to go downhill. I don't know what his take on it was, but he was brilliant bass player. At the time we really wanted somebody who could add that kind of energy and anger to the band, and that ability. But I don't know what the story with Algy was, really. He never seemed to be enjoying himself."

"Getting Algy in the first place," continues Scabies, "it was another bass player. Another day, another bassist. Captain, Dave and myself were pretty tight. We had been working together for a few years and we had our own way of thinking about the world and the band and what it should be doing. So when you suddenly get somebody who didn't really get it, then it became a problem later on down the road. And I think Dave was a bit fed up with him; Dave had had enough of kind of carrying it, you know?"

"And then I got sacked," recalls Algy. "The reason was because Scabies didn't want me in the band anyways—he wanted Paul Gray. It wasn't a happy time. And then I got beaten up. We did the video for "Smash It Up" and Scabies had his drum roadie hold me back. I was assaulted and then after that I wasn't fucking interested at all. I wanted to go, but I was getting paid and that's why I stuck around. After that they were basically waiting for when Paul Gray was available. I knew where they were going with *The Black Album*. I already knew, because I played on the demos, apart from the ones that Paul wrote with Rat Scabies. But no, I wasn't into that. I thought bollocks, I've had enough of this and I'm off."

Algy is right about that. The Damned had their eye on Paul, and were petitioning him to leave his current gig, Eddie and the Hot Rods. "We didn't think of ourselves as punk at all," chuckles Gray, asked about the legend surrounding the pub rock pioneers. "In fact, we didn't want anything to do with it. Billy Bragg once said, 'Eddie and the Hot Rods were the first punk band, and if anybody tells you otherwise they're lying.' To me, the punk bands were The Seeds and the 13th Floor Elevators and The Kingsmen. To me, punk started back in the mid-'60s with all those fantastic garage bands. That was punk, with everything on a budget, raucous, snotty, through equipment that didn't work very well and to hell with the consequences."

"When I joined the Hot Rods, we had a manager called Eddie Hollis, and he had the biggest record collection of anybody that I'd ever known. He lived in a caravan and this entire caravan was just full of albums. We'd go down the pub and come back, have a bit of a party, and he'd put on an album and he wouldn't just say to you who the band was and what the song titles were; he'd tell you who wrote them, who produced them, who engineered them, who the record company was. He knew absolutely everything; he was like a walking encyclopaedia. So he introduced us to a lot of music from that era."

"But half the band was from Canvey Island, and Dave Higgs, our guitarist... God bless him (died December 2013), he'd been in a band with Wilko Johnson. So he already had that kind of aggressive, snotty, minimalist guitar playing. And the time was right. We'd gone through the glam stuff that I loved, we'd gone through the rock band stuff like the Zeppelins and the Purples and all that, and music had got a bit disco-ish and very formulaic. The big rock bands were all playing on Persian rugs and charging vast amounts of money to see them. To someone that was my age, at 16, that just didn't cut it. I thought, well, where's the fun in that?"

"Then when Dr. Feelgood came along, that was kind of revolutionary and we embraced that spirit. So we got lumped in with that punk thing because we were playing the same pubs and clubs in London the same time as The Stranglers. The Jam had already started up, although they were a very different band then. None of us were aware of each other, really. It was a movement that morphed, without anybody really knowing what was happening until McLaren took it over and put his punk badge on it so he could sell all his clothing from his Sex Shop down King's Road, but that's another story. But yes, we embraced the punk spirit without subscribing to the punk clothing and all the gobbing that went with it. Eddie and the Hot Rods were a pop band. We were a young, fast, raucous pop band. And if you want to call that punk, then, you know, fine."

And that's not a bad description of The Damned at this juncture, although the band Paul was joining was both more punk and darker with their pop, but fully on board with pop tooling all the same.

The Black Album was recorded in May and June 1980 at Rockfield in Monmouth, Wales and issued on November 17th. It was a double album, with the 17:13 "Curtain Call" taking up side three, with some live tracks—all but "New Rose" being from *Machine Gun Etiquette*—taking up side four. These songs were recorded on July 26th 1980 at Rock City Studios in Shepperton as a special live gig for members of the fan club.

The North American I.R.S. Records version of the album consisted of sides one and two only, with different cover art, essentially a simplified, monochromatic version of the original. The UK Big Beat reissue of the record from September 1982 also dropped "Curtain Call" and the live tracks and was packaged in a plain black cover with the name of the band embossed, to mimic The Beatles' white album.

The original six live tracks were then augmented with four more and issued as a separate album called *Live Shepperton 1980*.

"We all had four-track portable studios and we all sent tapes to each other," explains Paul, on the assembly of *The Black Album*. "We then pretty much agreed what songs were going to be the best ones for The Damned collectively. We split the songwriting equally, which stops all that nonsense of, well, he's got four songs on the album so I want four songs on the album. We all brought stuff in, elements that were used and not used, and it became a melting pot. A lot of Dave's songs were pretty much worked up in the studio. Captain wrote dozens if not hundreds of songs—Captain is so prolific—and we all mucked in."

As alluded to, *The Black Album* would constitute the most stylistically diverse album from the band yet. "Yes," says Paul, "and that's because the songs that appear on any single or any EP or any album are the songs that are gathered at any one time. And they may or may not bear any resemblance to what went immediately before it or what immediately followed it. There's no kind of plan about, oh, we're gonna make this kind of record or that sort of record. It's entirely dependent on the contributions of whichever members are in the band at the time, and when we can get in the studio to knock them out."

"Everybody writes all sorts of different music and it's all thrown in the pot. And then we run through it, usually in the studio rather than in rehearsal, because The Damned have never been a great one to rehearse. Back then we'd normally end up down the pubs rather than rehearsing. If something works, then it was put down. There wasn't a lot of labouring, as I recall it. For the backing tracks, anyway."

Reflects Gray on playing with Scabies, "It's a weird way to be working as a rhythm section, but I don't think Rat really listens to what the bass is doing and I don't necessarily listen to what the drums are doing (laughs). Going back to the early days, the way that Rat and I worked in the past is that we both often played off the vocals or we'd take cues from them. I'm such a terrible singer, but I get all these ideas for vocal harmonies that if I had half a voice, I'd be thinking, oh, I'd love to sing that over top. Because I can't, because my voice won't do it, I seem to have adopted that melodic kind of thinking for the bass playing."

Summing up, Rat says that, "We had proved the point on

Machine Gun Etiquette that the band's audience would let us become more subtle. Little did we know (laughs). But of course when we went in to do *Strawberries,* it was the same feeling as we had during *The Black Album*. It was, 'Who's got songs, who's got ideas?' And, you know, let's record them. So it was a pretty straight-ahead and open way of working."

"It's a very organic animal, The Damned," agrees Paul. "There's no grand scheme, there's no grand plan and there never has been (laughs). The band has existed, with so many ups and downs, through a kind of sheer bloody-mindedness. But I thought the songs we had were cracking—and I still do. I think both those albums, *The Black Album* and *Strawberries,* stand up to this day—I'm incredibly proud of them. And I think it's testament to the band that they still have got a freshness about them."

****

Side 1

Wait for the Blackout (Scabies/Sensible/Gray/Vanian/Karloff) 3:55

The Black Album kicks off conservatively enough with a full-throated *Machine Gun Etiquette*-type punk rocker, meaning uptempo, violent at the drums, but artful of melody. As discussed, the band opted for a collective credit on the album, but it's Rat who writes the trunk to this one, with lyrics provided mostly by unsung punk Billy Karloff, a buddy of Rat's with his own band The Extremes, who were managed by Rat's dad. Dave assists on the words, with Captain composing the break sections.

Serious, sober, unshowy, the lyrics to this song essentially establish the Goth manifesto. And in 1980, with Dave in the band and with the collection of songs to come across this album and *Strawberries*, this puts The Damned at the ground floor, to the point where one could call them an important proto-Goth band, despite them strategizing none of this. To whit, not four lines in, daylight is to be diminished through curtains, with the promise of coming alive "in darkness."

Perhaps underscoring duplicity, the musical track is at the happy end of the band's melodic handbook, cheerier than "Love Song," "Plan 9 Channel 7" and "Melody Lee." Paul instantly distinguishes himself at the verse with a bass line high of note to the point of playing a harmonic, something we're pretty sure Algy wouldn't have done. The chorus has him complex, riffy and step-for-step with Captain, which carries on to the Cheap Trick-like break section where we begin to see the pains of production The Damned were willing to go through.

Chiswick in fact had assigned Alvin Clark to produce but the band had been bent on producing the album themselves, which they did, with the assistance of engineer Hugh Jones. Despite much of the usual drugging and drinking taking place at Rockfield, the guys devoted many sober hours to the actual studio work, with Rat and Paul generally most productive in the day and Captain and Dave taking the night shift.

Massaged into "Wait for the Blackout" are acoustic guitar embellishments and even tubular bells, across upscale arrangements. For example, the first break offers in fact two sections of new music, but when these figures are repeated later in the track, Dave adds a vocal to the quiet respite, which is then punctuated by dramatic stabs and then the bells, evocative of a Christmas night, followed by a Who-like jam of what is essentially a new or next musical passage. Captain eventually starts hitting Pete Townshend windmill chords, which gets Rat all excited as he doubles up the beat and then doubles down on his bash. As the song fades, we're left with a clean acoustic figure, taking us right into the next track.

Even though the song was essentially finished during the first week at Rockfield, it was still missing the guitar solo, as evidenced at a BBC session the guys did in October. This was remedied when a suitable solo was found and lifted from the break/outro section of a Damned song called "Some Girls Are Ugly Too," demoed at RMS earlier that year.

"Wait for the Blackout" was issued as a single but not until after the band had left the label, their contract expiring in April '81. Not expecting any promo from the members of the band, Big Beat nonetheless put the song out on May 6th 1982, backed not with a Damned track, but rather Elton Motello's minor (naughty) 1977 hit "Jet Boy Jet Girl," covered by casual offshoot act Captain Sensible and the Softies.

Lively Arts
(Scabies/Sensible/Gray/Vanian) 3:01

Like "Rabid (Over You)," "Lively Arts" is framed on a frantic and slamming high-speed four-on-the-floor beat from Rat that personifies pent-up energy. There are dropped beats and unexpected chord changes, Gothic and very English, as Dave sings a bemused Captain lyric about the class struggle between the poor and the rich and their lively arts.

Throughout, Hans Zimmer, producer of "History of the World Part 1," provides synthesizer sounds that are new to the band, taking the guys into the nascent world of synth-pop, even if for the rest of the song what we get is typical full-band Damned.

Like the first song on the album, "Lively Arts" saw belated issue as a single, Big Beat putting it out October 10th 1982 backed with "Teenage Dream" for the 7" and adding "I'm So Bored" to the 10" and 12" versions, both tracks being non-LP.

Silly Kid Games
(Scabies/Sensible/Gray/Vanian) 2:27

"Silly Kid Games" opens with a smart acoustic lick that sounds like Jimmy Page, who in fact had been briefly rumoured to be stepping up to produce *The Black Album* (which I can tell you right now, would not have gone well). But soon we're into something that sounds like a typical Damned song but done acoustically at very high fidelity. Captain writes this one and also sings it, making it the first Captain lead vocal on a Damned record. Dave had sung it as well, but it was deemed more suitable for Captain, who nonetheless has a similar singing style to Dave and a voice that is not diametrically somewhere else either.

More extreme than having Captain sing is the Beach Boys-like vocal arrangement at the mid-song break. This part modulates to a second piece of new music as the protagonist in the song takes his game show winnings—the song was originally called "Silly Quiz Games"—and bids adieu, presumably on his way to the airport to catch the first flight to Kampuchea. The amusing twist sounds more like a dare or at least a mischievous suggestion: Captain says the song was inspired by his love/hate relationship with English culture, in particular the custom of the seaside holiday fluffed up with silly kid games.

Drinking About My Baby
(Scabies/Sensible/Gray/Vanian) 3:28

Somewhat distressing, the heaviest, most punk song on *The Black Album* isn't particularly good, living or dying on a bad pun and then failing to get the benefit of the doubt because of an unimaginative vocal melody from Dave, who just follows the riff. Rat wrote this one top to bottom, and kudos for landing a song at the far end of a wide spectrum, but there's not much to it, with the earworm of a riff overstaying its welcome into the chorus.

At the positive, there's an incongruous but welcome solo keyboard intro, and once the song proper kicks in, Rat's drumming is infectious and rousing. Plus there are two other musical sections, one cozy and melodic, with Rat on fairly electric 12-string—this part is evocative of '60s garage rock, a genre that became a prime influence on the record—and the other gnarly and heavy metal with handclaps.

Later when the ascending melodic riff returns, so do the handclaps and all of a sudden we're in a happy New York Dolls place from here clear through to the end and all is forgiven.

Twisted Nerve
(Scabies/Sensible/Gray/Vanian) 4:31

Adding to the boost in music fan-ship The Damned got when Paul joined, Dave was bringing his own crate-digging predilections to writing sessions, exercising a growing love for what he called incidental music, or soundtrack music. And it wasn't just passive—the guys say he was writing more, was more engaged, and now that they were at Rockfield, he couldn't be as absent.

"Twisted Nerve" (working title: "Spy Theme") was pure early Goth as well as soundtrack music, minimal drums, grand piano, trumpet from Ray Martinez, a dark and murderous follow-up to "These Hands." It's also post-punk like Magazine, Joy Division, Echo and the Bunnymen, Chameleons UK and most adjacent, The Cure before excessive electronics.

Dave and Captain collaborated on the music for this one, but the riff, as such, comes from Paul, on plunky-effect bass, with Captain providing atmospheric palm-muted scratch sounds but also an ethereal guitar solo.

The lyrics are Dave's, with the paranoiac of the track shut in like on "Wait for the Blackout," but not likely to leave the lair for fear of the killer, who turns out to be our anguished protagonist himself, seeing in the window a reflection and not someone outside. His sense of panic is reinforced nicely by the accelerating chorus, en route to a closing summation where we hear the chilling phrase "twisted nerve" for the first time.

Hit or Miss
(Scabies/Sensible/Gray/Vanian) 2:35

If "Hit or Miss" sounds happy and pubby, traditional and even a bit mod revival, it's because Paul had brought it in, having penned the song for Eddie and the Hot Rods, who did a "slow, slightly bluesier version" of the song, according to my conversation with him.

Lyrically, this story of love gone wrong starts on the dance floor but ends in betrayal, from cheating to spending all of the guy's money. The brisk tempo is kept up throughout, with only a passing shot at a break outside of the verses and (too?) many runs at the chorus.

Captain solos gleefully, making a brief return at the racket at the back-end fade, where all of a sudden the chorus becomes "another shit or piss." Paul's performance on the track is a clinic in how to make the bass interesting to any casual music fan. As he'd often quip, he'd be a millionaire if he was paid by the note.

Although "Hit or Miss" wasn't issued as a single, it was picked up for radio play by a number of BBC DJs, plus it was used as a sort of double A-side billing situation along with the non-LP "There Ain't No Sanity Clause."

Side 2

Dr. Jekyll and Mr. Hyde (Scabies/Sensible/Gray/Vanian/Dadomo) 4:35

First there was "Silly Kid Games" and now "Dr. Jekyll and Mr. Hyde," two tracks that demonstrate Captain's success at writing these uptempo songs featuring vigorous acoustic strumming over strong bass parts and Rat being Rat.

Fortunately the production and the mix match for professionalism the performances from all involved, including Dave, who does a thespian job on yet another lyric (started by him and finished by Giovano Dadomo) that aids in the construction of a multi-dimensional psychological portrait of Dave when he's dressed to the Goth nines.

After a spoken word section where Dave sounds bemused at his split personality, we're back into another chorus, punctuated by Ray Martinez on trumpet, back for another track, turning this song nicely mod, evoking The Who, The Kinks and The Beatles, anything and everything British, including the royal family. But he's just part of a plush arrangement that includes the Keith Richards-like acoustic guitar to the right, clean and Byrds-like electric guitar chimes to the left and retro keyboard chords right up the middle. Not to mention soft and distant backing vocals, sometimes as choral oohs and ahhs, sometimes harmonised with Dave.

There are also a couple pensive instrumental breaks where the guys sound like Rush, who also come to mind at the intro before we hear Scabies, the direct polar opposite of Neil Peart but somehow equally busy back there.

Surprisingly, "Dr. Jekyll and Mr. Hyde" was issued as a single in the US and nowhere else. What's more, the uncharacteristic and almost proggy track (granted, ruthlessly edited down to 2:45) got picture sleeve treatment, rare in the States for a smaller label. The B-side choice was odd as well, I.R.S. going for a non-LP live rendition of the MC5's "Looking at You"—in other words, forget having DJs flipping the single and pushing the B, a happenstance that often resulted in a surprise hit.

Of note, *The Black Album* was the first Damned album to see issue in North America.

Sick of This and That (Scabies/Sensible/Gray/Vanian) 1:48

Punky, poppy and brief, "Sick of This and That" was originally called "White Cats," which was the name of Rat's somewhat promising interim outfit after Scabies had struck out with Rat Scabies & the Runners and Drunk & Disorderly.

There's something New York Dolls or even James Brown about the ascending show-biz chord sequence at the verse, but the amphetamine boogie "sick of the country" bit is all "New Rose." Once again, the guys are locked down tight on a quick number and then recorded perfectly, with guitars and drums to the fore, Paul less articulated and clacky here but instead loud and straight bass, Dave a bit distant and soupy, double-tracked. Bottom line, it's a fully integrated ensemble performance but it's Rat who sounds like he's having the most fun.

History of the World Part 1 (Scabies/Sensible/Gray/Vanian) 3:52

Despite being a prominent track on the album, "History of the World Part 1" is a complete enigma at the lyric end, with most listeners' ears really only perking up to the climactic "in the history of the world" high bit. The hooks are more musical, revolving around the classical-based pomp rock stops and starts, the incessant new wave keyboards and other production flourishes added by Hans Zimmer in August '80, working with the tapes at Nova Suite.

This earned him the footnoted "Overproduced by Hans Zimmer" credit on the album, with the rest of the record, including "Curtain Call," credited exclusively to the band. The melody for the song was helped along by Scottish artist B.A. Robertson, who was also recording at the studio at the time, this being Wessex in February just after Paul had joined, with the actual recording taking place at Rockfield in May.

The drumming is curious on this one, with Rat executing a four-on-the-floor clumped with tom fills. In fact Scabies had injured his hand and had to record some of the record with three operating limbs. On this song in particular he recalls overdubbing the cymbals, of which there aren't many, nor are they very loud.

"History of the World Part 1" was issued as a single on September 22nd, five weeks in advance of the album, backed with "I Believe the Impossible" and "Sugar and Spite." All three tracks were there whether you got the 7" or the 12", but only the 7" featured the swell Alan Ballard band photo on the back. The UK-only single managed a No.51 placement on the UK charts.

13th Floor Vendetta
(Scabies/Sensible/Gray/Vanian) 3:46

Adding significantly to the Goth quotient across the album is "13th Floor Vendetta," a dramatic almost classical piece, given the grand piano and sort of flamenco guitar flourishes. Also adding Goth cred is Paul's sullen bass line, recorded with bite, prominent in the arrangement as per one of the key definitive characteristics of post-punk, inside of which the first Goth bands dwell, in the shadows. Also placing it post-punk is the sort of drifting, wandering, inter-weaving essence of all these guitar and keyboard parts upon a rhythm track from Paul and Rat that is constant, albeit with wide spaces left at times to signify dynamics. Plus it's just two chords and there's no chorus or break bits, only a closing minute of electric piano and acoustic guitar that feels more like a coda to the song proper.

But first there's that title, which reminds us of one of the great garage psych bands of all time, the 13th Floor Elevators. In fact the song has nothing to do with Roky Erickson musically or lyrically, but rather is in homage to a 1971 Vincent Price movie called *The Abominable Dr. Phibes*, in which a renowned organist's wife dies, possibly due to medical incompetence, after which Phibes exacts his revenge.

Vanian says that the guys used to watch the movie all the time and were big admirers of Vincent Price, not to mention the cinematography and style of the film. But Dave's lyric offers only a snapshot, stressing Phibes' musical hobby, playing the organ as he boils inside at the injustice befallen him.

"13th Floor Vendetta" was one of the last things recorded for the album, invented at Rockfield and then worked on for real one day starting at eight o'clock at night, with Rat telling the guys to forget it, it's too late. But they persevered and had finished the song, from lyrics through mix, working all night until five in the morning, after which the guys had their breakfast outside by a big old oak tree. This made for one of the great memories of the session, and a lesson to the guys to strike whenever the creative irons were hot. To this day, Dave singles this song out as one of the proudest moments of his career.

Therapy
(Scabies/Sensible/Gray/Vanian/Hart) 7:39

Here's the most punk title on the album, attached to the most punk song with the most punk chorus, almost a precursor to D-beat hardcore as it were on all three counts.

"Therapy" is based on a poem by Fay Hart, who Captain had met at a

Dammed gig in LA in 1977. Hart had subsequently moved to London, where she wound up working at Stiff Records. Captain had fancied Fay's poem and asked if he could build a song around it, which he did, with Dave making a few adjustments to the lyrics along the way.

At the music end, Captain took the minute-long intro piece of unreleased 1979 Damned song "Don't Trouble Trouble" (which sounds somewhat like the beginning of Cheap Trick's "Auf Wiedersehen") and used it for the same purpose here, as part of an elaborate, jammy intro piece to a wholly unrelated song. Added are handclaps and some monstrous tone from Paul and his bass as the guys sort of sound-check away for fully a minute and twenty seconds until deciding to knock it on its ear.

But here comes Paul, breaking into "Love Song," and then, incredibly, staying with it as the guys build a whole new song around Algy's iconic bass part. After a few swift chord changes it's all over with fully three minutes to spare, Dave walking off leaving the guys to make a Who-like racket until engineer Hugh Jones mercifully fades them out and it's on to side three.

Side 3

Curtain Call
(Scabies/Sensible/Gray/Vanian) 17:13

"Curtain Call" began as a shorter, less epic piece of music written by Dave on his new harmonium back home in his apartment nearly a year prior to the band embarking on the trip that would take it to all the way to seventeen minutes. Dave's music was then hummed to Captain in pieces, with Sensible painstakingly transposing it to instruments, as he often did with Vanian.

Rat recalls Dave proudly showing him the lyrics for the song that Dave had in a notebook, something Scabies said that Dave rarely did. Eventually Rat lost patience with the time it was taking to do—after all, there wasn't much drumming on it—and so it got to the point where the guys could only work on it after Rat went to bed. Additionally, Rat's ire also helped push it along so it got finished at all.

Dave's lyric for the song is fairly involved and serious and beautiful, but it's not of a volume you'd usually find for a side-long song. In fact, so much of "Curtain Call" sounds like instrumental Hawkwind or Pink Floyd (think "One of These Days" crossed with "Echoes") that once these new age passages are set aside, it sounds like a proper song with lyrics, i.e. not much in the way of prog rock noodling and really no fat at all.

Vanian's words are descriptive and voluminous upon a simple theme, that of the performer at curtain call, mind racing as he steels himself to stride centre stage. Is there stage fright? Is it an adversarial relationship with the crowd? What's the point? The larger theme is akin to Shakespeare and "all the world's a stage," namely the idea that what the actor depicts on stage is a version of life itself. But one need not even go there, because there's so much to soak up from what he says just about the craft and the occupation, not to mention the fact that these questions are posed at curtain call, not spread to the hours, days and lifetime before approaching the stage door that afternoon and not particularly about what happens after the show has started.

As for the music, "Curtain Call" actually gets going pretty quickly, with the whole band cracking in at 2:30. But things shut down after a couple minutes and the song starts to sound like something from one of Rick Wakeman's 100-plus solo albums. The guys recall fondly the endless rolls of tape and the edits thereof, razoring, rolling onto spools with pencils, of opening up the harpsichord and hitting the strings with a hammer, mellotron parts, backwards parts, splicing in some of Rimky-Korsakov's "Scheherazade," the clapping crowd sounds... After this approximately ten-minute long middle section, much of it languished keyboard and synth passages as well as the experimental sound effects, the chugging full-band section makes an encore appearance. The song closes with the repeating synth loop that we heard earlier, at which time we might ponder that our actor upon the stage has finished for the night and his head has somewhat cleared.

Side 4

Recorded (with no overdubs whatsoever!) at Shepperton Studios in front of the Damned Fan Club.

Singles, B-sides, Bonus Tracks

I Believe the Impossible (Scabies/Sensible/Gray/Vanian) 2:54

"I Believe the Impossible" finds Captain imagining a better world like John Lennon, only in his punk paradise there are no workers, junkies, politicians, stranglers/Stranglers "dressed in black" or villains. Plus The Damned win because they are heroes.

This is not much more than an early demo with Paul, who frankly sounds absent. Nor is this a particularly rousing Captain vocal performance, monotone I suppose by necessity, and Rat's cymbals are not so much absent than... strangled.

Part of the song is Damned roustabout punk, but then it devolves into an unwinding hippie jam, where, granted, there are two guitar tracks plus bass and keys, with Rat doing some nice things with spaces and under-playing. Look for this track as one of the B-sides to the "History of the World Part 1" single issued September 22nd 1980.

Sugar and Spite (Scabies/Sensible/Gray/Vanian) 1:30

Apparently "History of the World Part 2" was so awful that, amusingly, it put Captain off ever writing bad songs ever again. "Sugar and Spite" was originally called "History of the World Part 3" but the label made the guys change the title—recall that "Smash It Up" had four parts.

It's not much more than Rat playing a tribal "Wipe Out"-like drum beat while Captain plays with the volume knob of his guitar. This is the second and final B-side to "History of the World Part 1," and you know, given this three-"song" taster to the new album, you would think any fan ruminating over the band during the month of October 1980 would be concerned.

There Ain't No Sanity Clause (Scabies/Vanian/Sensible/Dadomo)

Written and recorded in the spirit, the oeuvre and the temporal and physical space as the tracks comprising *The Black Album*, this was intended as a stand-alone single, a nice part of the market in which The Damned more than dabbled.

"There Ain't No Sanity Clause" featured music by Captain and a launching point by Rat, who lifted the phrase from a Marx Brothers bit seen and heard in *A Night at the Opera* from 1935. Giovanni Dadomi wrote the lyrics for the band about the band, getting so inside baseball with his references that it was hard to gather what he meant.

As for his central riff to this modest pirate song, Captain quipped that it's a bit too much like Magazine's "Shot by Both Sides"—not really, but one can see what he means, and it's nice of him to voice that credit.

THE
DAMNED
FRIDAY 13TH
EP
DISCO MAN
THE LIMIT CLUB
BILLY BAD BREAKS
CITADEL
ALL TITLES BY RAT SCABIES · CAPTAIN SENSIBLE · DAVID VANIAN · PAUL GRAY PRODUCED BY TONY (BROOZER) MANSFIELD
TOUR
NOVEMBER
Thu 12 NEWCASTLE, Mayfair
Fri 13 EDINBURGH, Odeon
Sat 14 SKEGNESS, Pavilion
Sun 15 SHEFFIELD, Lyceum
Mon 16 DONCASTER, Rotters
Tue 17 MIDDLESBROUGH, Gaskins Plus One
Wed 18 LEICESTER, De Montford Hall
Thu 19 BRADFORD, Tiffany's
Fri 20 COLWYN BAY, Pier Promenade
Sat 21 MANCHESTER University
Sun 22 READING, Top Rank
Mon 23 BRIGHTON, Top Rank
Tue 24 CARDIFF, Top Rank
Wed 25 BIRMINGHAM, Locarno
Thu 26 BLACKBURN, King George's Hall
Fri 27 STOKE-ON-TRENT, Victoria Hall
Sat 28 LIVERPOOL, Royal Court Theatre
Sun 29 BRISTOL, Locarno
Mon 30 DUNSTABLE, Queensway Hall
DECEMBER
Thu 3 PORTSMOUTH, Locarno
Fri 4 PETERBOROUGH, Wirrina Stadium
Sat 5 WEST RUNTON, Pavilion
Sun 6 LONDON, Lyceum Ballroom
NEMS

The idea here was to have a breakout seasonal hit, but the song is just not that strong, with shouty double-tracked vocals from Dave, with zero dynamics and with a recording that is not easy on the ears, unlike the almost creamy attendant tracks from *The Black Album*. The song was issued as a single on November 25th 1980 with an illustrated Santa on the sleeve but it failed to chart. Album track "Hit or Miss" got near equal billing, with the B-side being a live rendition of MC5's "Looking at You."

Disco Man
(Scabies/Sensible/Gray/Vanian) 3:20

The Tubes had "Slipped My Disco," Frank Zappa had "Disco Boy" and Kiss, ELO, Rod Stewart and others played it straight and tried the format for real.

The Damned's commentary on the subject is of course along the line of The Tubes and Zappa, and not resorting to a disco back-track like The Tubes to make the point. Captain's unreleased "Some Girls Are Ugly Too" was a second anti-disco diatribe from the band.

"Disco Man" hails from the *Friday the 13th* EP, issued on November 13th 1981 (a Friday) as a one-off with NEMS while the band, deep in debt, looked for a new deal, having left Chiswick over a number of small gripes, death by a thousand paper cuts. The band had to buy themselves out of the deal, with Rat's father John Millar collared to sort out the mess.

The EP tracks were recorded at Rockfield, with Tony "Broozer" Mansfield producing. Guy Jones hadn't been available and Captain was acquainted with Tony, who had been working on solo tracks with Sensible.

The idea was that each member was supposed to bring a track to the table and "Disco Man" was Captain's contribution. On it, the manager's son plays one of his pert, time-honoured four-on-the-floors, dropping a beat hither and thither, while Dave doesn't do much with the vocal melody and Captain massages in some vigorous acoustic guitar strumming to what is otherwise a full-band punk track, although moderate.

Helpfully, one day Rat had walked in with a copy of Family's 1968 debut *In a Doll's House*, pointing out, in his cryptic but inspired way, that the band should look at the track "Peace of Mind," which in fact is in (first) possession of the exact same vocal melody at the verse.

The song is noisy enough and Paul chugs along, climbing scales, but oddly it's the mild attack at disco (shooting fish in a barrel) and Dave's sing-song vocal that conspire to stop this one short of a winner. It's almost pulled out of the fire with the clamorous "Are you ready?" refrain, and indeed by the time the jam disintegrates, we are in somewhat of a happy Who place with The Damned sounding cool again.

Limit Club
(Scabies/Sensible/Gray/Vanian) 4:15

"Limit Club" was Dave's contribution to the *Friday the 13th* EP, the song written in tribute to Malcolm Owen from The Ruts, who had died of a heroin overdose. The lyrics are some of Vanian's best from the era, and the music was his as well, at least in its infancy, written on organ with Captain afterward assisting.

Speaking of organ, the Vox Continental played on the track by Captain was brought down to Rockfield by Roman Jugg, Paul's friend from Wales who would soon end up in The Damned.

The song is essentially a pensive, reflective Dave atop an aggressive, cutting bass line, with Rat back there providing a nice mid-paced groove with guitar and keys being incidental, although during the "laughing, laughing" section, the arrangement rises however briefly to Phil Spector levels. Paul appreciated what producer Tony Mansfield brought to the sessions, admiring his pop ear, his affability and easy-going nature and his ability to get sounds quickly.

As the song winds down, Rat drops out and the rest of the guys are left to weave a poignant coda to Owen's life, acoustic guitar, electric guitar, Vox Continental and gnarly bass again evoking The Who like The Damned have done so many times before.

Billy Bad Breaks
(Scabies/Sensible/Gray/Vanian) 3:53

Paul's told me that "Billy Bad Breaks" is the first song he ever wrote for The Damned, nicking the title from a character he had read about in a book about the cocaine trade called *Snowblind* and basing the music on a bass riff he calls simple, which in the hands of another might be, but Gray dresses it up until interest in this arcane corner of rock 'n' roll instrumentation is upheld and more.

Gray's lyric is as light-hearted as the music, more about a boy who can't help but make mistakes, and the vocal melody up top is sophisticated enough to make this perhaps the most memorable track on the EP, despite there being almost no guitar (acoustic can be heard but mostly in a rhythmic role) and a keyboard line that is braying and retro to the point of distraction. Like "Limit Club" there's a definite garage psych vibe, picking up where the likes of "13th Floor Vendetta" and "Curtain Call" left off.

Indeed The Damned, quite singularly at this point, seemed to have tasked themselves with drawing the line from heavy garage through psych and punk into a personal definition of Goth that was different from post-punk bands arriving at dark and atmospheric and bassy some other way, maybe up in Manchester, for example. It's as if the guys in The Damned all worked in record stores, which to my knowledge, none of them ever did.

Citadel
(Jagger/Richards) 2:48

Side 1 done with, flip over the EP and we get a cheeky Side A, with "Billy Bad Breaks" giving way to a cover of the Rolling Stones' "Citadel" from 1967's psychedelic send-up *Their Satanic Majesties Request*. Captain cherished his original copy with the 3-D cover art, and in a sense, one figures The Damned were comfortable enough in their own skins not to feel they had to cover something more obscure to look cool. In fact, Paul said the idea to do the song came up because the band had been playing it in sound check one day and liked the way it sounded.

It's a spirited rendition, reminding me of XTC psych alter-ego band The Dukes of Stratosphear, crunchy, rollicking, smartly appointed with old percussion and keyboard appointments. The song—and therefore the whole '60s revival jewel of an EP—ends with the band crashing out, leaving only backwards-recorded keyboard bleeps and blurps, a fitting introduction to the masterpiece of a neo-psych record to come.

Lovely Money
(Vanian/Sensible/Scabies/Gray/MacDonald) 5:22

Similar to their previous label deals, the band's signing with Bronze in May '82 was kicked off by a pre-LP single with neither "Lovely Money" nor its B-side "I Think I'm Wonderful" showing on the forthcoming *Strawberries*.

Issued June 4th 1982 "Lovely Money" demonstrates that The Damned could craft an enjoyable song framed on nothing more than the simplest of drum beats (much of it machine), along with thin, unadorned keyboard chords to suggest the tune. But this is where Dave and Paul take over, the two of them in cheery competition to see who can generate more interest, Gray through his hummable bass line, Dave through a reflective Goth vocal melody, again very British, on a Captain lyric about British tourism.

In fact Sensible was forty years ahead of public consciousness, because it's really about the statue debate raging today, about both glorifying and trivialising places like the Tower of London and various generals and majors, to quote XTC.

The song was recorded at RMS Studios, along with demos of a pile of songs we'd see on the forthcoming album. Owner of the place Randy MacDonald helped out on the lyrics, earning himself a credit. MacDonald also chimed in with a harmony part at the break that was too high for the guys to reach, while Captain accompanies Dave on some of the verse singing. Adding interest, there's also a spoken word part by Viv Stanshall from the Bonzo Dog Doo-Dah

Band (Bronze Records boss Gerry Bron used to manage them), playing tour guide for pretty much the back half of the song. There are also tinkling coin sounds and a keyboard solo.

"Lovely Money" was issued in the UK (reaching No.42 on the charts), Australia and much of Europe, all as a 7" and in the UK, also as a picture disc. Most versions include a "disco mix" version of the song as the second track on the B-side. Now more accurately called an extended version, this was always just the song with an extra minute-and-a-half of music at the end, distinguished by there being no drum beat—it's just Viv and keyboards—in other words, in totality, less of a disco version than the original.

I Think I'm Wonderful
(Vanian/Sensible/Scabies/Gray/MacDonald) 2:54

Here's yet another top-shelf non-LP track, "I Think I'm Wonderful" being tight, action-packed punk rock with a number of hooks, some ripping guitar soloing from Captain and Dave spitting out a mouthful of words.

The lyric is a paean to punk individuality and having the confidence to look different, get drunk and make noise. Perfect music back track for all that, I say, really fast but melodic, performed to perfection, locked-down rhythm section with Paul keyed in on Rat's snare and bass drum combinations, and much of the vocals being big pubby holler-alongs.

There's a brief *Machine Gun Etiquette*-worthy break which ends at 1:38 in a punctuated display of punk positivity that one can imagine in an alternate universe resulting in this anthem being played alongside "We Are the Champions" in football stadiums around the world. This is followed by more shredding from Captain, gleeful cymbal-bashing by Rat and Dave avowing over and over, "I think I'm wonderful," before a grand and raucous wind-up closes this gem of a lost single opportunity.

Teenage Dream
(Scabies/Sensible/Vanian/Ward) 2:33

October '82, just as *Strawberries* was about to come out, the band's old label Big Beat pumped out a spot of product in "Lively Arts," from *The Black Album*, backed with this song and "I'm So Bored." It was a picture sleeve issue, only in the UK, but as a 7" and a 10", and into 1985, adding a 12".

The song comes from Rat's old band The White Cats circa early 1978, pretty much fully formed (making the credit suspect), if a bit more pub rock of performance. The Damned's version is rendered live from back in 1980 with Algy on bass, kicked off by Captain announcing the song as "My Asshole's on Fire" after which Rat makes a big noise on his drums.

There's something very MC5 about the song (and not entirely directed at "Teenage Lust" from *Back in the USA*), especially with part two of the chorus, after a proggy and kind of belaboured sounding part one where a beat is dropped. The Dictators come to mind as well, especially at the gang-vocal closing bit. All told, "Teenage Dream" sounds like a track that could have fit just fine on *Machine Gun Etiquette*, while not particularly adding much to the cause.

I'm So Bored (Sensible/Scabies/Vanian/Ward) 1:15

This is The Damned's send-up of "I'm So Glad," as made famous by Cream—recorded in the studio with Algy, with live versions of the song also circulating. There are no lyrics beyond the title, and there is no music beyond the main refrain. It's hard to believe that the original penner of the song back in 1931, Skip James, isn't credited. But then again, thrice-removed, this bears zero resemblance to the original. Still, one supposes this scrap of performance art means a bit of something, being the musical equivalent of Johnny Rotten's "I hate Pink Floyd" shirt as well as an answer to The Clash's "I'm So Bored with the U.S.A." (of note, the Pistols also pointed out, in "New York," that "You're looking bored and you're acting flash"). As mentioned, "I'm So Glad" was the second B-side to Big Beat's belated "Lively Arts" single.

STRAWBERRIES
THE DAMNED
SIDE 1
33 ⅓ RPM
(1-5) Rock
Music Co. Ltd.
BRON 542
STEREO
℗ 1982 Bronze
Records Ltd.

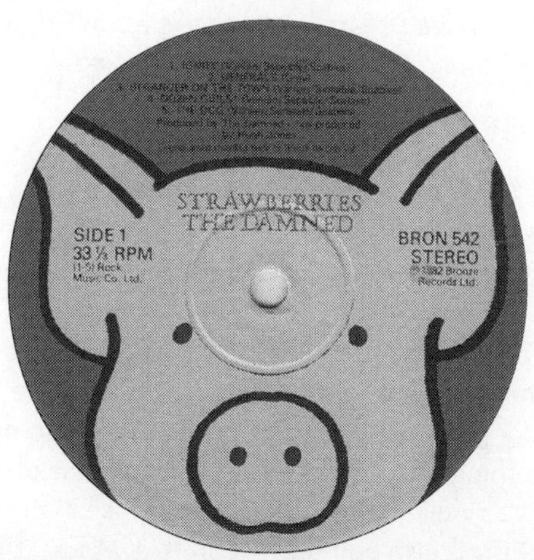

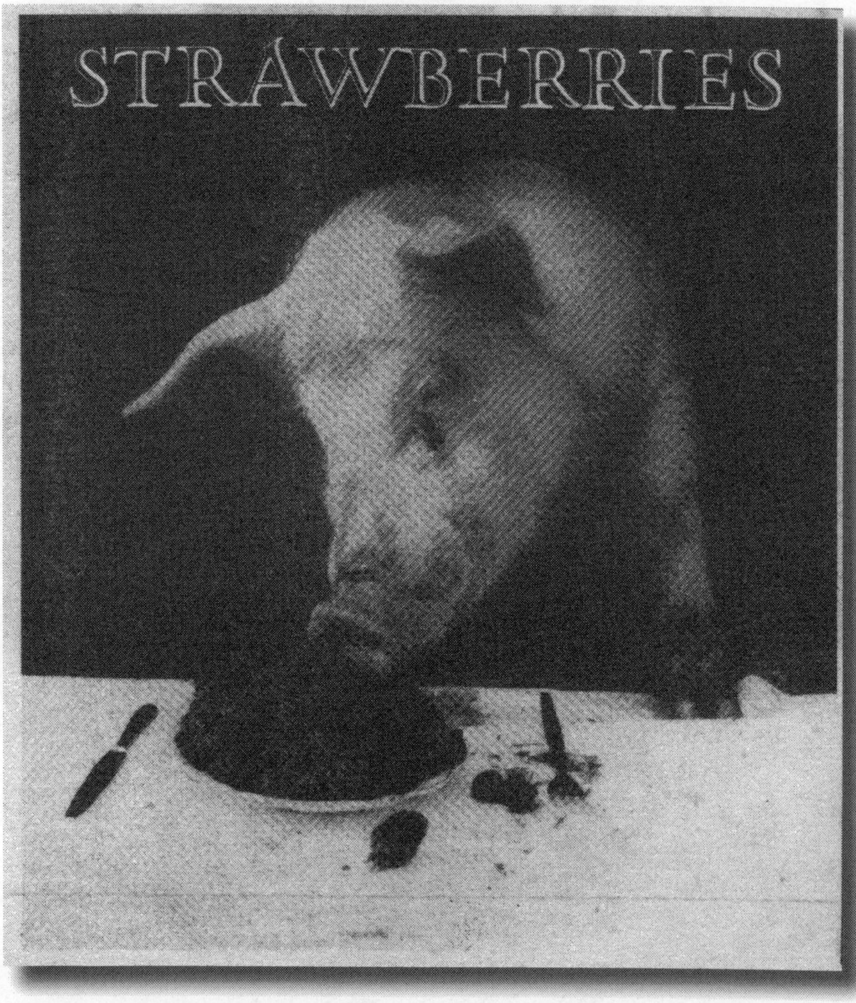

STRAWBERRIES

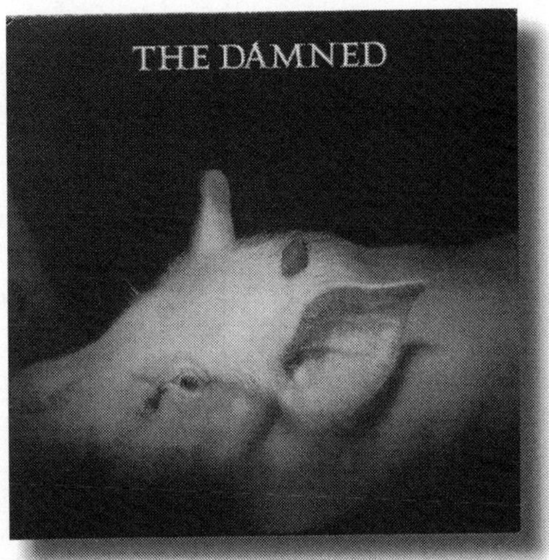

Strawberries

Buoyed by their experience spreading their leathery wings across *The Black Album*, The Damned approached the material for what would become *Strawberries* with the same intention, to expand the sound further, influences worn on their sleeves, the sky the limit, not at all reticent about being considered serious musicians and serious artists rather than punks with only punk ideals. The risk would pay off, with *Strawberries*, issued October 1st 1982, spending four weeks in the charts, peaking at No.15, the band's best showing yet. It seems there would be an appetite for a Damned that wasn't hard on the ears.

"Captain, Dave and myself embraced that spirit of *Nuggets*," recalls Paul, referring to the influential and pioneering garage and psych compilation, issued in 1972. "We loved that and those songs; we love The Elevators and The Seeds and the Chocolate Watch Band. Dave went on to form Naz Nomad after The Damned in the mid '80s, which was just that; they kind of modelled themselves as a pure *Nuggets* band. Once we discovered those *Nuggets* and *Pebbles* records, we'd go out on the towns, Milwaukee or Chicago or whatever, and come out with an arm-full of albums from that era. And we also loved the Vox Continental organ, which is that really squeaky "Louie Louie"-type organ, and we used that a lot on stage. That record is in the same spirit as all that, a free-for-all teenage spirit without worrying about record companies and sales targets and A&R people and all that stuff. It was making music for the fun of making music. And that's what we love, the cheesy, fuzzy guitars and wah-wahs—it's just great."

On *Strawberries*, as with the previous record, the band's embrace of garage rock is complicated. The expected connection forward to punk is expected and addressed, but then there's the more high-fidelity flourishes (including the use of sitar, cello and brass), not quite prog but more uptown than psych, again, arriving at something like nascent Goth rock, which comes from the songwriting, specifically the chord changes and vocal melody choices.

"Captain uses some lovely chord tunings and chord inversions," notes Gray. "And at my end, I mean, I ludicrously over-play a lot of the time. But nobody's actually told me not to. It tends to work with the band's way of working, luckily for me. Captain's also got great ways of combining rhythm and lead playing at the same time. I just really like the way he puts chords together. He's a melody man. The same as me. We both got a shared love of pop, you know, cheesy pop, any kind of pop. And I think that comes out in the way we approach playing our instruments."

The critics would indeed pick up on the idea that *Strawberries* was the poppiest Damned album yet, and again, there weren't a lot of complaints because the songs were so good, and varied internally as well as in relation to each other. Then there was Rat, also sympathetic to the power of hook.

"Yes, well, I follow the melody line and the vocal," explains Scabies. "It's really what dictates what I play. I also follow what happens with the guitars, because I'm a big guitar fan. And Paul's a great bass player. You kind of forget what made something work and why it was good. I just really enjoyed his playing and the realisation of how well we locked in together. I guess you'd call it empathy."

"I'm a great try-er of everything," continues Scabies. "There aren't any rules. I probably played riffs on guitar when writing that Captain found utterly un-guitarist-like. Because everything I was doing was just using two fingers or one bar chord up and down the frets. I didn't really have that ability to switch chords or the understanding of how to do it. But what that meant was that I came up with things that were sort of unusual, not what a guitarist would do necessarily, and I would do the same thing on keyboards."

As for the odd title of the record, "From what I remember," explains Paul, "we were in the studio roaring with laughter. I had just done a harpsichord thing as a link piece and I was playing it. I believe it was Captain who was in there guffawing with laughter and he said, "God, harpsichords, The Damned, it's like giving strawberries to pigs." In a way that he was saying, 'Are they gonna appreciate this kind of stuff?' But of course The Damned have used string quartets and brass. But that's where the album title kind of came up: what on earth are people going to make of it? Is it going to resonate or go over their heads? And happily, I have to say from memory, it pretty much resonated."

It wasn't quite like that, corrects Rat. "I know the story very well; I was there. And it was Captain that said it. He used to get really fed up with all the gobbing and people throwing beer and piss, you know, just being punk rockers. In those days, it was a lot wilder than it is now, well, than it has been for a long time. And I just remember him wiping the gob off his guitar and going, 'I'm fucking through. These assholes don't appreciate us. It's like giving strawberries to pigs.'"

Concerning the front cover, where a pig with a strawberry on his head stares out at the prospective buyer, Rat recalls that, "*Strawberries for Pigs* was gonna be the album title originally, and then somebody with some common sense said that's a really bad idea (laughs). That picture was an accident. They had done that whole mock-up thing with the tiles and the pig and the strawberries you see on the back, and as the photographer was stepping over to get in with the pig, the camera went off accidentally and that was the shot. There was only one of them, with the strawberry on the pig. The rest of them all looked like the back cover, which I thought looked pretty good. But the accident was the one we decided on."

Early issues of the album went so far as to have a strawberry-scented sleeve. "Quite funny," remembers Dave. "It backfired though. One kid—he was in the papers—he couldn't play his Damned record unless he was wearing a mask because the strawberries would bring him out in hives. It had a picture of him putting on the record in these household rubber gloves."

"There are so many things on *Strawberries* that I really love," sums up Rat. "'Stranger on the Town' was one of my favourite tracks on it and I think 'Life Goes On' is really good as is 'The Dog.' A lot of tracks on that album I think are really great. Recording it, I'd gone through a lot of different drum kits on that album, but I ended up doing most of it with a really cool Slingerland kit. It had this black chrome finish and it played really well. I really loved those drums. I tried to swap them for a Pearl kit, but then I just came back and just said, 'No, no, I want mine back.' But I only wrote one song on *Strawberries*, which is 'Under the Floor Again.' I sat down with the guitar and said to the guys, 'Here's what I've written.' That was influenced by *Satanic Majesties Request*, Rolling Stones. It's one of my favourite records anyway, but I just remember having that around. I was probably trying to steal something from it but ended up with 'Under the Floor Again' instead."

The band recorded at Rockfield, beginning in August, with Dave not showing until later, despite telegram entreaties to find him and get him to work. Engineering was Hugh Jones, who earns a co-production credit on seven of the album's tracks. There was a sense that Jones was asserting himself a little much, having just experienced the Top Ten with Echo and the Bunnymen as the producer of *Heaven Up Here*. Roman Jugg was officially made a member of the band during the sessions, although his credit on the album reads, merely: keyboard solos. He was quite disconcerted about the tensions he saw during the sessions, noting that for long periods only he and Dave and Captain were present and engaged.

Eventually relations soured between Paul and Rat, first over Rat not wanting "Pleasure and the Pain" on the album, and then over songwriting credits, which, throughout the ensuing history of the record, have been significantly altered. On the original vinyl there's a pile of songs with everybody credited except Paul, and then two songs credited *only* to Paul. Odd. "Yeah, I thought that when I saw the credits as well," laughs Gray. "Yeah, you'd have to ask the drummer about that." Relations steadied for a spell and then there was a switch in studios, to Farmyard, where the band finished up the record, self-producing the remaining songs.

"The studio dynamics were a little bit different, slightly more intense during *Strawberries* for various reasons," notes Paul. Reticently—Gray would leave the band in February '83. "And maybe that helped make it the album that it is. Rockfield is only thirty miles away from where I live. It was the perfect place for us. God knows how they didn't chuck us out, shooting tubular bells at 5AM in the morning with a shotgun. Most studio managers would have had a heart attack and said like, 'Be gone, you bunch of yobbos.' But not them. 'Oh, it's The Damned shooting tubular bells again.' They took everything in their stride. We had food fights with the lovely ladies who used to come in and cook. They used to always wake Captain up with the Hoover in the morning. He'd roar out bullock-naked and chop up the Hoover cable with his Stanley knife. And they took it—it was really good-spirited. Half the band, me and Rat, worked reasonable hours, and then Captain and Dave would get up at six or seven in the evening and keep the poor engineer up until five in the morning or even later. I think we drove him to a nervous breakdown. But I think probably any of the songs on either *The Black Album* or *Strawberries* could've been interwoven, couldn't they?"

"But that's because there's never been a conscious effort to say let's do this album like this or this album like that. It's whichever songs people come up with at the time and you chuck them all in a pot. That's what we did; the songs that work best as a band are the ones that end up on the record. That's a natural progression with musicians and writers and influences and all of that. It would be pretty boring to come out with the same stuff album after album. Which extends to my playing. When I pick up the bass and play on a given track one day to the next, it's never played the same. I just have fun with it and play it differently. I think that's one of the great things about The Damned. That's what makes it such good band to play with. Nothing is set in stone. Everything is slightly wild and on the edge—anything can happen."

****

September 25, 1982 SOUNDS Page 31

*****Indispensable ****Worth buying ***Worth listening to **Boring *Junk

ALBUMS

Spread the word

*THE DAMNED 'Strawberries' (Bronze BRON 542) ****½*

IT'S ALMOST like a Republic serial of the Forties. Just settle down, dim the lights and revel in the monochrome crackle of an endless cliffhanger.

'The saga of the Damned! The story so far . . .' Perilous Pauline would have nothing on these guys.

'Just how will our ghastly heroes cope now that the vile Captain Sensible, self-proclaimed most revolting man in the world, has been catapulted to fame by an undiscerning horde of Marmite encrusted infants? Will Croydon ever be the same again?' Thrilling stuff indeed.

'Strawberries' is the latest installment in the story of the Damned. It's their first album in over two years (has it really been that long?) and their most audacious yet.

Somehow 'Strawberries' (crazy title, I wonder what the story is behind it?) manages to indulge both Dave Vanian's darkly obsessive Gothic vision and the good Captain's psychedelic whims without sacrificing any hard rock sensibilities. The result is an album as heavily stylised as a baroque crypt. I think if Roger Corman ever gets around to cutting a record it might well turn out like this.

All things being equal (which of course they ain't) 'Strawberries' should be the LP to grant the Damned the recognition they've courted for so long. With an enthusiastic new label behind them as well as Sensible's newly acquired notoriety and loot (happy talk!!) they should finally be able to dump that stubbornly persistent second feature/B movie tag and move up into the major league.

I don't mind admitting it's something I'd love to see happen. Let's have no more cries of 'Quick Igor, the shovel.' The Damned don't deserve to be buried.

This is certainly their most accessible album to date, with a grand sense of scale that almost borders on the pretentious. Hugh, whuzzat? The Damned being pretentious. Huh, whuzzat? to the right album here? I think fairweather listeners might well be surprised at just how mellow the band are sounding these days.

Should they pick this up hoping for a re-run of the magical, metallic shambles that was 'Damned Damned Damned' they'll be sorely disappointed. Even devotees of 'Machine Gun Etiquette's' rawhide rowdyism will find little here with which to gird their loins.

'Strawberries' is the Damned at their most melodic and subversive. Themes hinted at on their last epic 'The Black Album' like 'Wait For The Blackout' and 'Twisted Nerve' are resurrected and embellished with an even brighter pop gloss.

But that's not to say 'Strawberries' is out 'n' out wimpham (perish the thought). The opener, 'Ignite', strategically placed to lull you into a false sense of security no doubt, boasts some rigorous rock guitar and 'Bad Time For Bonzo' hits home like a HM Monkees track.

It's just that to these ears at least the emphasis now seems to be on style rather than muscle. 'Pleasure And The Pain' is a typical example of the album's low key approach.

Despite his dramatic career turnabout, Mega-duck Sensible usurps the vocals on only two of the tracks which is about par for the course: the LP's throwaway closer 'Don't Bother Me' the weird beat of which punctuates the entire second side and 'Life Goes On', a curiously dour piece wherein he apparently mopes the absence of his beloved Dolly Mixture.

The excellent 'Generals' is somewhat more lively, a champion slice of wonderhorse pop that simply brays for life as a single. There's also an endearing teen melodrama with 'A Dozen Girls' as well as odd-ball psychedelia in 'Under The Floor'.

Perhaps the only track I'm not that bowled over by is 'The Dog', which I dislike in much the same way I disliked 'Dr Jekyll and Mr Hyde'. I dare say it could turn out to be a similar showstopper live.

'Strawberries' is a jolt to the system. A bright and exciting treat that just demands to be eaten. The Damned are back in town. I guess the saga continues.

STEVE KEATON

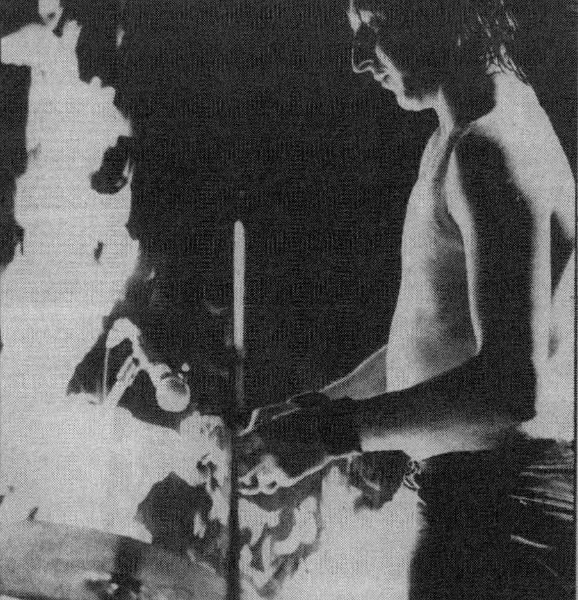

RAT SCABIES seen preparing his fifteenth greasy fry-up of the day

Mick Young

*DEPECHE MODE 'A Broken Dream' (MUTE STUMM 9)**½*

DO YOU ever get the feeling that some urchin has popped all the party balloons at the synthesised picnic? It has all been getting just a little drab lately, even though these keyboard stars had been promising you (and themselves) fun, frolics and fulfillment with a little help from their electronic friends.

'A Broken Dream'? Well, if you still believe that through the sole use of 'synthesised sound' there is some salvation from the tired tradition of smutty rock and roll (which may be 'smutty' but it was never *programmed*) then my little spring chickless, you most certainly are *dreaming*.

Although there is not that much left that one can do with the good ol' gtr/drm/voc plaything, at least in terms of a brand new format, if 'A Broken Dream' is a fair sampler of what else is on offer, then the market place (a plug for all you nouveau businessmen) is becoming a bare and empty space.

The main problem for Depeche Mode is that the use of synthesised sound, to the exclusion of almost everything else, within a pop song is rather limited. The reason that Yazoo — to pick a slightly obvious comparison — manage to make their songs succeed on more than the perfunctory 'nice tune' level, is the way the hard synthesised beat is juggled against Alison's vibrant vocal style.

David Gahan's voice serves the instrument — barely intruding, always obeying, never giving any *orders* — instead of playing off against the flat sheen of the Moog.

Listening to Gahan on 'A Broken Dream', you know that he is not a boy who is likely to make a fuss, shout at people or make any kind of nuisance of himself. He/they will merely sing you a lullaby, and there'll be sweet dreams all round.

The songs of Depeche Mode are not *bad* — there are many that I wouldn't even let near my record collection — and they are, pathetically at times, *nice*. But, is that all there is? If you want Beatles melodies chucked through a home computer, then I'm sure that a fourteen old schoolboy with a Casio 'mini synth' could satiate you.

It is possible to accept this calculated kind of blandness when it is just a three minute stab at the charts, because then you know that it isn't going to last that long. But the very attempt to put together a whole LP's worth of these songs shows their shortcomings to what is becoming an (hopefully) increasingly critical world.

Ah well, it's only rock and roll (ha! ha!). Good-night, sleep tight, make sure the bugs don't bite.

CHRIS BURKHAM

*THE PSYCHEDELIC FURS 'Forever Now' (CBS CBS 85909)*****

I SEEM TO have been listening to this album for the whole of my life. *"It's so ethereal, it's just like sleeping gas . . ."*

The Furs are a gradual infiltration, a hazy intoxicant. Some of my friends and colleagues — notably McCullough and Slattery — will tell you that the (Eric) Psyckes are a group with no fun, no function, no finesse and no future. This is merely wishful/wilful thinking on their part.

The Psychedelic Phurs are as useful and as functional as you allow their music to be, and — as my friends know — I'm very permissive! I like to use 'Forever Now' in hundreds of little ways, just as I use Simple Minds, UK Decay, Yazoo, KaS Product and Dexys.

Often I merely use them as a prelude to sleep, so that the most inspiring of music not only illustrates my dreams through the day, but inspires new dreams by night: Fall asleep with 'Forever Now' and that's no insult and phuck a phurl

But it's this question of music's phunction that is important, which is why the Psychos are more than just a shower to be ripped apart. They know how to pursue a good idea and build on it, so that a sense of undulating progression rather than swashbuckling adventure is the essence of their drama.

Within their deceptively languid flow of music and words, there lurks an effortless reservoir of graceful determination — and humour — which plucks the Psychkes from anonymous mediocrity and may yet herald a success story.

The single, 'Love My Way', is only the tip of it all. Encouraged by Todd Rungren's wide production, the Furs are opening up and out, *flowering* in an *overpowering* yet smoothly commercial vein — it's all rather like Sixties underground groups having hit singles . . . Yardbirds, the Move, Small Faces, the Beatles even. It's a good move.

As it is, 'Forever Now' (a title to match even 'New Gold Dream' in terms of ambition and optimism) has an engaging firmness that suits its poppiness.

'Run And Run', apart from leaping out as a probable next hit single, features the best opening line I've heard all year in *"Go on get Tarzan, go on get Jane, go on get Superman, get Lois Lane"* in that hoarse drawl of Butler's that is admittedly ridiculous, but hypnotically so!

Much of the wordplay is a delight, but delivered in such an offhand, casual style that it often eludes ready appreciation. Like the music in which it is extravagantly couched, it benefits from constant acquaintance, though side one's closing 'Sleep Comes Down', a sort of 'He Said She Said' meets 'Hello Goodbye' is an immediate pond of tranquility.

Like the intentionally Psychedelic sleeve and accompanying poster, the music sometimes contrives to camouflage the heart in flowery deception, but the truth is . . . 'Forever Now' is a phlawed masterpiece despite itself. Use it.

JOHNNY WALLER

Side 1

Ignite
(Vanian/Sensible/Scabies) 4:53

Strawberries kicks off with a scampering punker, music and lyrics by Dave. What is instantly notable is how the song is full band but doesn't sound particularly punk or heavy or powerful, but rather claustrophobic and suddenly frantic about it, due to the galloping bass line, but mostly due to surprise restraint from Rat, who holds the song back from grooving through one of his four-on-the-floor beats, the fastest he's ever attempted. At the chorus, Paul plays the same note separated by an octave, lending the song a sort of comically fast and not weighty cognitive dissonance.

Lyrically, Dave as vampire is preparing for an evening out just as he was at track one on the last album, but with more energy and optimism this time, commanding and attacking the night rather than, pale and weak, requiring it for survival.

Arguably (of course) the song is twice as long as it needs to be. Already at the halfway point we've heard everything, including lots of soloing from Captain. Yet now the band sees fit to drop into jam mode, at which time Captain stomps his wah-wah to no great effect. The long disintegration of the song is no more musical or useful, the end effect being the least appreciated song as far as this writer is concerned, across one of the top two or three Damned albums of all time.

Generals
(Gray) 3:24

It's Paul that supplies "Generals," an innovative, driving track of dark Stranglers-like melody, framed upon a smart, busy bass line (followed quite closely by Dave's vocal) and pumping electric piano. Captain is placed unobtrusively in the mix, firing off freight train licks. There's an epic and elegant musical break at the halfway point in which Simon Lloyd provides a sax solo and some additional backing brass (certainly trumpets). Rat's drums reverberate around the arrangement in Phil Spector wall-of-sound fashion and then we're back into the song's final verse. There are some fierce sax runs during the closing rounds of the chorus, with Captain chiming in as well, Rat closing things off with a bit of military snare.

Paul had told me that the verse melody of "Generals" was inspired by "Waterloo" from Abba, and that the lyric is about the race to take Berlin, the fall of Berlin to the Russians and in general the futility and legacy of war. One of Paul's best memories from the early part of his career—both with The Damned and Eddie and the Hot Rods—was going to Berlin and getting up early ("if I managed to get to bed at all") and heading out to Checkpoint Charlie, aghast at the difference between East Berlin and West Berlin.

"Generals," backed with "Disguise" and "Citadel Zombies," was issued on November 25th 1982 as the second and last single from *Strawberries*, however

Page 56 SOUNDS October 2, 1982

THE DAMNED

THE NEW SINGLE

DOZEN GIRLS

3 TRACKS ON 'B' SIDE, BRO 156 (NOT FROM THE ALBUM)

TAKEN FROM THE FORTHCOMING ALBUM

STRAWBERRIES

BRONZE RECORDS LTD.

THE DAMNED

DAMNED-TOUR 1982

Sunday	3rd October	READING	Top Rank
Monday	4th October	BRIGHTON	Top Rank
Tuesday	5th October	PORTSMOUTH	Guildhall
Wednesday	6th October	HITCHIN	Regal
Friday	8th October	BATH	Pavilion
Saturday	9th October	PLYMOUTH	Polytechnic
Sunday	10th October	CARDIFF	Top Rank
Monday	11th October	LONDON	Hammersmith Odeon
Tuesday	12th October	BIRMINGHAM	Tower Ballroom
Wednesday	13th October	BRADFORD	Caesars (formerly Tiffanys)
Thursday	14th October	NEWCASTLE	Mayfair
Friday	15th October	GLASGOW	Tiffanys
Sunday	17th October	SHEFFIELD	Lyceum
Monday	18th October	MANCHESTER	Apollo

the song failed to chart. As well, capitalising on the band's moderate success at the time, Big Beat issue the archival *Live Shepperton 1980* album.

Stranger on the Town
(Vanian/Sensible/Scabies) 5:14

One of the big reasons people love *Strawberries* so much, "Stranger on the Town" is an easy-on-the-ears slice of pop confection, (northern) soulful given the brass arrangements, ancient keyboard tones and one-and-three beat. It's mod and mod revival for the same reasons, as well as a bit psych, and despite doing so much is effortlessly memorable due to its cloud-breaking chorus. Dave had brought this one in, with Captain turning it fully musical. So it's fitting that as the song progresses, they charmingly duet, making the modulations at the end a rich listen, like Dexy's Midnight Runners or full-production story-telling Kinks.

It's got quite the opening as well, with three huge show biz chords and stadium rock Rat fills giving way to lonely bass chords and then the riff, which is played in unison between bass and two keyboard tracks. Then we're into gorgeous brass with Captain texturing as Dave begins his lightly film noir story of a drifter rolling through town, no doubt with a toothpick between his teeth and smirks instead of answers.

Dozen Girls
(Vanian/Sensible/Scabies) 4:34

Here's another one that sounds like a Dukes of Stratosphear *Psonic Psunspot* track. In other words, "Dozen Girls" sounds like psychedelic music that didn't exist at the time, like punk had to happen for it to be born. The end result is a joyous, carnival-esque punk, with the keyboards evoking vintage Monty Oxymoron, to criss-cross even more time-travel into all this.

"Dozen Girls" goes back to 1981, when it was demoed with Billy Karloff on vocals, Karloff also helping with lyrics and, logically, vocal melodies—both he and Paul Gray were added to the credits up into the official CD reissue of the album.

The song begins and ends daft. At the start, Captain plays a keyboard run that sounds like something you'd hear from the organist at a hockey game. This is followed by a gnarly guitar riff that's very similar to the Flamin' Grooves' "Slow Death," which just drops away as the band breaks into the pent-up energy of the song proper. At the end, out of nowhere, we learn that the ladies' man marvelled at throughout the song has thermal underwear (there's a debate whether Dave slips in a "purple" in place of "thermal" here and there). Over and over we're told this while keys and guitars jam away over a climactic wind-up, ending in a barrel of laughs and a comedic solo drum beat proposed and then faded.

"Dozen Girls" was issued as an advance single from the record, September 17th 1982, but failed to chart. For the single, the thermal underwear refrain was replaced by a roll-call reading of a dozen girls' names, with a prominent horn line that is not on the album version (there are other slight mix alterations as well). For the picture sleeve, Bronze stuck on the pictures of women that were the victims of an American serial killer, suggesting an entirely more sinister and of course unintended reading of the lyric.

The Dog
(Vanian/Sensible/Scabies) 7:25

"The Dog" is the full-on Goth rock classic of *Strawberries*, kin to "Dr. Jekyll and Mr. Hyde," "13th Floor Vendetta" and "Curtain Call" from the album before, and "Pleasure and the Pain" and "Life Goes On" later up the track list. No surprise that this one originates with Dave, with the lyrics describing Claudia from Anne Rice's hit 1976 book *Interview with the Vampire*. A small girl with her hair in ringlets (and importantly, as Dave has pointed out, "an adult mind trapped in a childs body"), Claudia is a paranormal temptress skulking dark New Orleans alleyways with a crushed chrysanthemum in her hand and vampiric death in her black heart. As is typical of this type of Damned song, the pervasive keyboards evoke *The Phantom of the Opera*, a suitable cultural touchstone given the visual presentation of Vanian as well as his thespian vocal delivery.

Inside of this one is a creepy instrumental break dominated by Paul playing bass chords across all manner of dissonant percussion whack driven forward by Rat on EKG bass drum. Afterward, as if there's nothing more to be said, the band lapse into a sweeping unwinding of the song, punctuated by jazzy piano atop more bass chords, the beat dissipating then building and dissipating again, replaced by the snarling dog of the titling, which in itself adds an extra layer of meaning and metaphor to the tale.

Side 2

Gun Fury

(Vanian/Sensible/Scabies) 2:57

On the back cover and on the label of the record on the original vinyl issue of *Strawberries* it's "Gun Fury," while on the lyric sheet it's "Gun Fury (or Riot Forces)" as crooned in the chorus. Captain's lyric is in fact about his disdain for the heavy-handed tactics of the cops at various demonstrations of unrest across Britain, Sensible protesting like a true punk and activist, a role with which he was increasingly comfortable and confident as he progressed past the pure mayhem of his persona as it existed across the first three album cycles.

Dave's almost pastoral delivery of the lyrics are set to an equally ancient and folky musical track in 5/4, inspired by the Pentangle 1969 song "Light Flight." Geometric piano lines weave in and out with Paul's hypnotic bass line and Byrds-like guitars from Captain as Rat swings in the background, recorded beautifully. There are percussion appointments, some quite electric soloing from Captain, plus breaks taken for a recurring unrelated riff from Captain using a chorus effect. As the song ends, here comes some more incidental music, reminding one of another old wyrd folk band, Trader Horne, who did much the same thing on their one and only album *Morning Way*, from 1970.

Pleasure and the Pain

(Gray) 4:23

This second track brought in by Paul had Gray writing the song on his old upright piano at home, was influenced by the likes of Blues Magoos. As Gray explained to me, the lyric can be interpreted as physical pleasure and pain in a relationship, or the emotional pain of a relationship ending, regardless of who ends it.

Unsurprisingly, the bass riff plays as much of a role in the melodic structure of the song as does the assertive piano chording, the Stranglers synth line or Dave's wistful vocal melody. There's a musical break where we get a rhythmic cello part, suggested by Captain and played by his girlfriend at the time, Rachael Bor. She's soon joined by Sensible who plays a brief keyboard solo, making that three keyboard parts going at once, before we're back into another run at the chorus. At the close, the cello returns, playing a slow line across the top of the track, finishing off what has been another bold move at taking the Damned further and further away from the chaos years.

Of note, however, the band never played "Pleasure and the Pain" live. Not only would Paul be gone anyway, but Rat disliked the song so much, thinking it sappy, that he and Paul actually got into a physical fight over it, with Rat knocking Paul out, sowing the seeds for Gray's quick exit from the ranks.

Life Goes On
(Vanian/Sensible/Scabies) 4:09

The most popular Damned songs on Spotify are "Neat Neat Neat" and "New Rose" by a wide margin, "Smash It Up" fourth with "Life Goes On" coming in a surprising third place. The song is indeed a classic, kicked off with an iconic bass line which ten years later we'd be hearing all over the radio as part of Nirvana's "Come As You Are."

In fact that bass line dominates, underneath a lead vocal from Captain, who also provides the memorable plinky and muted guitar riff heard occasionally across this dreamy, melancholic track about perseverance—or at least about putting one step in front of the others, passing those open windows. Elsewhere the song is kept rolling and surging by plush keyboard textures and additional clean guitar licks from Captain, while Rat sits back, even half-timing the beat for the repeat run at the first verse late in the song, a nice contrast to the break section, where he double-times the beat.

Of note, "Life Goes On" is preceded by an elegant thirty-second spot of renaissance music played on a harpsichord, in later life known as "Missing Link." With respect to inter-song incidental music, this one is by far the most evocative of what was done between songs on Trader Horne's *Morning Way*, which I always pictured as the perfect soundtrack music for the bustling speakeasy scene in *The Shining*, at which The Damned should have been the house band.

Bad Time for Bonzo
(Vanian/Sensible/Scabies) 3:29

The Ramones had "Bonzo Goes to Bitburg" in 1985, but here's an English band chiming in timely on the election of Ronald Reagan, famous to this point for being the Governor of California and also starring in the 1951 comedy film, *Bedtime for Bonzo*.

The song integrates nicely with the rest of the album tracks, adding to the half that are punk on the surface, but sophisticated melodically, with a nod to garage rock. Here through the R&B call-and-response structure in a minor key punctuated by vintage keyboard stabs, as well as the clean guitar tones applied to Captain's note-dense hard rock riff. Further underscoring the band's concurrent side-scholarship of '60s music, there's a vocal vamp at the 2:03 mark that is a quote from The Human Beinz' (via the Isley Brothers) 1968 hit, "Nobody but Me"—both the Ramones and the Dictators also drew inspiration to this song. There are some further vocal harmonies at the chorus and also at the close where the rhythm section drops out for a spot of sleepy-time music, at which time Bonzo lies dreaming and scheming. Cue the grandfather clock, the end.

Under the Floor Again (Vanian/Sensible/Scabies) 5:29

Right when the guys were thinking up stuff to write about, along came the story of Norman Green from Wigan. Having apparently burgled an 86-year-old woman's house and having the occupant die from fright, Green went into hiding back in 1974 with the help of his wife Pauline, living in a 21"-tall space under the floor of his living room. He would come up for air at night, as well as for food and beer with the aid of his wife, the only one who knew where he was. Not even his six children had a clue, although that's hard to believe, because some of the locals seemed to be in on the secret, seeing him going for walks in his wife's clothes during his exercise breaks at night. He eluded police for eight years until a tip came in and the jig was up, with Green emerging with two feet of hair and a beard like Rip Van Winkle—all charges were dropped.

Dave found the story hilarious and wrote this churlish song about it, surreal enough to need the services of Captain and his newly purchased sitar, which is heard a lot throughout the song, while Paul plays like Barry Adamson from Magazine. The last two minutes sound like heavy Pink Floyd, slow and brooding with a dramatic stadium rock solo from Captain. The effect is to make the listener think seriously for a moment about this preposterous tale, in parallel with Dave's lyrics, which similarly humanise Green and make us think about how human beings can make bizarre decisions when their backs are up against the wall.

Interestingly another Norman Green, also from Wigan, was charged with double murder of two children in 1955 and was hung by Britain's most well-known executor Albert Pierrepoint.

Don't Bother Me (Vanian/Sensible/Scabies) 2:10

That irresistible, loping drum track we've heard as incidental music early on the album returns and lingers. Once the listener is about ready to wander off in boredom, here comes Captain for his second lead vocal on the album and suddenly those drums have a purpose. When he sings low and quiet and in an English accent like this, it's easy to mistake Captain for Dave, but this lyric is quintessential amusing Captain. Even though it's easy to imagine both he and Dave writing a song around this theme, one gets the sense that the Captain of this particular lyric doesn't want to be bothered because it's bound to wind up a disappointment for the botherer. As well, you get the feeling that he knows this from experience, having bothered people and found out they were just a bother.

Underscoring the possibility of some level of illuminating insight being transferred, there's a gorgeous modulation at the halfway point that makes the song suddenly sound like a Christmas carol, or at least seriously crafted and no longer a novelty tune, given Captain's extra energy in making his point coupled with some very sober and delicate guitar playing. "Go away. Not interested!" says Captain, as the record comes to a close.

Singles, B-sides, Bonus Tracks

Take That
(Vanian/Sensible/Scabies) 2:47

Here's an underachieving punk rocker that seems like an exercise in testing out electronic drums and drum effects, even though most of the track finds Rat as spare as he's ever been on a full-throttle rocker. Dave sings this a bit like Elvis, telling the tale of some hard-done-by kicking post warning that he'll figure out a way to win in the end, and hopefully at society's expense. The song just gets more daft as it wears out its welcome, roughly at the half point, with Captain turning in a meandering solo harsh of tone amidst more percussion experiments. The guys rally somewhat and cooperate on a closing bit of new music, culminating in a bunch of absurdist—or at least place-holding—"la la la la ooh"s.

Mine's a Large One, Landlord
(Vanian/Sensible/Scabies) 1:15

This might sound like someone just goofing on a cheap organ in the showroom, but there's actually four different tones or parts contributing to the instrumental comedy of the song, which might have served, chopped-up, as some of the inter-song hijinks back on the official *Strawberries* album. The title of this one should serve notice that once the needle drops to vinyl, what you're gonna be hearing is an instrumental. And the fact that this is The Damned should serve notice that if it is an instrumental, there's not going to be much to it. Indeed thus far there's been nothing in the catalogue that sounds inspired by the likes of "Frankenstein" or "YYZ," but then again, wait until the end of this one and there's a couple bits of window-dressing, betraying the fact that someone must have spent an hour or two putting this together.

Torture Me
(Vanian/Sensible/Scabies) 1:24

"Torture Me" is a dark and impactful ballad featuring Captain solo at a piano for all of 1:24 delivering tragic lines in the support of animal rights, Captain being a vegetarian since being illumined at the house of Crass. He's as thespian as Peter Hammill here but smoother of delivery, getting dangerously theatrical when he goes high for the "And if I can suffer more" closing dagger. "Take That," "Mine's a Large One, Landlord" and "Torture Me" are all B-sides on the "Dozen Girls" single, issued September 17th 1982.

Disguise
(Sensible/Scabies/Gray/Vanian/Jugg) 3:28

In conjunction with the band playing some local shows in October in support of *Strawberries*, Captain Sensible found himself a minor pop star through his No.1 smash single "Happy Talk," a cover of a Rodgers and Hammerstein show tune from the movie *South Pacific*. Subsequently his attentions were elsewhere when the band was sent back to the studio to cook up some B-sides for Bronze's "Generals" single slated for issue November 25th.

Paul didn't make himself available either, so it was down to Dave, Rat and Roman Jugg to enter Roundhouse Studios and come up with the goods. "Disguise" was written by Roman—both music and lyrics—and is a straightforward grooving pop song, if a bit under-produced.

The bass line is simple, Dave's vocal a bit tired, and there are too many fills from Rat for a song that might have sounded better straightened-out and ascribed some gloss. Still, there's a tenor and tone from the band we've not really heard before, with Roman's lyric being sober and mysterious, like Dave's dark conceptual tales but somewhat less pointedly Gothic. The end result is something like The Stranglers meets The Church, with dulcet harpsichord sounds from the former and a seductive grower of a chorus from the latter.

Citadel Zombies
(Sensible/Scabies/Gray/Vanian/Jugg) 1:58

"Citadel Zombies" is a full band musical track saved from being a straight instrumental by virtue of the title being repeatedly sung throughout, with feeling, multi-tracked and with harmonies. There's not a lot to the music but it rises to the level of song without lyrics at least, given the guitar, bass and drums backing plus a keyboard melody line up top. There are also guitars making elephant sounds across a cinematic musical break which morphs slightly, becoming the bed for a brief bit of aggressive guitar soloing, which then continues throughout between the vocals. "Citadel Zombies" followed "Disguises" on the backside of "Generals," with the two tracks representing Roman's first couple of song credits with The Damned.

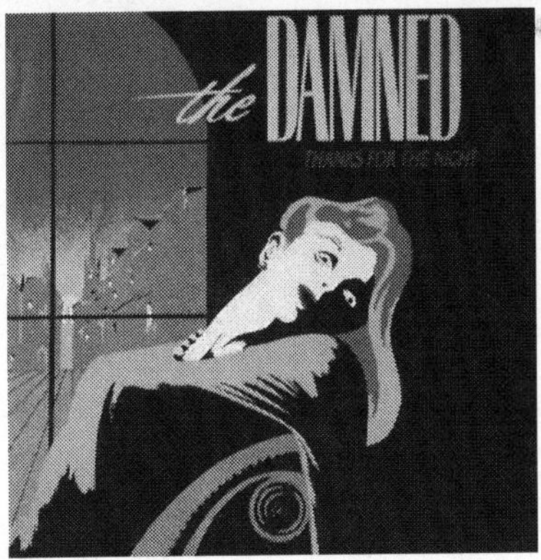

Thanks for the Night
(Sensible) 3:30

Best of both worlds or neither, "Thanks for the Night" is a song forged in limbo, by a band with a fifth wheel, surprisingly, that of Captain Sensible, who would be around as an official member for this single and then be gone all the way up until 2001's *Grave Disorder* album. In essence, this is the work of the four-piece from the next era—Dave, Rat, Roman and new bassist Bryn Merrick—with Captain almost guesting, away from his frivolous solo career.

Captain actually wrote the song, but back in 1981. The band was rehearsing at a studio in Wandsworth, along with potential hire at the keyboard position, Pete Saunders from Dexy's Midnight Runners. There were riots going on outside the studio and Captain's lyric focuses on the attendant looting, taking a positive view on the chaos, the opportunity, the fun and the fire, along with the act of activism inherent in being out there stealing for the cameras. The title therefore bears no sexual connotations or vampire vibes. Instead, the sort of diarist of the song is thanking the night for providing the shroud of darkness for an exciting night out, at which consumer goods have been secured as well.

The trundling but somewhat awkward and hobbled musical track bears a resemblance to "Ignite," which is why there was no way both songs could co-exist on *Strawberries*—there's even "The fires ignite" in the lyric—but Dave's vocal melody takes it to a different place, as does the chorus. Dave in fact sounds strained on the song, forced into a high range. As well, the song's production, by American unknown Hein Hoven, is stuck in the mids, not particularly high fidelity and certainly nowhere near the standard set by *Strawberries*.

Despite a rigid four-on-the-floor beat from Rat, the rhythm actually makes a tricky switch-over, most graphic from the guitar intro into the intro with rhythm section, then into the first verse, thanks to added beats to the bar, something that apparently tripped Paul Gray up back when the song was being written.

In fact confusion reigns even before we hear Bryn and Rat, with two guitar parts working against each other at the 12-second mark of the song. All told, "Thanks for the Night" is a bit of a frustrating play, especially within the context of the band having to put it out themselves, May '84, with no record deal in sight and no full-length album from the band going on two years.

Nasty
(Scabies/Sensible/Vanian/Jugg/Merrick) 2:51

Here's a punk rocker scared up for British goofball comedy show *The Young Ones*, where, on the episode aired May 29th, you can see the Damned performing it as part of a scene with some punks trying to elude the clutches of a pretty hapless looking vampire, a middle-aged Dave Vanian as it were. Dave's main memory of the visit concerns the band getting covered in fake chemical cobwebs, which were impossible to wash off and left white spots on the skin.

The fascinating part of the scene is the sartorial presentation of the band itself. Captain is off to the left looking like a healthy and successful version of his now public domain cartoon character, while the rest of the guys are clearly on the way to the upscale Goth rock persona they'd present during the *Phantasmagoria/Anything* era—even Rat's donned a top hat for the occasion.

As for the song, "Nasty," written by Roman, was recorded January 19th 1984 at Elephant Studios in Wapping. The vocal melody and the riff draw a line back to "I Must Be Mad" by The Craig, a Birmingham garage act that featured on drums, Carl Palmer. The curious phrase "video nasty," used in the chorus, refers to horror movies, a profusion of which were suddenly being made available for rental given the new technology at the time. Ergo there was a debate on about banning the worst examples.

You can really tell the difference in bassists, with Bryn lacking Paul's acrobatics. It doesn't help that the song has one speed, basically a quick D-beat feel. It's almost as if everybody decided they were going to be punk on it, from the raw and pubby gang vocal in the chorus over to the guitar solo, which is manic and noisy. Little did we know this would be the last hurrah for The Damned as punks for a long time.

Do The Blitz
(Scabies/Sensible/Vanian/Gray/Jugg) 1:55

"Do the Blitz" had been around for a while, with the band having played it live, hence the Paul Gray credit. It kicks off like Eddie Cochran's "C'mon Everybody" but then becomes modern with the B-52s keys (imitating horns) and Rat's uncharacteristically straightened-out beat. Up top Dave channels his inner Elvis (like Glenn Danzig, later) over what is a classic "dance craze" song format. There's a little boogie woogie to the riff, which carries into the old-time rock 'n' roll guitar solo, with the nod to the past also evoking the early '70s glam of Mud and even "Ballroom Blitz," particularly with Rat's snare at the chorus.

The Damned/ Charge Hammersmith Odeon

[illegible]

WINSTON SMITH

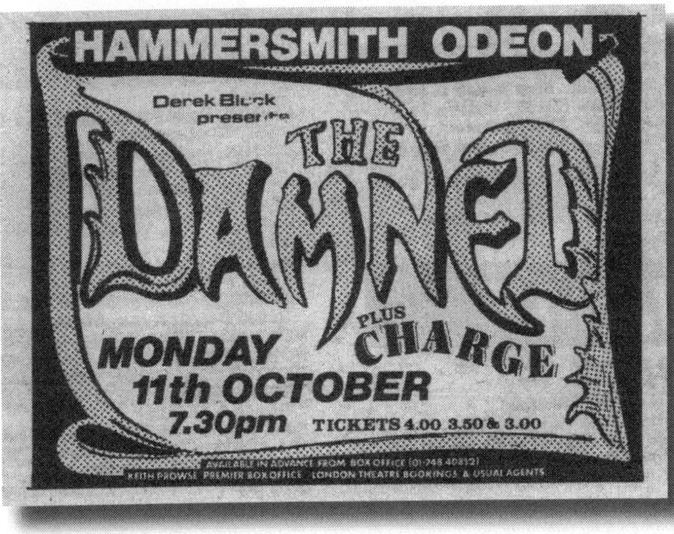

Page 42—New Musical Express 20th July, 1985

The Damned

Phantasmagoria

The Damned 'Phantasmagoria'.
Includes the hit singles 'Grimly Fiendish' and 'Shadow of Love'.
Only **£4.99** album or cassette.

HMV

The Worlds Best Music Stores.

STORES IN: OXFORD STREET · TROCADERO, PICCADILLY · BEDFORD · BIRMINGHAM · BOLTON · BRADFORD · BRIGHTON · BRISTOL · CARDIFF · COVENTRY · DERBY · EDINBURGH · ENFIELD · EXETER · GLASGOW · GLOUCESTER · GUILDFORD · HULL · LEEDS · LEICESTER · LIVERPOOL · LUTON · MANCHESTER · MIDDLESBROUGH · NEWCASTLE · NORWICH · NOTTINGHAM · OLDHAM · PLYMOUTH · PORTSMOUTH · PRESTON · SHEFFIELD · SOUTHAMPTON · STOCKTON · SUNDERLAND · SUTTON · SUTTON COLDFIELD · SWANSEA · WOLVERHAMPTON

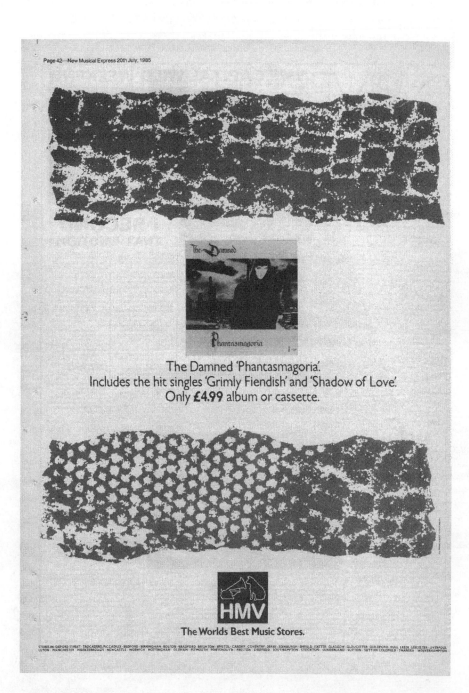

Phantasmagoria

"Roman brought a huge nose to the band, even bigger than Rat's," laughs Paul Gray, now departed from The Damned and onto an ill-fated run as part of UFO in their nadir. "No, I met Roman where we both lived in Wales, and he was a bit of a Damned fan, and I invited him to come around and have a beer. I had a four-track at the time, porta-studio, and when I was away on tour with The Damned, I said, well, come in and feed my cats, and knock some demos for yourself out if you like. He ended up playing a few bits on some of the things I was writing and I ended up playing a few bits on the songs he was writing. And when the time came that we needed a new keyboard player for The Damned, I suggested Roman. So he came into the band that way. Then after I left, he brought Bryn Merrick in, who he had been in a band with. That became kind of the Goth period of The Damned, which I didn't really have anything to do with. But Bryn was a lovely chap. You couldn't help but really like Bryn. He was a mischievous chap but he was a lot of fun. Really great bass player as well."

Roman Jugg of course had entered the fray earlier, but now he was key to the band's continuation, because Captain was about to leave the band, calling Roman on August 24th 1984 and telling him he was out. With gigs slated, Roman quickly moved over to guitar which would turn out to be his official lot. Signing with MCA on October

10th would be the new four-piece, consisting of Dave, Roman, Bryn and Rat, who had fallen completely out with both Sensible and Gray, beginning with the Rat's accosting of Paul—pleasure and the pain indeed.

"Roman contributed a lot," notes Rat. "He started hanging out with the band and was friends with Paul Gray. He used to feed Paul's cats when Paul went on tour. And then we found out that he was a very talented guitar player and also a very talented keyboard player and also a great songwriter. The thing with the way I write and the way that Dave writes, they need interpreting, and an interpreter is what Roman was really good at. He'd say, 'Well, how about something like that?' And he'd turn it into something that had proper structure and thought. So on that level he was great. And he was one of the few guitar players that the Damned had that could absolutely play the whole catalogue; he could play 'New Rose' just as readily and very well as he could 'Smash It Up.'"

"And Bryn, totally brilliant as a player, but with a totally different attitude and technique to the instrument than Paul. With Paul it flowed; there was a bit of free-form, a bit of maybe drifting in and out of time with each other and then coming back in, that looseness that the band has or can have. But with Bryn, he was much more rigid, which meant I had to tighten up. Working with Jon Kelly and suddenly having to work with click tracks and stuff also introduced the same element. So Bryn was absolutely perfect for that. Plus he was a fun guy to have around (laughs)."

It had been decided within the ranks that the band's survival was bigger than any one member, and that they were going to get serious and put the booze-fuelled antics aside, much easier now that Captain wasn't around to egg Rat on. It was also decided that The Damned were going to concentrate on writing hits, something that their new big shot MCA was happy to hear. Things would get off to a great start with the demo sessions at Pathway as well as the launch of an advance singly in "Grimly Fiendish" that would reach No.21 on the UK charts and be the subject of a posh video. The song would see release on multiple formats, as was the sneaky norm of the day, designed to fudge the numbers for chart success.

The pursuit of a Goth image (and first-foot-forward song to match) came mostly from Dave and Roman, but everyone agreed, from Rat through (new) management and the label, that a new direction was called for in order for the band to survive.

"Generally, we listened to a lot of our critics and we were very aware of what the last album sounded like and what it had done," muses Rat. "But moving on, that's what a musician does. If you just keep on repeating your last trick, you become staid and boring, and it's not why we do it. It's certainly not why I do it."

"Until *Phantasmagoria* we never really saw any money at all," adds Dave. "It was just enough to live on and get by. We had everything, the usual mismanagement, people appropriating funds, just stupid things we should have learned from. But I never gave it up. There had been times I thought maybe I'm going to have to, but luckily enough, I've always managed to scrape by. But believe me, there's been some tough times where you just think, why do I even bother?"

"*Phantasmagoria* was influenced by the garage bands of the '60s," continues Vanian. "There was a golden era, especially in America, from about '62 onwards, that was just this amazing amount of bands that wrote incredibly different diverse music. The Seeds and the Shadows of Knight did not sound like the Left Banke. And you had great moments like the Mamas and Papas, all of those vocals bands you had, with great melodies. There were so many different flavours of music; it wasn't all the same."

"And it wasn't just the songs," continues Vanian. "It was the production techniques where everybody was learning how to use stereo for the first time, going from mono, trying different things out. So producers were trying radical ways of making music. Shadow Morton was doing great things with The Shangri-Las using sound effects which hadn't really been done, these rich sort of orchestral parts. Very much, in the Phil Spector mode, obviously. So when you listen to the radio from those eras, you hear a vast difference in styles of music. To me, nowadays, production's gone all flat, where everything sounds upfront and in-your-face. It sounds great, but it sounds similar to a record you've heard before. But back then, Motown didn't sound like The Animals and the Stones didn't sound like The Beatles, not just within the music, but the production side as well. That, for me, was what the '60s were great for: a really golden era of experimentation, trying to push the boundaries in so many different ways."

"Being in The Damned wasn't like being in a pop group," continues Rat. "But when it came to *Phantasmagoria*, in the contract it was, ah, this *is* a pop band. Instead of being four individuals, there was now more focus around the image of the band. So we got to wear those funny clothes and grow our hair and play that game for a while, which was good fun to do. I didn't always enjoy the challenge of making *Phantasmagoria* and *Anything*. We worked with some really great people like Jon Kelly, who produced the albums, but it was a learning curve, about getting it right and making things sound good and putting stuff together. But when you work with somebody as experienced as that, it's difficult not to."

The sessions proper were conducted at Pete Townshend's Eel Pie studio in Soho, commencing in mid-April '85. Antithetical to how the record sounds, most of *Phantasmagoria* was played live with minimal overdubs, because the band had routined the songs well and even played some of them live. The extra challenge was that the band's songs were no longer bathed in noise but rather now steeped in atmosphere. Sounds would have to be dialled in perfectly for it to work.

"One day we were there," recalls Rat, "and Jon was rubbing his chin and going, 'It's the drum sound.' And I'm like, 'They sound all right; what's wrong with them?' He said, 'You can hear the heads are plastic.' And as soon as he said it, I could hear it (laughs). And that changed the whole feel of just the tonal thing you get with the drum kit, what you can do with the real sound. Before we always worked in smaller studios. When you can suddenly hear something in a different way, with a bit more clarity, you begin to understand that the real sound of what you're doing is important. We always used to depend a lot on the desk, and EQing: 'Well, it's not a great sound, but it'll be all right when we put some compression on it,' that kind of thing. It's really what studios are for. But working with Jon Kelly, it was, 'What you give me is what comes out, but I'll make it bigger and better than what it is.'"

Reinforcing the grey music enclosed was the stunning image used for the front cover, with the entire presentation being as far from *Machine Gun Etiquette* as possible. You couldn't make a more Gothic rock cover, given the typestyle used, the title, the temptress in a graveyard under thunderheads. This was in fact Susie Bick, later to be married to Nick Cave, yet another Goth icon. She is pictured plotting something in Kensal Green Cemetery, Harrow Road. On the back there's a crow, but as if it was deemed necessary to complete the circuit on the front, that same crow is reproduced there in red silhouette, so now we have blood too.

"That was a Bob Carlos Clarke photograph," explains Rat. "He was a renowned fashion model photographer in London. And the thing was he would only take one picture. He wasn't like a lot of others who would usually shoot off dozens and you'd go through choosing the right one later. He would get everything absolutely perfect beforehand. But this one, he'd already done it. It was just such a totally cool picture and he'd never done anything with it. Like most artists, he would have stuff lying around. And then he photographed us for the inner sleeve, so I mean we did actually get our pictures taken by him. But even the small airplane on the back cover and the whole mood of it, again, reflected absolutely what we wanted to say."

Asked to pick a favourite on the record, Rat explains that, "We all had a lot of ideas for those records. Roman and I spent a lot of time sifting through things and working it out, just sort of saying, 'Well, if you go in this direction…' But I thixnk on *Phantasmagoria* it's probably 'Shadow of Love' that still stands out for me. There are a lot of drums on it and I like the tune, the way it moves around and the little breaks in it. It was almost like a snapshot of the band at the time, through the mood of the song and the lyrics, almost a summary of exactly what we were about at that point in time."

****

Side 1

Street of Dreams
(Scabies/Vanian/Jugg/Merrick) 5:36

It's sax, from UK session treasure Gary Barnacle, and three errant bass notes, that conspire to announce the new Damned, in other words, introduce to the world what is a new band, let alone introduce a new song or even a new album. Barnacle stays as the band heats up, en route to the first verse, framed on tribal drums, across a song that will have to stand as the rockiest thing on all of *Phantasmagoria*.

Dave's lyric further fleshes out the Goth manifesto, portraying the song's haunted men as tormenters inside of one's dreams or Goth ghoulies out at night in the real world. A glimmer of hope for these "seekers of unlikeliness" comes through strength in numbers, "a thousand voices sweet and clear," as well as the image of holding one's head up high when walking the street of dreams, the street of aspirations.

The song is thoughtfully constructed, with a tension-building pre-chorus, an anthemic chorus, a surprising techno-industrial break and an entirely different break later, where Dave does a spoken bit, accompanied by castanets and Spanish guitar from a session player added by Jon Kelly after the band had already hit the road. Also prominent in this section is Bryn on bass, recorded with the same sort of articulation and bite we got with Paul. On top of a couple of key changes, as the various instrumental sections progress, there's a modulation, culminating in a squealing Barnacle sax solo over Rat going nuts hitting everything in sight.

Shadow of Love
(Vanian/Scabies/Jugg/Merrick) 3:49

It's Bryn and Rat that are to blame for The Damned delivering a country western tune, with Bryn coming up with the defining bass line to the song as a joke, and then Rat sealing the deal with his swing snare beat. "Shadow of Love" actually began with a piece of music written by Captain, who nonetheless has been scrubbed from the credits. The chorus came from Roman, the break riff from Rat, but the main frame of it came from Captain, who was just leaving the band when the first demo sessions were happening at Pathway, August '84.

All told, given Dave's sort of paranormal-level seductress lyric, where the hour is late and there are doors and mirror and candles and prayer, the song comes off more "Ghost Riders In The Sky" than strictly country western—this is country like The Cramps are country, with a shared evocation between the two being Elvis and rockabilly.

Keeping the song dark are the chimey, echo-drenched guitars, Dave's low-register vocal and the attendant ghostly back-ups. And then there was the video, which featured the band playing in a dollhouse, outside of which lurks the temptress, a Gothic beauty very much like the one on the cover of the album.

Mirroring the lyric, we have a mirror, mirroring the band. The candle is now a candelabra. There is fire as well as a black cat with glowing white eyes. Roman and Dave compete for who has the biggest hair with Rat not far behind and Bryn running a distant fourth. There is a profusion of psychically generated wind to help with the measurements, lest we not be sure.

"Shadow of Love" was issued as a single on June 10th 1985, making it the second song to be released before the full album would see the soul-crushing light of day.

There'll Come a Day
(Jugg/Merrick/Scabies/Vanian) 4:13

"There'll Come a Day" represents a hypnotic combination of the themes of the two pleasing and painful nightmares that came before it. "The torch of love is a burning flame" and it seems to have burned our protagonist from "Shadow of Love," who, like back in the "Street of Dreams," is holding his head up as he emerges from his lair "into a brand new day," amusingly waiting until the skies are overcast.

With harpsichord keys like Dave Greenfield and thuggish bass like J.J. Burnel, this one's even more perfectly post-punk than the opening two tracks of the record, but consistent of upbeat rhythm, also evoking The Stranglers with its nod to '60s garage rock—a direct reference is early buzz guitar classic "Dirty Ol' Man" by The Electras from 1966. But there's also Hammond and there are harmonies, as well as a modulation and artsy guitar soloing from Roman that touches on the blues and on rockabilly, Jugg proving his versatility but still within a tight frame of austerity that was of the times and of the chimes.

Sanctum Sanctorum
(Vanian/Jugg/Merrick/Scabies) 6:22

From the title on down, "Sanctum Sanctorum" is about as Goth rock as one can get—on an album full of the stuff—and yet The Damned are not one of the first names that comes to mind when running down the list of top Goth bands. Makes sense, obviously, because it's only one of many things they do. Still, few actual Goth bands went this far from rock instrumentation to explore those feelings of dread (and dead). "Sanctum Sanctorum" starts with rain, thunder, pipe organ, ghost woman wailing, more rain, more thunder, and then Dave crooning low and alone over classical piano—and we know what he looks like.

Vanian's lyric depicts a feverish dream state, perhaps between sleep and waning wakefulness, with the protagonist tormented by the thoughts of a love interest. Dave wrote the song about Patricia Morrison (Rainone), who he'd been having an affair with despite his marriage to Laurie. In 1997, in Las Vegas, Dave would marry Patricia. Veteran bassist of a number of bands including The Gun Club and Sisters of Mercy, Morrison would also join the family business, enjoying an eight-year run in The Damned from 1996 through 2004, a period that included the recording of the *Grave Disorder* album.

"Sanctum Sanctorum" was written in the studio once the band got to Pathway where they conducted the album's demo sessions. The originator of the idea was Dave, but Roman worked closely with him, writing on an upright piano. Indeed there are no bass and drums in "Sanctum Sanctorum" until the halfway point (and no guitars at all), where the band break into a hypnotic and swinging waltz and we hear Dave's rich baritone, intensifying the drama. Soon we're back into the uneasy peace, accompanied by violin, and after another round of the swirling loud stuff, we get more ghostly female pining, set to *Exorcist*-like piano.

Side 2

Is It a Dream (Scabies/Jugg/Vanian/Merrick/Sensible) 3:27

Over to side two of the original vinyl, and The Damned offer up the breezy, Julian Cope-like "Is It a Dream" (no question mark), which was one of the earliest written songs on the album, reaching back a year to when Captain was still part of the team hence the credit. There's a John Peel session version which Rat prefers, but in truth, it's not much different than the final, which perhaps exhibits more influence from producer Jon Kelly, who had brought to the band Fairlight technology and the attendant austere synth/keyboard vibe that has not aged well.

Rat says that because the band had been playing "Is It a Dream" live, this was the easiest song to record for the album, with the guys knocking it out in a day. But there's not much to it anyway. The chorus is a slight variant to the verse, with the pre-chorus doing any of the heavy lifting. The break is brief and behaved, with the highlight being the "Like a fly in a cup of tea" simile. After this, Rat switches to a four-on-the-floor with Roman sticking in some noisy guitar soloing that adds little to the song, strafing and comment through to the end, although at one point he works in a quick run that reveals the guitar hero within. Rat doubles up the beat at the close of the tune, but again he sounds anything but punk. Then everything stops and Dave queries, "Am I dreaming?" Not sure, but we're all sleeping.

"Is It a Dream" was issued in "Wild West Express Mix" form as a single on September 9th 1985, reaching No.34 on the charts. This version is almost twice as long with a bunch of ambitious extra parts added, plus it's punchier with more guitars and more clearly heard piano.

Released in various formats in a number of countries, the single's main B-side was a live version of "Street of Dreams," recorded July 11th 1985 at the Woolwich Coronet. Other B-sides include a 4:13 version of "Curtain Call," a cover of the Sex Pistols' "Pretty Vacant" and a cover of the Troggs' "Wild Thing," all recorded at the same gig. Further rolling out the red carpet, MCA produced two separate videos for the song, one with the band performing to the track out in a field, the other a classy multi-camera performance clip, both using the shorter album version of the song.

Grimly Fiendish (Jugg/Vanian/Merrick/Scabies/Jackson) 3:47

The "Grimly Fiendish" lyric is inspired by black-cloaked "rottenest crook in the world" Grimly Feendish (sic) of British comic strip fame, created by Leo Baxendale in the mid '60s. Vanian calls Feendish an *Addams Family* rip-off, but notes that the British character had fangs and that bats flew out of his mouth. He's perfect for a Damned song and given extra dimension here, partially through the thoughtful words said and what is left unsaid, through the typical sketchiness of the band's spare lyrics. What we get are essentially the reflections of Feendish/Fiendish along with those of his accusers as he stands trial.

The sympathetic portraiture is set to a soundtrack that is as perfectly English as it is perfectly moustache-twisting fiendish, framed by the harpsichord-like saloon music at the beginning and the 1920s speakeasy trumpet later on, bell included, courtesy of Willy Algar. As for the English side of things, what we get is a cross between The Kinks, The Jam, Madness and music for British sitcoms, culminating in the "bad bad bad boy" section, which sounds like a Victorian nursery rhyme gone Goth.

The Jackson credit of the song pertains to Clive Jackson, a.k.a. The Doctor in Doctor and the Medics. It was at his place that the lyrics were finished, says Roman, "in an acid-soaked environment," but the song was pretty much written by Roman at the music end, who also was in on the lyrics, sharing Vanian's love for the cartoon character from the British papers.

The band were initially shocked and disconcerted by Bob Sargeant's production on the early days' version used for the single, choosing not to use him for the forthcoming album. Still, they ultimately wound up with a sound not so much different from Sargeant's courtesy of producer Jon Kelly.

"Grimly Fiendish" was the advance single that got MCA all excited about what The Damned might achieve all dressed-up and looking like Grimly Feendish. There were various remixes, with the track reaching No.21 in the charts, the band's highest placement since 1979. The front sleeve of the single featured a suitably occulted Bob Carlos Clarke photograph called "Crown of Thorns," with each member of the band signing 1,000 copies, for a total of 4,000 copies each signed by one band member. Available was a white vinyl version plus a gatefold sleeve. Musically, across all permutations, all we got extra was album track "Edward the Bear" plus the various remixes of the A-side.

Making the cinematic and expensive-looking video for the song (with the band dressed to the nines in Victorian finery), at one point Dave had been carrying a torch down a dark and freezing-cold stairwell and his big hair caught on fire, prompting staffers to jump on him and smack him on the head until disaster had been averted.

Edward the Bear
(Jugg/Scabies/Merrick/Vanian) 3:34

Brought in by Roman, "Edward the Bear" is even sung by him, Roman capably playing the Captain role, the cleaner, more adolescent voice lent further mischievousness due to the choice of singing in an English accent. Jugg says the song is about growing up, with references to Captain himself. The band had intended the song to remain a B-side, but the label stuck it on the album against their wishes, due to, granted, the band coming up short on material.

Part of the band's reluctance, one imagines, might have been because it's a bit of a lift from King track "Baby Sign Here with Me," which somewhat incensed Henry Badowski who wasn't happy he didn't get in on the credits, having written and sung the root song. One wonders as well if the band was reticent to include it because Roman is singing a tad wobbly, not to mention that the track doesn't fit the Goth mandate lyrically, being a bit sunny and mainstream and in fact too similar to "Is It a Dream," once more Julian Cope coming to mind.

Sax, keys, rainy Byrds guitar, octave-jumping bass line, pretty harmony backing vocals... such is the melange of sounds that places this innocuous ditty inside of the sonic mandate for the record, one that makes *Phantasmagoria* so different than the previous five albums, most specifically because there are no punk songs and thus nothing dominated by guitar with distortion pedal, no power chords. We also get uniform production values and arrangements because of this, given the tight range of instrumentation and sounds, the odd bit of brass window-dressing notwithstanding.

The Eighth Day
(Scabies/Jugg/Vanian/Merrick) 3:44

Amusingly, the bleakest lyric across the record is placed upon another one of the record's bounciest musical beds, Rat putting the snare on one and three like a pubby mod revival song, with Roman and Dave sending it further in that direction with very British melodies. Lyrically, Dave is strident and poetic here, substantial, as he describes the apocalyptic events that God will get up to after his day of rest is compete. Mountains rise, seas boil, there's acid rain, "pure white heat" and "crimson mists." Cheerily stated, Dave also expects a "dancing devil knocking on my door," set to a chorus that sounds like R.E.M. or The Church.

Trojans
(Merrick/Jugg/Scabies/Vanian) 4:47

Phantasmagoria closes with a gorgeous instrumental, although "Trojans," written by Bryn, wasn't intended to stay that way—Dave was supposed to come back into the studio to do a vocal for it but didn't bother. In that respect it's not your standard action-packed instrumental, but quite spare and languished, perhaps at the music end the regal equivalent of "Sanctum Sanctorum." There's something Pink Floyd-like about the song, given the sax solo and the soft rock underneath that particular section, and given Roman's bluesy electric guitar licks as sort of colour commentary or vocal substitute like David Gilmour might do. "Snowman" from Rainbow's 1983 album *Bent Out of Shape* also comes to mind.

Toward the end of the song the band triple up on the beat, over which simple and stark grand piano notes team up with synth pop keyboards. As the album winds down, Rat chucks in some extended rolls around the kit as bar-ending fills to remind us what The Damned once sounded like, at least as far as the drummer is concerned.

Singles, B-sides, Bonus Tracks

Nightshift
(Vanian/Jugg/Merrick/Scabies) 2:25

The self-produced "Nightshift" is an atmospheric and tribal post-punk rocker with pure punk tooling like the soundtrack-only "Dead Beat Dance" and unlike the album at hand, *Phantasmagoria*. It's the key and proper B-side of the various short snappers that show up across the clutch of remix single versions of "Shadow of Love," specifically on all versions, but the only song to show on the 7" issues from the UK and from Germany.

Unfortunately like "Dead Beat Dance," it's a little rushed and substandard, although it does manage to form a handshake in a dark garage between punk and Goth, with a little Who-like noise and Cramps horrorbilly added to the cauldron. Which is the perfect noir setting for the lyric, spare as it is, about a guy who works the nightshift, heading into town at night, a "father never seen in the day."

Let There Be Rats
(Scabies) 2:12

"Let There Be Rats" is a "Shadow of Love" B-side, but only available on the UK double-7" single version, on the second record, backed with "Wiped Out." In fact neither track is part of the 7", 10" or 12" versions. The song lives up to the potential of its title but no further. It's a semi-proper song with a jaunty comedic punk rock riff, along with a vocal of which the entire lyric equals the title, although it's said with feeling, in a gang vocal.

In between, Rat sort of mildly and musically solos on the drums, pitter-pattering on his toms, the beat kept going with his foot on high-hat. The song manages a musical modulation, at which time we get a brief guitar solo and an elegant wind-up which sounds like an Oi! band playing a Christmas carol while Rat does one of his usual concluding rackets.

Is this a Damned song? Sort of. Rat had issued the track on a solo single issued by Paradiddle Records back in February of '84 when he though The Damned were doomed. This was the A-side, backed with "Wiped Out" and "Drums Drums Drums," with The Damned uncredited. But here it is on a Damned single, not attributed to Rat as the artist (only as the writer), on MCA with the same swanky overcast sky record label making it look all official.

Wiped Out
(Scabies) 1:38

"Wiped Out" is the B-est of Damned B-sides, put all the way to the back of the attic of the "Shadow of Love" double-7" version as track No.4. Like "Let There Be Rats," it's a lift from Rat's obscure solo single. It's similar to that song as well, a near-instrumental positioned to showcase Rat on drums, even if he doesn't really want to do much beyond "Wipe Out," i.e. playing "music" on the drums and not soloing as such. "Wiped Out" is sort of "Secret Agent Man" surf music, with guitar, bass and drums and cheesy vintage keyboard sounds. It's the kind of thing Rat would do on his full-length 2020 album *Sparkle*, as part of a duo with Billy Shinbone.

Would You
(Mason/Scabies/Jugg/Vanian/Merrick) 2:31

Not to be confused with "Would You Be So Hot (If You Weren't Dead)" from *Grave Disorder*, "Would You" is a country and western piss-take featuring Rat's soon-to-be-wife Vivian Mason on vocals (and lyrics), hence the Mason in the credits.

Over lo-fi strummed electric guitar and living room organ drum beat, Mason asks if she would be loved with three eyes, getting sick in a bucket, had fake teeth or walked on a wooden leg. How about if the neighbours laughed and called her Peg? If so, then her prayers have not been ignored. There's also a perfunctory country twang guitar solo, but also a dog barking. "Would You" would be part of all 10" and 12" permutations of the "Shadow of Love" single and none of the 7" versions. The song probably stands as the biggest liberty taken ever with respect to a declared Damned B-side.

Dead Beat Dance
(Jugg/Scabies/Merrick/Vanian) 3:51

As the story goes, Big Beat Records were on tap to issue in the UK the soundtrack album to comedic horror movie *The Return of the Living Dead*, for which there was to be punk music (the movie was a US production, with Enigma issuing the album stateside). Big Beat exec and Damned producer Roger Armstrong knew Dave would be into it but the contribution had to be turned around in two days. Bryn had brought in a 1979 song from his old punk band Victimize called "The Day I Met God," written by Bryn and Andy Johnson. Dave wrote some new lyrics, the band straightened out the previous four-on-the-floor beat and this scrappy B-grade punk song was born.

"Dead Beat Dance" was recorded at an erstwhile *Phantasmagoria* demo session, hence its completely different (and self-produced) sound from the forthcoming album—quite tinny actually, with Rat's drums sounding particularly weak. Bryn happened to be away when the song was recorded, so Roman played both the bass and guitar, peeling off a ripping Captain-like solo, which is followed up by a Theremin solo. Dave's zombie lyric ends at this point too, with some sampled maniacal laughter and the introduction of Doctor Death amidst dovetailed backing vocals. The whole thing collapses into an anguished scream after a typical Rat drum rave-up.

The Damned got pole position on side two of the soundtrack album, joining what is mostly a Gothic punk cast of bands, namely 45 Grave, The Cramps, SSQ, Tall Boys, TSOL, The Flesh Eaters, The Jet Black Berries and psych legend Roky Erikson.

Eloise
(Ryan) 5:10

Garnering much press attention and excitement from the fans over the course of touring *Phantasmagoria* in late '85, The Damned were in a position to have a third single launched. MCA wanted to try "Is It a Dream" and the band didn't want a third single at all, or rather, if they had to, Dave in particular wanted to do something new. In the end, they did both.

Dave had it in mind as far back as 1976 (as evidenced in a Sniffin' Glue interview Rat recalls seeing), to one day cover "Eloise," an insanely orchestrated baroque pop hit back in October of '68 performed by Barry Ryan and written by Barry's twin brother Paul. Not hard to see why the song was a hit, vaulting to No.1 in 17 countries around the world.

First off, it was practically "Bohemian Rhapsody" in terms of its musical and vocal arrangement. Second, it's got a hooky melody but a complicated and fresh one (or two or three). Third, it's got a rhythmic pattern where most of the music stops for the verse, which is then punctuated once and then punctuated twice—never under-estimate the appeal of a good air-punch.

The Damned recorded the song in two sessions, beginning on October 14th and 15th at Music Works and finishing up November 23rd and 24th at Eel Pie—Jon Kelly producing, with a mix at Swanyard. The second session took care of the vocals as well as all the faux orchestration, which Roman put together using a Yamaha DX7 and an E-mu Emulator. Essentially what he dials up fit into four categories: synths, harpsichord-like keyboards, strings and simulated angelic vocals, although most of the backing vocals are real and somewhat Beach Boys-like, as heard on the 1968 original.

The value in the song comes from the song itself, with The Damned's version being typically punchy and modern using '80s production tropes, but largely faithful to the original where it matters. Essentially, in this form, "Eloise" would have dovetailed in nicely with the rest of the songs on *Phantasmagoria*. It's psych, it's dark pop, dramatic, very English and the lyric tells of a torrid, obsessive love that causes restless nights, loosely the theme of everything on side one of *Phantasmagoria*. Rat has said he liked to imagine that the song was about a transgendered schizophrenic, with Eloise in fact being a second personality trapped within the song's restless protagonist.

"Eloise" was issued on January 27th 1986, essentially right between the two MCA albums. The song became the band's biggest hit ever, reaching No.3 on the UK charts. There were a number of different formats and mixes, including an "Extravagant Mix" that took the song close to ten minutes long. The "No Sleep Until Wednesday Mix" pared the song down to seven minutes. Played up, always, was the song's big stabs, which, again, proved the value of a purely rhythmic hook.

Temptation
(Jugg/Scabies/Vanian/Merrick) 4:05

"Temptation," written by Dave and Roman like most of the band's material during this era, was recorded at the same time as "Eloise" and used as that song's main B-side, showing up on all versions of the single. It's an ambitious track, influenced by the Doors, with Dave throwing Jim Morrison shapes over dark but jazzy beat generation keyboard and bass for a minute-and-a-half before Rat joins in, channelling John Densmore.

But then at the 2:30 mark, all of that is put aside as the guys board the good ship Hawkwind for a little interstellar jam, framed by a sinister guitar riff that sounds like signature Dave Brock. Rat begins playing a tight uptempo four-four, but then as Roman starts ripping off howling guitar licks on top of the riff, Scabies responds in kind, letting loose until the fade, fully four minutes and three distinct movements after this obscure gem of a B-side had begun.

Neatly, at the lyric end, "Temptation" reads like an intensification of the "Eloise" joint, which in turn, as discussed, fits perfectly thematically with the literary totality of *Phantasmagoria*. In fact, the cover image used on the picture sleeve of the "Eloise" single—an oddly androgynous but definitely frantic Dave character with a comely woman either *as* his nose or attached to his nose—fits equally with the B-side as it does the A.

Beat Girl
(Barry/Peacock) 2:21

Helping make the "Eloise" single three for three with respect to quality, The Damned craft a studious cover of "Beat Girl," composed by John Barry for the 1960 beat generation teen flick of the same name. "Beat Girl" per se is orchestrated and instrumental, but the version emulated closely here is that of "The Beat Girl Song" with Adam Faith on vocals (lyrics by Trevor Peacock), Faith having co-starred in the movie.

It's a perfect song for The Damned given its dark surf rock terrain, representing a type of nascent hoodlum garage rock more likely to show up in any given B-grade horror flick of the day than at a beach party. Dave's glowering vocal reinforces this notion of impending menace, which comes to fruition when his drummer suddenly goes into a wild solo, effectively blowing up the song.

THE NEW SINGLE

OUT NOW ON 7″ & 12″

ALSO AVAILABLE

AN EXTREMELY LIMITED
EDITION COMPACT DISC
SINGLE FEATURING
ALONE AGAIN OR, ELOISE,
IN DULCE DECORUM
& PSYCHOMANIA

ALONE AGAIN OR IS TAKEN FROM
THE DAMNED ALBUM "ANYTHING"
(ON RECORD, TAPE & CD)

·THE·
DAMNED
Anything
THE NEW SINGLE ON 7'' & 12''
FROM THE FORTHCOMING ALBUM "ANYTHING"

Anything

The narrative around the band's second and last album for MCA is that, in essence, it's the difficult second album. As the concept goes, you have your whole life to write and routine the songs that go on your first album, and the second one is a hurry-up affair. That's what happened here: *Phantasmagoria* was the product of a relative stirring, steeping and simmer, vaguely conceived before there was a record deal and then nurtured into being. *Anything* had the band harried, from constant gigging (including a US tour) and from TV appearances and press demands back home, partly because of the "success" of *Phantasmagoria* (more in the public consciousness than in hard sales) but also because of the very real success of follow-up non-LP single "Eloise." MCA demanded more.

"We'd been on the road for pretty much ever since *Phantasmagoria* had come out," recalls Rat, "and before then we never really stopped touring. So we didn't really have a lot of time to write. You need to get away from it and stop and get bored again before you start picking up instruments and doing stuff. When you've been doing it with that sort of intensity, you start to get numb to it. So you need to get away. And of course we hadn't really had much time or chances to be doing that. That's why we covered 'Alone Again Or,' because it was a good track and we didn't have anything better. So why not do it?"

Jon Kelly was back producing—you tend to go with the same producer again when you've had break-out success the last time and nobody has killed each other—but the guys would be whisked off to the rural Puk Recording Studios in northern Denmark to piece the album together, writing almost everything in the studio, working from June to August of 1986.

"Anything," "In Dulce Decorum," "Gigolo" and "Psychomania" had been demoed in rough form, but mostly without lyrics. Past that, there were only bits and pieces, adding to the frustration of the technical problems encountered when the band first got to Puk, resulting in a week of downtime. Then Dave was away, due to a family emergency with his wife, and then once he got back, Rat took off for a few days. As well there wasn't much to do around the studio, so the guys concentrated on improving their snooker game and riding three-wheeler ATVs, along with Go West who were recording at the studio at the same time.

As for the direction of the material, there were no radical shifts there either. "It was a funny time," muses Dave, "because, obviously, by the time *Anything* came out, Captain had been out of the band for a while. It was Roman Jugg playing guitar, and we split the writing between us. Those two albums are very much Roman and myself's influences and music. So they're more melodramatic, with the orchestral things coming from my side, really. When I worked with Captain we still had that, but we'd do it in a different way."

There were tensions concerning material as well, with Roman dismissing Bryn's ideas and Kelly dismissing Rat's, with the label siding with Kelly, who, more than the other guys, wanted to keep things in line with the Gothic direction of *Phantasmagoria*.

Dave was most integral to the vision and success of the band during this period, but he'd still be hard to track down at times, and when he was away, the band would only venture toward getting backing tracks down, wanting him to be there for important decisions.

"He wrote quite a lot of the lyrics and contributed greatly to the artwork and the image of the band," says Rat. "Everything from *The Black Album* album cover to the title of *Phantasmagoria* and tracking down Bob Carlos Clarke and getting the logo right and stuff like that, all mixed in with trying to turn in the right record, I guess. But yes, he could be awkward sometime. He wouldn't turn up for days on end. Incredibly, we wouldn't see him for some time. But he was always great with gigs. In my experience, I think there were only two occasions where he didn't turn up, which wasn't bad. It was trying to get him into the studio or get him to do interviews; that was always the hard part. Because if he didn't have something solid to do, if he didn't know exactly what he was doing or if he didn't like the idea of what he was going to be talked into doing, you couldn't get him to do it. I don't blame him. But he could come in and just be completely brilliant. Thing is though, you'd maybe have to wait for awhile for him to come in."

Having run out of time (and shekels) at Puk, Jon Kelly resigned himself to mixing the record in September at Jacobs Studio in Surrey, a small facility with dodgy acoustics. Any influence the guys in the band could have on the proceedings was now over with, not that they ever worried themselves with mixes too much to begin with.

Anything was issued on December 1st 1986. The home country got a gatefold sleeve with a little black-and-white pop-up picture of the guys, once you cracked the gate. There were printed lyrics and a merchandise order form. In North America, the extras were stripped away. The album cover, although containing the same elements, was rendered in monochromatic gold sculptured relief, against the original UK colour illustration. The album certified silver in the UK for sales of over 60,000 copies, reaching No.40 in the charts, with all four of the singles from the album charting as well. It didn't do much business stateside.

History has not been kind to *Anything*. On the one hand, critics, fans and the band alike look back fondly on a period when the band were a semi-thriving operation, part of the machine, above the radar as it were. On the other hand, the narrative that has simplified and ossified over the years (in no small part thanks to the band saying as much in interviews) is one that positions *Anything* as the weaker second part of a two-part story, with the enthusiasm over the band's reinvention now dissipated and replaced by a certain amount of jadedness and exhaustion.

****

Side 1

Anything
(Jugg/Scabies/Merrick/Vanian) 4:47

Anything cracks wide open with the record's headbanging title track, indeed the closest the band would get to heavy metal since the *Machine Gun Etiquette* days. A palm-muted chug, accompanied by bass begins the proceedings, with Roman adding some oohs and aahs (and not always in tune), along with Rat who provides random bursts of violence. Then we're into the song, and all the excitement wrapped up in The Cult's "She Sells Sanctuary" and "Rain" and other rockers on *Love*... well, The Damned are bringing it right here, along with the same children of the night fashion sense. We can also draw a line back to "Street of Dreams" from the previous album—*Phantasmagoria*'s lead-off track would be its rockiest as well.

Doomy, sophisticated, uptempo, groovy... "Anything" has got everything, including Dave bringing the menace through a bit of a bullhorn technique, with his angry vocal phrasing, as has been noticed, sounding a bit like Iggy Pop on his *New Values* classic "Five Foot One." Tempering him are ethereal female vocals courtesy of Suzie O'List, but nothing can stop this juggernaut, not the gunshots, not the yelp of pain after the "I'll make my girl scream" line of enquiry, not Jon Kelly's industrial ear candy, not Roman's classy country twang guitar solo. In fact, the song never breaks tempo, with the inevitable fade being the only solution.

"Anything" was issued as the album's first single, November 6th 1986, a month in advance of the album—the band had wanted to go with "In Dulce Decorum" but were over-ruled. The key B-side would be non-LP track "The Year Of The Jackal," with various remixes of the A-side showing up across the different formats. After the success of "Eloise," the song's No.32 showing in the charts was viewed as a let-down.

Alone Again Or
(MacLean) 3:38

The original version of "Alone Again Or," written by Bryan MacLean, served as the opening track and centrepiece of Love's classic 1967 album *Forever Changes*. Ironically, the last big cover of it was on the 1977 album *Lights Out* from UFO, whose bassist when The Damned were pondering a version was none other than Paul Gray.

It's a much better choice for The Damned though, given the band's love of Love, along with the recent single success with "Eloise" and the fact that this particular slice of scholarly '60s music sounds similarly baroque and Gothic all at once just like "Eloise" and much of the band's original oeuvre since *The Black Album*.

Picked partly because of a dearth of material, Roman also says he wanted to do it to try out a new guitar he had recently acquired from a Danish luthier; no doubt this is the one heard playing the rainy Byrds-type signature hook. As well there was the problem of Dave being in America right in the middle of the recording sessions and therefore unable to write. To be sure, Rat picked up the slack when it came to write the lyrics needed for *Anything*, but it was much easier to do something already written—indeed Roman even performs a co-vocal with Dave (it's mostly Roman) on this gloomy Gus of a song. Amusingly, Rat had never heard "Alone Again Or" and thought it was something Roman had quickly cooked up.

It's a professional, glossy rendition we get from The Damned, bright and lively at the production end, faux orchestration, almost braying percussion, highlight being the guest trumpet parts from Kurt Holm. If the drums sound loud, that's because the band recorded them in the hallway that separated The Damned's studio from Go West's.

"Alone Again Or" was issued on April 6th 1987 as the album's third single and as the first CD single to come from The Damned, an item that also included amongst its four track "Eloise" on CD for the first time. The regular 7" single had for its B-side a version of "In Dulce Decorum" recorded live at the Hammersmith Odeon, November 12th 1986. The Damned enjoyed its first single release in the

States in five years, when MCA issued the song backed with the studio version of "In Dulce Decorum." The song's No.27 placement gave the band their last Top 40 placement to date. Here in the modern era, based on plays on Spotify and the like, "Alone Again Or" is far and away the most enduring song from *Anything* by a magnitude of ten-fold.

The Portrait
(Jugg/Scabies/Merrick/Vanian) 3:50

"The Portrait" feels like another track stuck on *Anything* from necessity, given Dave's absence (and his semi-apologetic acknowledgement that he was away), with the song being wholly Roman's thing. What we get is a creepy and quiet lo-fi piano piece, accompanied by wind sounds, with Mellotron eventually added to the dreamy dance. The composition charts a nice through-line back to "Trojans," similar of mood, but more of a full band performance.

"The Portrait" was inspired by an unsettling fantasy film from 1948 called *Portrait of Jennie*, in which an impoverished artist in Manhattan meets a young girl, paints her portrait, and then watches her grow up at an accelerated pace, falling in love with her, afterward witnessing a sort of paranormal happenstance envelope her with respect to the experience of time. The song contains a creepy, nursery rhyme Jennie sings in the film, which got left off the album due to legalities, but included at the front of what's called the extended version of "The Portrait," used as a B-side on the 12" version of "Gigolo."

Restless
(Jugg/Scabies/Merrick/Vanian) 4:57

A deep album track no one ever talks about, "Restless" really anchors the band to its recently new and profitable mandate, that of Goth rock. There are the dual male/female vocals—Dave singing with Suzie O'List—but more than that are the chimey guitars, with Roman being so comfortable in this field, underrated, almost forgotten as a key creative in this space and time of spiky and teased and dyed black hair.

And then there's the tribal drums, which dominate the mix through performance and accentuated reverb. Rat is an unlikely participant in this realm, one dominated, chronologically, by Joy Division, Killing Joke, Siouxsie and the Banshees, The Cure, Echo and the Bunnymen, New Order and concurrently at the time Sisters of Mercy and The Mission, a curious pairing that weirdly gets joined by The Damned in terms of being perceived as a bit Hollywood, a bit corporate, a bit 12" mix.

Lyrically, "Restless" is pure Goth, with an interesting rural harvest moon-type vibe, with our protagonist restless (like the Wyeth painting) and looking to move on, watching his father work hard but broken by the bad times all the same. He wishes to be back at the idyllic childhood he experienced back at the house on the hill (cue the Audience), but he's now corrupted, "walking in the footsteps of the beast." It's a perfect marriage of doomy music and word, and fortunately for any fan of *Phantasmagoria*, another welcome track that keeps us medicated and dream-fevered in a suspended state of static electricity under gauzy grey skies.

Side 2

In Dulce Decorum
(Jugg/Scabies/Merrick/Vanian) 4:47

Continuing the exercise of matching tracks up to the last record, *Phantasmagoria* had "Sanctum Sanctorum" and now we've got "In Dulce Decorum," both, additional to the Latin titling, being musical tracks that explore the Goth rock space.

Dave's lyric is inspired by Wilfred Owen's World War I poem *Dulce et Decorum est* with the title translating as "It is sweet and fitting" which moves onto "pro patria mori," or "to die for one's country" in the original Latin ode by Horace. Welsh rockers Budgie also referenced Owen's poem, issuing a compilation album called *An Ecstasy of Fumbling*, which is a direct quote from the work.

Dave's devastating lyric (completely different from the poem, more like another scene of the same horror show) speaks of a young World War I soldier on the front lines writing to his mother, indicating that judging from what's happened to his friends he's not long for this world. He writes that he sees the face of the enemy and realises that the two of them share the same fate. "In Dulce Decorum" actually opens with an excerpt of a Winston Churchill speech given to the House of Commons as the Battle of Britain was ramping up on June 18th 1940, which of course means we've got a Second World War artefact at the front of a song about the previous conflagration.

As for the music, the song is built on a thumping four-on-the-floor beat with busy high-hats along with a prominent post-punk bass line. There are also atmospheric signature post-punk electric guitar lines with individually picked notes, along with a track of acoustic guitar strumming. Up top, Dave sings in a range somewhat out of his comfort zone, capturing the anxiety and fragility of the letter soon to be sent off to mum. Roman supports on vocals, his more youthful and arguably more English voice also underscoring the story line, his tone and timbre perfect for the patriotic musings (set to very proper English melodies) as well as the monk-ish chanting of the choral Latin.

"In Dulce Decorum" was issued as a single but a year hence, essentially in support of *The Light at the End of the Tunnel*, MCA's two-LP compilation album released on November 30th 1987—underscoring that fact, the picture sleeve cover design for the single bears similarities to the jacket used for the album. The song reached a middling No.72 on the charts, with the hits and rarities package reaching No.87. An instrumental version of the song can be heard on the *Miami Vice II* soundtrack album, with the song also showing up briefly in a third-season episode of the hit cop show. The single's B-side was "Psychomania," with the 12" version adding an extended version and dub mix of the A.

Gigolo
(Jugg/Scabies/Merrick/Vanian) 6:02

A clear single pick from the record, "Gigolo" is the most upbeat song on *Anything*, sounding like an optimistic XTC, finally about to execute a commercial breakthrough with "Mayor of Simpleton." But also like Andy Partridge might do, the song is quirky and inscrutable with a complicated pedigree, based in a couple of ways on the Syd Barrett solo track from 1970, "Gigolo Aunt."

First off, The Damned's chorus is framed somewhat like Syd's, while also literally using the phrase "gigolo aunt" like Syd did. Second, Syd's keyboard riff is revived here and used for the extensive intro, where The Damned put a bunch of (madcap) laughing and talking over the key line along with some spare guitar. This goes on for two minutes, in the creation of a piece that sounds like a mid-'70s Pink Floyd song collage in tribute to Syd. Then we switch gears completely into Roman's rainy "(Don't Fear) The Reaper" technique, followed by Rat's stadium rock drums and into a song that sounds like a follow-up to "Eloise," in other words a remake of an old and very English hit single.

In addition, the first verse of Syd's song reads like a précis for the vibrant Gerard de Thame-directed video created to promote the Damned track, basically a description of a black-and-white Dave immersed in a scene of wondrous colour. In the video, it's raining cats and dogs in a sort of *Alice in Wonderland* scene, Dave—looking debonair with moustache—singing with a bunny perched on his hat. Again, it's all very XTC-like, in the delivery of an opaque lyric only elliptically about a "gigolo aunt," which I gather has something to do with a female gigolo who doesn't dole out sexual favours for money, but rather for the power.

Apparently the band wasn't happy with all the heavy production work that went into this one, and tried to rectify it with a remix and a redoing of the bass line when back in England, an alteration that didn't get used. In any event, the song dovetails sonically with the rest of the record's tracks, underscored further in its Britishness by a return visit of Kurt Holm on trumpet along with vocals from Roman in addition to Dave.

"Gigolo" was issued as a single in a number of formats and vinyl colours (plus a version missing the circus music intro), backed with "The Portrait," also in regular and alternate version. The song got to No.29 in the charts.

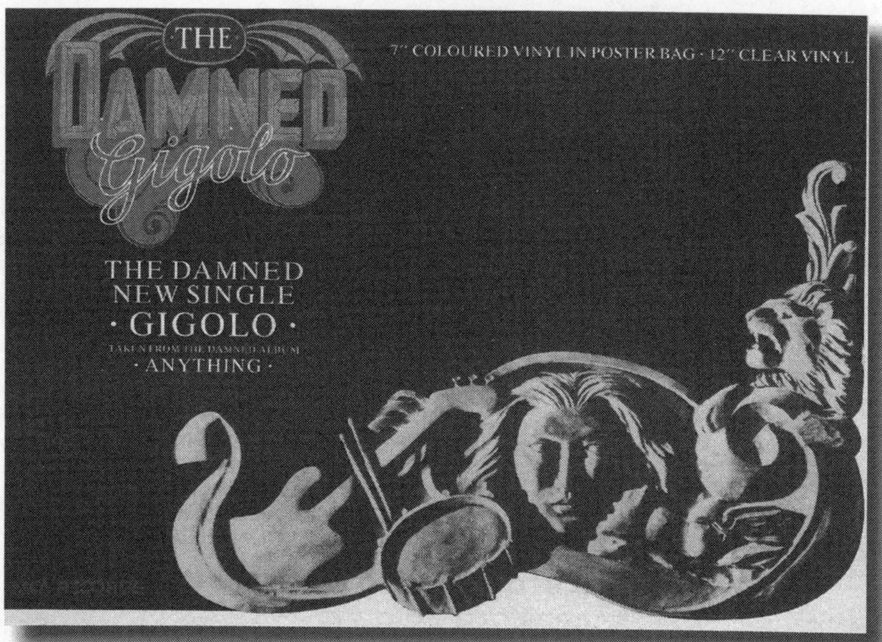

The Girl Goes Down
(Jugg/Scabies/Merrick/Vanian) 4:35

It's as if The Damned enjoyed doing "Beat Girl" so much that they wanted to write one of their own, "The Girl Goes Down" sounding like that song musically as well as lyrically, with the added twist in this one being that our comely go-go girl is tracked through town to the point where she goes down some stairs to some mysterious place that sounds a lot like hell with dancing.

When the song was played live, girls were invited up from the crowd to dance in the cages used as part of the elaborate set, less Gothic this time, instead themed like a travelling circus show to go with the front and back cover imagery used on *Anything* (not to mention the couple of minutes of circus music at the front of one of the album's marquee tracks, "Gigolo").

Tightrope Walk
(Jugg/Scabies/Merrick/Vanian) 4:21

The circus theme from "Gigolo" is back, only this time the dramatic orchestrated intro music of "Tightrope Walk," with Dave as carnival barker, supports a true circus theme with the ensuing song being very much about a tightrope walker. As Dave starts singing the verse, all he has as support underneath him is a pulsating keyboard throb designed to resemble low brass, along with tinkly player piano-like window dressing. The only percussion we hear is an echo-drenched bass drum accompaniment, slowly like a heartbeat.

Cinematic effects help turn the song into the second piece of soundtrack music on the album, alongside "The Portrait." There's a sophisticated but spooky instrumental break, dominated by cutting synthesizer, before Dave is back into the troubled contemplation of the walker and the job before him. The song ends with a funhouse flourish which makes us wonder if today's show has been a success or not.

Psychomania
(Jugg/Scabies/Merrick/Vanian) 4:03

The last song on *Anything* is a James Brown-type show-biz raver, brisk and swinging Friday night beat, braying horns (made from keys) and lots of open spaces into which Dave sings like Elvis. But there's a chuckle of a disconnect with the lyric, which is yet another painful paean to a witchy Goth seductress like Laurie and Patricia. I could imagine this mournful bank of images crooned low to the accompaniment of nothing but a church organ at 3AM, but here it is set to music that is the punchiest and most action-packed and indeed the most baldly accessible across the entire album, no English eccentricities to be had, no nods to crate-digging in the dusty psychedelic rock section of the record store.

Affected by the energy, Roman turns in his wildest axe solo on the record, after which the band turn in a surprise of a melodic break, with synths and Rat bashing away, until we get to the intensifying big wind-up, all horn section and modulation, with the song ending *Anything* like "New Rose" or "Love Song" or "Looking at You" ends a chaos years Damned show.

Singles, B-sides, Bonus Tracks

The Year Of The Jackal (Jugg/Scabies/Merrick/Vanian) 5:52

Proving the band's very real dilemma concerning the dearth of material at the time, all they had for new music to use as B-sides was "The Year Of The Jackal," an instrumental track written and performed entirely by Roman. But it's a corker, Jugg giving the long track a Moroccan flavour and using all sorts of novel and aggressive sounds across the song's hot desert expanse.

For percussion, what he's provided is a big processed bass drum sound alternating with echoey, processed high-hat. Up top there's spare piano tinklings, hypnotic, simple bass, wind and sort of wind chime sounds. At the halfway point he hits some huge chords and then brings in looping and pulsating guttural synths, raising the temperature. It stays hot and anxious toward the end, which arrives very gradually, across a long fade.

"The Year Of The Jackal" was used as the main B-side to "Anything," along with "Thanks For The Night (Rat Mix)" and one (or more) of the various remixes done of the A-side, depending on the format and permutation.

Fun Factory (Sensible) 4:00

The Damned had lost their MCA record deal for the number one reason anybody loses their deal when things are actually looking pretty good—the guy that signed you leaves the company and you are looked upon as "that guy's" project. Then they broke up, trying out different band configurations, and eventually drifting back together to do some shows.

Captain had a label called Deltic Records, which soon would crash in flames, almost costing him his house—he said he had bailiffs at the door and lost £25,000 on the venture. But before that happened, he got it together to release this *Strawberries*-era track from late 1982 that the guys had thought was lost forever. The idea had been to release it as a single back then, but then Bronze went bust.

"Fun Factory," written by Captain (who also does a bit of singing), is a fairly long and involved pop rocker, light on its feet, psychedelic but happy about it. Its chief distinguishing factor is that Robert Fripp provides the atonal, highly processed soloing during the intro of the song, quite far from the two or three things he's known for.

The King Crimson icon had been in the studio with the guys and scheduled to do more, but this is all they came up with, although Fripp ended up joining the guys on stage for a few songs at a show on October 11th 1982 at the Hammersmith. To be sure, he's gone after this unrelated intro passage, but later on there's a whacky keyboard solo to keep us entertained, along with a heavy break section. Otherwise, it's essentially the rapid-fire delivery of the inane chorus that maintains momentum.

"Fun Factory" was issued in late 1990 as a 7", 12" and CD single. The 7" included a Captain Sensible song, remixed, called "A Riot on Eastbourne Pier." The 12" and CD-single issues included that track plus two additional Captain solo selections, "Freedom" and "Pasties."

Not of This Earth

Put all your reservations aside—please, I beg you, for the sake of the children—this is a Damned album, and for three good reasons: it's got Dave, it's got Rat and it sounds like one.

And here's how we get to this place. After losing their deal, The Damned actually broke up and then reformed with the original line-up, actually managing to record, in June 1990, a wackadoodle of a song called "Prokofiev."

Then things dissipated once more, with Brian quitting after a spat with Rat, resulting in Paul Gray coming back and Captain switching over to guitar—the *Black Album / Strawberries* line-up was indeed together again. But then Rat sacked Captain and that proved to be the death of the band once more. As Scabies puts it, things were getting stagnant, the money wasn't great and, intriguingly, he wanted to try something in a grunge direction and Captain wasn't having it.

This sent both Dave and Captain back to their solo careers and Rat into a new situation writing with guitarist Kris Dollimore from the well-regarded Godfathers. Next to Rat's new cabal, at Kris' behest, was James "Moose" Harris of New Model Army fame.

Dave Vanian was asked to join but the day he swung by, Rat had invited this hippie violinist to the session, who, once he started playing, drove Dave from the studio without saying barely a word. Rat ended up scuttling the project after trying to rebrand the thing with a different singer, maybe Robbie Williams or Joe Strummer, as was bandied about.

Next Rat started writing with Alan Lee Shaw, who had worked in Brian's solo band, with Rat calling back both Dollimore and Moose. Shaw had shown Rat demos he had of "Testify," "I Need a Life" and "Shadow to Fall" and he was instantly impressed.

"Those were from one session I did," explains Shaw. "I'd been in Brian James Gang. I also did Brian's solo album, played bass on that, and we did that in Brussels in 1990 and we did a tour in Europe. And some of the people that we met on that tour, some French people, they had a studio in London and I did all my demos with them, all the songs that are on that album, in one session in about 1991."

Explaining why they fit so well as Damned songs, Shaw says that it's because his songwriting "tends to the dark side, being about frustrations—'My desire is your frustration'—people who let you down, sort of snake in the grass/dodgy people, plus relationships. I'd been working with Brian since 1977 on his various projects, and Brian and I are very similar in attitude. Brian is a very dark writer. I won't say those songs were written for Dave but it did fit his profile."

Dollimore would be the reconstituted Damned's lead guitarist with Shaw playing rhythm. Vanian was asked to join again and this time said yes. This new line-up of the band—as valid as the previous one essentially, being the same two originals plus two new guys—participated in the world, doing a BBC session and touring the UK and the US and even Japan. Things went so well in the Far East that Toshiba signed the band to a record deal, which resulted in the first version of this record to emerge, on November 8th 1995.

Even before this, Cleopatra in the States had shown interest, having issued in 1993 a compilation called *Tales from the Damned*; hardcore label Victory Records was interested as well.

In the summer of 1994, the band convened at the studio of famed German producer Conny Plank and did the basic work on the record (backing tracks for nine songs in a week), finishing up back in England at a number of studios over the course of the following three months. Producing was David M. Allen, who had worked with The Mission, The Chameleons and most substantially The Cure. Affirming Dave's instincts, all of the songs came from Rat's writing partnership with Shaw, save for the addition to the album of "Prokofiev," credited to Rat and Brian. Shaw had brought upwards of thirty song ideas to the party, essentially overwhelming any other suggestions.

But bad blood courses through the story of this album, with the band somewhat disowning it or ignoring it, demonstrative through claims on an earlier version of the official website that *Grave Disorder* was the band's first album since *Anything*, and that this particular piece of Damned history was "not intended for release in this form" (today, at the site, the record just sits along with all the others with helpful links on how to go buy it).

The main sticking point was that as the album was being mixed and readied for release, Dave found out that he wasn't going to be credited as a songwriter. Vanian threatened legal action and Rat, boss of the band at this point in every way (which also was causing problems), held his ground. Dave responded by publicly disowning the record as well as coming up with the story—surprising to all—that he thought he was making a demo and that the *real* album would have Captain on it.

In fact it was Shaw who was most adamant about not sharing credit, given that he had already done so quite generously with Scabies. "Rat did talk to me about it and said that maybe we should roll Dave in on this. But I said, look, he honestly hasn't changed anything about my lyrics; he's created nothing on the writing side of things. And I did offer to have him help, and if he would've helped he would've got a credit. But he didn't. I just felt it wasn't right that he should get any credit. But then again Rat could've given him some of his credit, which he didn't do. He wanted his 50-50 with me."

As for the title, Rat had always intended that the album be called *I'm Alright Jack and the Bean Stalk*, based on a saying used by a friend. But that was considered by Toshiba to be too awkward, with *Not of This Earth* used instead. When Rat put the album out himself in the UK in 1996, forming Marble Orchard Recordings with former Damned tour manager Henry McGroggan, the original intended title was used, which was also the case for the Swedish and German issues. Cleopatra in the US went with *Not of This Earth*, as well as different cover art. Most reissues are called *I'm Alright Jack and the Bean Stalk*.

Back to the bad blood, it's no surprise that The Damned had actually broken up by the time *I'm Alright Jack* even saw the light of day, with the first issue of the album being November '95 and the band being kaput that August. Apparently Rat didn't want to tour so much, while Dave wanted to keep working, to pay for his divorce to Laurie.

This sent the front man back to his struggling "gothabilly" project Dave Vanian and the Phantom Chords, who had managed to get a full-length album out in April of that year. But the Phantom Chords had always been part of the problem as well, with Dave prone to blowing off Damned dates to concentrate on the Chords. Record deal negotiations also got scuttled along the way, when Dave would demand a deal for the Chords in exchange for him signing as part of The Damned.

But I prefer to conveniently forget all that, because like I say, *I'm Alright Jack*, to these ears, is a fine Damned album.

"My whole idea about this album was to get back to the roots, to get back to the first album," opines Shaw. "That was always my favourite, the *Damned Damned Damned* album. When I saw The Damned in '76, '77, they just blew my mind. I'd never seen a band quite like theirs. Their on-stage presence affected me as much as when I saw the MC5 play—there was just this chaotic explosion when they'd come on stage and The Damned were like that and it blew my mind. That's how I really appreciated The Damned and that's why I wanted the music and the production to echo that first album. I didn't want all the synthesizers and stuff that they had done before; that wasn't my idea of what The Damned were about. My idea was to have that explosive MC5 feel in the songs."

"But I don't think we got that from David Allen," continues Shaw. "I wasn't very enamoured with him. I wanted Rick Rubin to produce the album. At that point in time The Damned still had quite a bit of a reputation and I think we could've got him. Also the guy who did Nirvana, Butch Vig. Rat was negotiating with Victory Records at the time and they had some connection with him and they had written him in as the producer of the proposed album but that fell through. So Rat got his friend, David M. Allen to do it. I wasn't really for it but my hands were tied, because Rat was managing the band at the time. It's a good production but it didn't have the fire and the raw action that I would've liked to have seen. We did a live album called *Molten*

Lager which is closer to the production I would have preferred. But David smoothed out the edges, made it more MOR for want of a better word."

"I think it was what it set out to be," reflects Rat, "which was a reasonably strong kind of middle-of-the-road album. You know, I knew that there weren't any 'Smash It Up's or 'New Rose's on it, but I thought the songs were pretty good, the band was good and I think we did a good job making the album. That album was really supposed to keep the band alive until we moved on to the next project. That's what we were thinking at that point. So I never thought of it as being an amazing record, but I do think it's a really good record; there's some great stuff on that. Some of the musical things are obvious. It's hard to talk about it in a nonbiased way, but putting it together and making it, I just remember at the time it was all about Offspring and bands like that who were really starting to break through. So the big temptation was to try and sound like that—which I think would've been a real mistake. So I decided what we had to do with that record was to be anything *other than* that American sound, and instead, really sound like an old-fashioned British band."

****

I Need A Life
(Scabies/Shaw) 3:20

Like I say, whatever you want to call this thing, it's absolutely, explosively a Damned album. To be sure, it's Alan who had "I Need A Life" early on, but first off, the lyric is perfectly suited to Dave, all about life-giving and life-taking love-struck obsession, salient right now as Dave transitions from Laurie to Patricia (I suppose transition is the wrong word).

But it's the music that makes a statement. An intro with owls and birds and other effects over a slow blues suddenly erupts, with Scabies driving this hard-tailed and tightly-wound punk rocker. Rat is so excited about a new Damned album that he decides to do a "Ballroom Blitz" snare thing at the verse once in a while, or more accurately, when he's not joyously peeling off the extended fills missing from the previous two sombre records for MCA.

All around him are disciplined guitar lines that lend a sense of class and geometric structure to the song, the result being classic old Damned but professionally so. The James Taylor Hammond parts are an afterthought, but a good one, suggesting that for comparison, "I Need A Life" should be looked at as part of the *Black Album / Strawberries* family more than that of the first two albums.

In the end, The Damned's version of "I Need A Life" isn't all that different from Alan's original demo (issued as a single in 2020 on Blighty Records), with Shaw sounding a fair dose like Dave, in terms of both voice and the punky, Iggy Pop manner in which he uses it.

Testify
(Scabies/Shaw) 2:56

"Testify" fit perfectly the MC5 and Stooges vibe Rat had in mind for the ensuing Damned record, somewhat underscored by this idea that Alan's writing was as influenced by those bands as it was The Damned itself.

Like both of those '60s bands, The Damned create a wall of sound, Rat not so much playing a beat but soloing, behind constant chording and a Dave singing laconic like Iggy. The clean guitar intro (courtesy of Alan) reminds one of

James Williamson as well, but like the first song, the intro is rudely interrupted by a new Damned rocking out well beyond what they had done during their off-brand New Romantic years.

At the lyric end, what we get is a sort of religious revival meeting, maybe in a tent, maybe as part of the travelling carny show used as a setting for the *Anything* album and tour, maybe with rattlesnakes.

The American issuer of *Not of This Earth*, Cleopatra, have always been prone to remix projects, and thus the following year issued the *Testify* EP, which included two pretty cool overhauls of "Testify" (UK Subs Mix and Nosferatu Mix), along with two mixes of "Shadow to Fall," one each of "I Need A Life" and "No More Tears" plus a 1985 live version of "Looking At You" by MC5, who turned out to be the primary influence on the clanging show band spirit of *I'm Alright Jack and the Bean Stalk*.

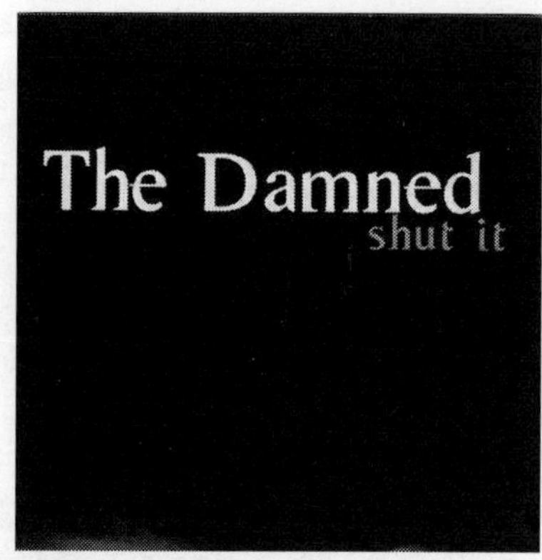

Shut It
(Scabies/Shaw) 2:48

Same key as last time and same hepcat MC5 energy generated when Rob Tyner and Wayne Kramer are channelling James Brown and slaying some headliner from the UK who dares come to the Grande and think they own the place.

Once again we're in the world of boy-girl politics, with Alan writing the perfect song for Dave's situation. The lyrics are in your face but no more than the lip-of-the-stage music, with Rat punctuating the one-beat harder than he ever has on a song that is not so much fast but immediate. Come solo time, now we're in a Ron Asheton zone of psychedelic tone, although the effect is fleeting, subsumed by the jackhammer rhythm and Dave's repeated pleas for peace and quiet—as Shaw told me, any of the fiery, uptempo guitar hero solos on the album are from Kris, with Shaw playing the slower and moodier stuff.

Is it all too much of a racket? Damned fans indeed complained as much. But then again, did we really want more of *Phantasmagoria* and *Anything*? To be sure, this was a Damned circling back upon itself, with Captain, frankly, expendable as long as Dave and Rat were there. Fortunately, as the album progressed, the trilogy of opening loudfastrules rockers would remain that, a statement to be expounded upon, across a record that wound up varied enough for the discerning Damned fan to appreciate.

In the US, Cleopatra issued "Shut It" as both a CD single and as a red vinyl 7" single. The 7" featured the LP version and a Die Krupps Mix, with the CD adding "Shadow of Love," recorded live at the Woolwich Coronet on July 11th 1985. In '97, Cleopatra included a Paul Raven mix of the song on their multi-band two-CD *Industrial Mix Machine* compilation.

Tailspin
(Scabies/Shaw) 4:13

The newly constituted Damned offer a change of pace with "Tailspin," but the contemplative *Phantasmagoria*-like song would cause problems for other reasons. As it turns out, whilst recording at Jacob's, Moose wasn't around to do his bass parts so Rat called in none other than original Sex Pistols bassist Glen Matlock. He did his thing and Moose wasn't pleased, nor was Dave. There was also the matter of Moose and Glen showing up at the same time to do overdubs. Moose eventually re-recorded some of the bass, but the damage was done.

Lyrically, we're still on point with the idea of burning and intoxicating obsession, Dave playing the part well over music that ranges from the downright delicate (and somewhat light rockabilly) and the punky, all of it at the same mid-paced tempo blown up by a hyperactive Rat, who is slowly turning this record in to an album all about the engine room.

Of note, "Tailspin" is the song on the record that Alan figures is his proudest moment (the title track a close second), with Shaw pointing out the various parts and the myriad of emotions the listener goes through. As well, these are his guitar solos, with Rat and Shaw having assembled most of the song in Rat's attic studio rather than at Conny Plank's in Germany.

Not of This Earth
(Scabies/Shaw) 2:55

Subconsciously for some and consciously for others, here's where those complaints of samey-ness across the expanse of *I'm Alright Jack* gather validity and obviousness. "Not of This Earth" sounds like a pastiche of "I Need A Life" onto "Shut It" with a bit of "Testify," Rat revisiting his military snare beat across similar BPMs, the band performing in a familiar key using the same admirable urgent punk-type arrangement and sound picture.

Providing contrast, there's a bit of the blues to this—and The Doors, and a Bo Diddley beat—and additionally, we're off the woman problems and onto a portrayal or portrait of a standard "snake in the grass," which, across Damned history can reference any number of cracked actors. Further hallmarks of uniformity, however, are the ever-present keyboard accompaniment, sometimes quiet, sometimes prominent, and the relentlessness of Rat, snare tuned tight, rock-hard, every whack rendered in hi-fidelity to match the disciplined guitar lines of Kris and Alan.

Of note, Alan—again, writer of everything—took offense to the insulting "theme guitar" credit in the liner notes, chalking it up to Rat being Rat which indeed is the same as Rat being Captain. He admits that it's a bit his fault though: he used to use the term theme guitar repeatedly to describe riffs, and Rat just picked up on it and credited him as such as a bit of a prank. What's worse, as the booklet is configured, only four members get (faux) pictured and named twice, leading one to believe that Rat's intention was to present the official band line-up as a four-piece consisting only of Vanian, Scabies, Dollimore and Harris.

Running Man
(Scabies/Shaw) 5:06

Despite the late-period Doors vibe of "Running Man," the song brings something new to the catalogue, this bluesy hard rock thing, exemplified by Dave's rulebook vocal melody as well as the clean lines of the guitar soloing and attendant licks. Rat creates an excellent groove with his smartly placed snare whacks, eventually doubling up on the beat to underscore the title of the thing. Other than tinkly bar-room piano though, there isn't much to the song to justify its length, with the lyric lacking the inscrutability the band regularly get up to, whether it was a Dave or a Captain or even a Rat joint (less so Roman). The concept is apt, because sung by Dave, it reads like a summary of the band's preposterous career arc, even if some of the lines are clunky.

My Desire
(Scabies/Shaw) 2:48

Different key, but with "My Desire" we're back to the same sort of velocity and Rat-dominated workout we've heard repeatedly already. In fact, Dave sounds rushed, underscored by all the rhythmic punctuations—this is one of those rare occasions where a slower version might have worked better. There are some nice touches though: the guitar line at the beginning sounds like horns, there's a wah-wah guitar solo, there are not one but *two* Hammond organ solos (one after a modulation, both pretty far back in the mix), and the Rat fill at the nine-second mark is arguably his best ever (!), introducing a song that is in fact the most fun from a drum point of view thus far, on an album pitter-pattered by heart-palpitating percussion.

Never Could Believe
(Scabies/Shaw) 4:57

Change of pace, "Never Could Believe" is an uptempo ballad that sounds like psychedelic Beatles, which is almost a genre in itself, a type of Beatles tribute that countless bands in the hard rock field try eventually, sometimes with sitar or at least lots of chorus on the guitar. The cosmic lyric from Shaw supports the choice of this meandering Hammond-coloured musical track, but it also reads like a continuation of a "Street of Dreams" modality of thought. Even the phrasing fits; in fact, one can envision a mischievous and drunken Damned one night firing up the music for "Street of Dreams" with Dave stepping up to the mic and singing the "Never Could Believe" lyric.

This one goes back to the earliest days for the band getting these songs together. On November 29th 1993, the guys did a couple of radio sessions, with "Testify" and "I Need A Life" being played at both of them and "Never Could Believe" only at the second one. At that point the big descending guitar line was more prominent to the point of it sounding like a power (or power pop) ballad, also made more energetic through Rat soaking the place in crash cymbal. During the guitar solo on the BBC session, Kris fires off a bit of a lick in homage to his old band The Godfathers, but on the studio version, most of the guitars come from Alan.

Moose, citing an example of Rat's dictatorship over the band at this juncture, says that he thought he and Scabies had put together the perfect backing track in Germany at Conny Plank's place, but that once back in England, Rat had called him back into the studio to re-do some of his parts, the implication from Moose being that if anything, the extra work made the song less good.

Heaven... Can Take Your Lies
(Scabies/Shaw) 3:49

Weirdly, this might be the most Damned-like lyric on the album, all psychically discombobulated and anxious about it, enigmatic like Brian James. The ellipsis in the title adds to the tension because it's hard to find anything right about it (Shaw has no idea why it's there, chalking it up to Rat again). The throwback to the debut album at the literary end fits because the music track sounds like something from *Raw Power*, with the song driven by a garage rock an' rootsy James Williamson riff (maybe less of a riff, more of a lick), Dave doing a monotone Iggy and Rat swinging like Scott Asheton.

Having said that though, calling something a throwback to the Stooges or MC5 or The Doors implies a certain conservativeness of structure, and "Heaven... Can Take Your Lies" suffers from that, coming off as "unremarkable," maybe even worse due to the dull chorus. Indeed, any variation from the root riff lasts a bar or two at most and then we're back and (IMO) not happy about it.

Shadow to Fall
(Scabies/Shaw) 3:02

If "Heaven... Can Take Your Lies" swings, then "Shadow to Fall" is a Damned shuffle (albeit with a counterbalancing four-on-the-floor), with Rat pulling out once again his "Ballroom Blitz" beat, heard also on "I Need A Life" and "Not Of This Earth." And yet again, the touchstones are bluesy, dark Doors for the verse, along with MC5 come chorus time, with the guys putting a smart show band yet garage rock set of chords together for the punctuated choral apex.

Is this gothabilly? Could we picture either of these last two tracks on a

Cramps or even a Misfits or Samhain album? Maybe so. Like many songs essentially adapted from heavy blues, nothing much happens, and there's a sense of the wheels falling off once we get to the handclaps, after which the guys just make a bunch of noise until it gets old.

But credit to Alan Shaw, this is another fine Damned lyric, so squarely along the recurring themes on this record and leaping to the others concerning having one's head dented in mentally by life's obstacles, The Damned curse as Dave calls it, only half-jokingly. Further credit to Alan as well, given that in most cases he would actually sing the lyrics first, with Dave watching on and then taking over, no doubt influenced by Alan's phrasing and melodies.

The Leather Strip Mix of this song on the *Testify* EP, after a bunch of distorted synth noise, amusingly breaks into the actual "Ballroom Blitz" beat, before settling into what is essentially a new industrial version of the song, with Dave re-doing the vocals, cutting back on the throttle, somewhat straightening out the vocal melody.

No More Tears
(Scabies/Shaw) 5:14

"No More Tears" finds the band putting a sophisticated twist on a slow cocktail-jazz type song, eschewing the expected three-four waltz time and going with a four-four that is fully novel, with the snare landing on the "and" after the two and then again on the four—bizarre. Dave, getting inside of the depression-themed lyric, croons this one almost down to a whisper, with Rat later on underscoring the delicacies of his vocal and Alan's clean jazz guitar with grace notes on the snare, suggesting a shuffle feel. All told, the interplay between drums, guitars and Hammond are icy smooth and professional, making this a real gem on an otherwise shoot-'em-up album. "No More Tears" was never played live, although the guys tried it out at a couple of sound checks.

The Spahn Ranch Mix of the song on the *Testify* EP is practically a new song, pure synths with doctored vocal, new melody pretty much, and for a beat, the synth version of the snare lands on the three—all told, very little to do with the original.

Prokofiev
(Scabies/James) 3:24

Not exactly the expected way to announce a reunion with Brian James, The Damned write what is essentially a Hawkwind song that is more Nik Turner and Simon House than it is Dave Brock. Essentially what we have here is a one-chord jam put together by Rat and Brian in Rat's attic-bound home studio back in June 1990. "Prokofiev" was issued as a 2,000-run single the following year, as low-key as is humanly possible, representing some sort of marker for the doomed few US live dates carried out in September '91 by the reunion version of the band with Brian and Captain, meaning the exact line-up that made *Damned Damned Damned*.

The A-side of the non-picture sleeve single is a version of the song (named from Russian classical composer Sergei Prokofiev) that includes a claustrophobic, smothered, nightmarish, overlapping Dave Vanian vocal. The brief to Dave from Rat was not to work anything out, just go for it, don't think about verses or choruses. The B-side and the album version are the same length, but the album version has gone through a remix. There's also an 11-minute 2014 version. None of them sound anything like Brian James-era Damned. Popular description of the song points out the idea that "Prokofiev" is built on some sort of loop of the Stooges' "Gimme Danger," but the resemblance is tenuous at best. In any event, here it is tacked onto the end of the *I'm Alright Jack* album bearing no resemblance to what came before.

Singles, B-sides, Bonus Tracks

It's a Real Time Thing
(Vanian/Sensible) 0:30

Here's the first thing worked on by what was essentially the *Grave Disorder* version of the band, namely Dave, Captain, Monty and Patricia, plus drummer Spike T Smith, working with producer Hugh Jones from the *Strawberries* days. Smith would soon quit to join Morrissey's band. He would be supplanted by Pinch, who Spike had recommended as his replacement. What we get is a swell, well-executed slice of garage psych confection and four short lines about the nagging march of time that is all of thirty seconds long, created for the Fat Wreck Chords compilation, *Short Music for Short People*, described on the cover as 101 bands playing thirty-second songs.

It was The Damned's participation in the project, issued June 1st 1999, that caught the attention of Offspring's Dexter Holland, who, after requesting and receiving some promising demos, then signed the band to his Nitro Records label. Unsurprisingly, Holland was already a fan, with The Offspring having covered "Smash It Up" for the *Batman Forever* soundtrack four years earlier, which, according to Captain, helped him stave off bankruptcy for another year.

Grave Disorder

The ramp-up toward the first Damned album in six years found the band shuffling their musical chairs while languishing without a deal very much like last time (first album in nine years) indeed, disenchanted, on fully three different occasions before that. We have the bust-up with Rat, who, it must be said, brought *I'm Alright Jack* to market through sheer force of will, building a cracking band that could have served the brand with distinction, only to see it fall apart.

You reach rock bottom when you are fighting over the price of handing over the name, and that's what happened next, with Rat asking £50,000 and settling on much less. The ultimate thorn to Scabies was Dave patching up relations with Captain, but that would be as far as it would go with respect to old members back. Although for a spell there, Paul Gray was the band's bassist, only to be replaced by Patricia Morrison, who joins in 1996 (as mentioned, Dave and Patricia are married in Vegas in 1997) and therefore by the time of *Grave Disorder*, is fully road-tested, not that she's a novice, having been in many serious bands herself over the years. Festivals,

Australia, Japan (first time ever for Captain)... this period may look fallow, but The Damned were a working band. There was just no label deal and no record.

Also soon part of the fray, after working through two drummers, was Andrew "Pinch" Pinching, founding member of English Dogs, who, along with Patricia, will be instrumental in righting the band's business affairs and making the machine run more professionally on the road.

The way we get to Laurence "Monty Oxymoron" Burrow, is through the Captain connection, and is in fact part and parcel of the story with respect to Dave and Captain reacquainting and reacclimatising. Dave had once again found his Phantom Chords project disintegrating but the guys had managed to pull off one show, at The Mean Fiddler in London, with Captain, whose solo career was going a bit better by comparison.

New to Captain's band was Monty on keyboards. By virtue of Captain and Dave playing together on the same bill, and importantly catching up with each other and even interviewing together, notice was taken and live dates were offered for a band called The Damned. This first re-configuration was essentially Dave with Captain's solo band, which was Captain, a drummer called Garry Priest, Monty Oxymoron and Paul Gray. Switch out the drummer (a couple times) and put Paul to the curb somewhat unceremoniously and we have the band that makes *Grave Disorder*.

The band then signed with Nitro—five years old and home to a number of quality US punk bands at this point—in 2000 and set about recording the album with producer David Bianco.

To set the scene, Captain describes Mad Dog Studios in Burbank as a "big kind of warehouse room," with everybody looking at each other with headphones on. He says he was always wired on caffeine by the time he got to the studio because the place they had breakfast every day, Frank's Diner, would keep topping up your coffee but only charge you once, something that Captain hadn't heard of before.

Early songs tested on stage would include "Democracy?," "song.com," "Thrill Kill" and "She," all fairly hard-hitting like the last album. But *Grave Disorder*, issued August 21st 2001, would end up offering so much more with respect to both quality and quantity, all housed in professional digipak packaging with foil printing and an extensive inner booklet.

"Thank you, I'm glad you said that," Dave told me with a chuckle, when I complimented him on the visual presentation back in October

2001 during a pre-gig interview in Toronto. "We had to fight tooth and nail to get that. It wasn't really expensive either. It's just that we wanted people to understand what we were doing. The record company didn't want this sleeve. I designed it with a few people; Vince (Ray) obviously did the front. It was tough, and in the end that took longer than it took the album to make (laughs). But it was worth it, worth it that we stuck to our guns. And people have complemented us, so that's good."

"The main thing is that *Grave Disorder* is the first one I've worked on with Captain in twelve years," continued Vanian. "So in some ways, it's like we've started the day after we did *Strawberries* or *The Black Album*. It's been quite weird to pick up again. It didn't feel like twelve years had gone by. It's quite bizarre but it's been a lot of fun. He's been off doing his "Happy Talk" and his Punk Floyd and all his solo stuff. We're all still a little bit hungry (laughs). We haven't been sitting back in our thirty-room mansions and getting loads of money yet, so I think there's still a bit of that. I'm like any working stiff. I have to pay the rent. But the main reason I'm here is obviously because I enjoy the music that we do. That's why this album is good. I don't think it's good because technically we thought about it and spent years at it. It's more a case of, we just love music. I'm hoping, as anyone does, that this album reaches a wider audience. Because I think that's the thing about The Damned's music: it's always been made for any eclectic cross-section of people, not just one audience. Although sometimes that goes by the wayside because of the punk tag, I imagine."

Underscoring the shared point about the album's versatility, Dave opined, "I feel that this album came out as a strangely balanced album. The songs could be from other albums, but that wasn't intentional. We didn't realise that until we were five or six songs into the album. The only difference with this album as opposed to some of the others is that we knew what we were going to do when we went into the studio. A lot of the albums have had two or three experimental tracks when there's been perhaps only a guitar line or an idea on the piano so people were tearing their hair out thinking we're never going to get the songs done. And those sometimes come out as some of the better songs on the albums. So that was kind of strange. We just went in and did it; we were on a tight schedule. But we didn't set out to do anything any differently than we've ever done. The band have always written songs that are quite funny and political or whatever, but also have an edge to them."

"We've always tried to experiment a bit," added Captain, "and this is a progression, I suppose. It doesn't sound like anything else we've ever done, but you can obviously tell it's the same band. We've just done it for ourselves, really. If people like it, then that's fantastic. Maybe if we would have crafted the records for whoever was buying records at the time, then maybe we would have sold more records and made more money, but that's never really been us. Thankfully we've survived for a while because there's always something creative going on in the band. It's always buzzing with ideas—we've never done the same thing twice.

And in 2001, Captain was still enjoying the road. "I do nowadays, yeah. The secret is not to smash too many hotel rooms and too many guitars, because one, you end up penniless at the end of the tour, and two, you also end up in the police station occasionally. So we try to rule that out of our touring experience nowadays, which isn't to say that we don't occasionally get thrown out of bars. That first beer of the day is always a magic moment for me—still. At this ripe old age, the first beer just always tastes fresh."

Offered Dave in closing, "The one thing that has always kept The Damned together... it sounds like a cliché, but when things have been the worst, there's always people who come to see us. There was a time when we weren't actually legally allowed to release a record, and the only way we could actually stay alive was to tour. We were playing shows that were packed, with people around the block and stuff. But no new records coming out. And in England there was particularly that time when the press were suddenly saying, 'Oh, we don't want The Damned around anymore,' and we were mauled by the press. Other people were playing to half-filled venues and they were getting front-page press, and we were packing these places in and getting no press whatsoever. So that was very helpful to us—it's the people that kept us alive and that's happened right up until now. Even though it's been ten years or so since a proper Damned record came out, the audiences have still been coming. That's why we have that big thanks to the fans in *Grave Disorder*—that's actually a very heartfelt thank you. Because the record industry has not been our friends, really (laughs)."

****

Democracy?
(Sensible) 3:21

I'm sure it was unintentional given the bad vibes around the last album, but "Democracy?" sounds like an *I'm Alright Jack* song, from the production through to the tempo, right down to its life as a big drumming and drummer's song. Only this time it's Pinch filling the fills, proving that Rat is replaceable—if I'm to be brutally honest, everybody is replaceable in The Damned, as in almost every band, save for the lead singer. But no, it's no surprise that if Captain and Dave wanted a drummer like Rat, he or she could be found. In fact, any drummer worth his salt who doesn't play like Rat, if told "Play like Rat," could do so on the very next song jammed, provided he knows his Rat on record. And on *Grave Disorder*, they have a drummer who is playing like Rat—Pinch says this actually constitutes slowing down versus what he had to do in English Dogs—and he's even mic'ed up and mixed like Rat. Ergo there goes a Damned album with no "Democracy?" is a Captain song about how neither revolution nor voting changes anything, and how even in proper democracies, it's still crap, a case of voting for the lesser of two evils. This is set to a song with only three parts: verse, pre-chorus and chorus, with the latter two firing along at an effortless punk clip while the verse has a sort of machine gun roil and then into a bit of an awkward scale-climb of a riff. Massaged in are light, unobtrusive keyboard washes from Monty and even a track of acoustic guitar. The opening of the song, and therefore the album, gives us tolling bells like "Black Sabbath," but this is Big Ben, the tradition of it all underscored by a rough radio-sourced audio clip from the House of Commons from decades earlier.

The backing vocals are the smoothest of the Damned canon, on a song that offers one thing kinda new—more so as the story of the album is built—and that is catchy, mainstream melody, which would attract a few hoots and accusations that The Damned might be biting on the surprise success of SoCal pop punk as a thing.

"Democracy?" was written early enough to have been one of the tracks demoed with drummer Spike T. Smith in the band. It was also the song chose as first (and only) single, emerging as a picture sleeve promo CD single in July '01, a month before the issue of the album proper.

song.com
(Vanian/Sensible) 3:39

Grave Disorder develops along a melodic punk theme with "song.com," but the band introduce a few rich features, including Monty's first keyboard solo ever, a Hammond affair, even if he's not particularly high in the mix. Elsewhere, there's a nice chorus effect on the guitar over the tribal-drummed verse, and then nods to the Beach Boys in the chorus. Nicely, the song's above-surface messaging is about how fun this new thing called the Internet is, while barely behind that is the idea that it's no replacement for reality. In that light, talking about surfin' the net while quoting the Beach Boys takes on new meaning. Besides the ooh-oohing, late in the track Captain strafes the place with a little Dick Dale surf guitar lick.

Adding substance is a second completely new break section, where the chords are darker, more pensive, underscoring the implication in the words that the Internet can be a place of outward directed deception as well as self-deception.

To be sure, 2001 is a good five years into the life of the Internet, so it's already a little dated to be talking about this (let alone how it comes off today). But the guys were pretty enthusiastic about the whole thing, Captain expressing in interviews optimism about how it would help spread the word on smaller bands, decrying Metallica for suing Napster and talking about how it's allowed him to find stuff he might have missed, like a reunion Cowsills album!

Thrill Kill
(Sensible/Pinch) 5:37

Strength to strength, "Thrill Kill" takes us back to the fecund creativity of *Strawberries* or even "Curtain Call," all Gothic and rocking and full up with interesting sounds, even film noir movie samples (in contemporary interviews, Dave talked about how he got into music through film soundtracks). The lyrics are Captain's and even this is a throwback, to Brian James, really spare and inscrutable, threatening, but then again, is this kill "a fantasy crime?"

Sensible credits Pinch for coming up with the music, which just proves the bench strength of the band. We've heard that Pinch and Patricia really took the reins of Damned Inc. (and for a second time on the album, a bass riff can be heard alone in the intro and integral throughout), plus we've discussed how Pinch is filling Rat's shoes. But here he is, as Captain has explained, writing songs on a *Playstation* (four of them, he says), using a program called Music 2000—of note, *Playstation* is name-checked in "song.com."

No surprise then that Pinch gets to play a lot—and that snare is tuned so tight—even though the song is not structured particularly like a drummer's showcase tune. Monty opens the proceedings taking us back to *Phantasmagoria*, as does Dave with his deep and menacing vocal, as does Captain with his various sophisticated Roman Jugg sounds across the expanse of this nearly six-minute-long song without many parts. Indeed there are no solos per se,

"Thrill Kill" being more about layers of sound creating texture. Along the way we get harmony backing behind Dave for the chorus, a classy two-fisted high-hat pattern from Pinch, and then by the end, a sort of avalanche of sound, culminating in sirens, which suggests that this "black night" "cold kill" might have been the real thing after all.

She
(Sensible/Vanian) 4:27

Traditional in so many ways, "She," first off, is a tribute to Patricia from Dave, which he's specifically done before. But then it also reads as a standard Damned Gothic temptress lyric, similar to songs Dave has written generally, i.e. not about Patricia, or songs written by Brian or even Alan, in both cases always more tenuous because of brevity or vagueness. And speaking of Alan, "She" is in that *I'm Alright Jack* wheelhouse in terms of its gothabilly death 'n' roll structure, with the vocal in particular adhering to blues rules like call and response, emphasised by the bull-horn effect on the response.

And like a good chaos years Damned song, the drums dominate—it certainly isn't Monty, who continues to be distant in the sound picture—Pinch playing up a storm using a nice array of cymbal sounds. As for special moments, the band do a verse with just vocals and drums, followed by a verse where only bass is added. The first break ain't much to look at, but later on the song shifts into this repeated "she, she, she" mode, with a bit of soloing from Captain added. The last minute of this pattern converts to half-time, with the band gradually getting quieter, Monty playing piano rather than organ, Captain going acoustic, Pinch getting jazzy and Dave now ruminating, reflecting, admiring.

Looking for Action
(Vanian/Sensible/Pinch/Morrison/Burrow) 4:04

Why do bands do this to us writers? Back cover sez "Lookin for Action," the lyric's got the line "Lookin' for action baby, yeah?" and the title in the booklet is "Looking for Action." Let's throw up our hands and go with that last one, although there's a sense of consistency that on the *Warped Tour 2002 Compilation*, it's the anti-grammatical way it is on the back of the digi.

In any event, this might be the heaviest song the band has ever done, an equal to a half dozen in the writing, but with this power-packed production and Pinch attack, the no-nonsense metal guitar and the fat, prominent bass, it vaults to the top. Above the mayhem, an exasperated Dave expresses a beat generation need for speed, utilising a conversational beat poet cadence, but shouting as much as he is talking.

As if suddenly aware that they are in the process making hardcore history here, the guys decide to go for a second record, creating the loudest, noisiest, most molten and apocalyptic end-of-song wind-up in the history of rock 'n' roll—and that includes live albums. Everything we need to know is over and done with by the 1:50 mark, but we get fully two more minutes of mayhem, everybody on ten and to a man (and woman) passed-out by the end save for Captain, who's flat on his back for last thirty seconds torturing his amps like Ted Nugent on *Double Live Gonzo*.

Would You Be So Hot (If You Weren't Dead?)
(Sensible) 4:13

Here's Captain taking on the legend of John Lennon, reminding people that the beloved Beatle who preached a "love philosophy" could be difficult and selfish and quite nasty to people, including his own family, notably Julian. In fact the guys were going to call the album *Mercury Retrograde*, because of Lennon's obsession with returning from wherever he was and hiding away at the Dakota every six weeks because of the bad luck that comes with the astrological period of Mercury retrograde. For this, Captain seems to harbour a little bit of sympathy for Lennon—he most certainly includes himself and Dave among the slightly mad—musing in period interviews that so many great artists could be a little loony, and that we should maybe cut them a bit of slack given their genius.

At the music end, "Would You Be So Hot" is in a rock 'n' rollsy an' rootsy camp with "Idiot Box," "Generals," "Pleasure and the Pain" and "Life Goes On," relaxed with a bit of Keith Richards to the riff and rhythm. Monty plays both piano and organ, while a typically active Pinch drives the song along, at one point playing a Keith Moon-like drum break that is nicely phase-shifted.

Like "She," eventually the song collapses into half-time, spending the last minute-and-a-half in a jazzy instrumental place, with Captain soloing for much of it, first meandering and textured, then raising the intensity for greater note densities higher up the fret board. Amusingly, the tradition across the album thus far is maintained, with solos (from Captain and from Monty) being quietly upstaged by the arrangement upon which they're placed.

Absinthe
(Vanian) 4:17

A song about the glowing green fairy seems like a natural for The Damned, and now is as good as ever. So the band set about putting together a dark and delicious Goth rock musical track sufficiently unlike anything else on the album thus far, aligned with what we might hear on *Phantasmagoria* or *Anything*.

At the outset there's the pouring of the dodgy wormwood elixir, a *Bram Stoker's Dracula* movie sample about it, plus green fairy wailing and wind, all set to a musical rendition of ice tinkling in a glass. It's a lot of ear candy, but as always on this record, once the music starts, it's uncluttered. Dave was appreciative toward producer David Bianco for this, for his live sound, but also his versatility to work with different styles and not to over-produce in the addressing of any of them.

Then we're into the mid-paced track, Dave crooning, piano from Monty, who does a nice descending scale at one point, exemplifying the surrender to intoxication (and hopefully not permanent brain damage). The "round and round" break is complex and dramatic, a bit Spanish sounding, as is the punctuated last verse before a relaxed slide into oblivion. At the close, the green fairy seems harmless enough, although one gets the impression her ultimate goal is to inflict madness, friendly until the worm turns.

Amen
(Sensible/Pinch) 7:55

To open the record we got Big Ben and members of Parliament and now we've got church bells and an evangelist, who are quickly replaced by a reverse-fade drum beat, Dee Dee Ramone bass and very fuzzy guitars as The Damned deliver some pretty direct punk rock, but with a bit of UK hardcore to it as well as very English melodies. A nice touch is the recurring church bells and evangelist clips throughout, as well as the monk-ish chanting, which come off somewhat amusing like Jonathan Richman. Captain's soloing makes use of wah-wah, and not for the first time on the record, some of it accompanied by the chanting as well as a tribal beat from Pinch.

Lyrically, "Amen" is your typical screed against religion, notably TV evangelists with their fear-mongering and general non-scientific belief. It's the band's new "Anti-Pope" as it were, with Captain decrying in period interviews that Prime Minister Tony Blair shouldn't be doling out money to Catholic schools when it should go to the regular public school system.

For the fourth time on this record, a song has a significant back third or so that is some form of a coda, this time with a complete disconnect. "Amen" proper ends at 5:20, after which we get more than two minutes of an instrumental keyboard showcase, consisting of an electronic drumbeat with synths and piano as well as splashing wave and seagull sounds and a woman's voice intoning, "It's so simple; it's fast, it's free, it's easy." Near the end we get a little mild clean guitar soloing, but we never do hear from anybody besides Captain ever again. Strange.

Neverland
(Sensible) 3:31

It's Michael Jackson's turn to get poked by Captain, with "Neverland" covering the hair on fire incident, Michael's monkey, even Lisa Marie Presley, but "at least he's marginally better than the boss."

But perhaps more so compared to his portrait of John Lennon, Captain's sympathetic to Michael, seeing a sad and lonely figure that missed out on childhood. Sensible in fact took his run at Michael five years earlier, including the song on his 1996 solo album *Mad Cows and Englishmen* (when it was all perhaps a little more newsworthy—Zappa was skewering MJ back on 'Why Don't You Like Me?' on 1989's *Broadway the Hard Way*).

However, Dave pointed out the song as worth doing, no doubt attracted to the catching vocal line, with the thrice-said word at the end of each verse line. And so here it is, pretty much intact save for Pinch's hilarious double-Rat drumming behind the lead-up riff to the verses. The song is pretty much straightforward upbeat pop punk, with a brief mellow break where we get the opining about the marriage to Lisa Marie. But there's lots of squalling, pealing soloing from Captain, which only seems to excite Pinch who solos right along with him.

'Til the End of Time
(Sensible) 3:51

Helping keep *Grave Disorder* eccentric in totality, The Damned go for a sort of icy electronica track, with synths, vibraphone tones, occasional guitar (at the end, Captain's most innovative on the record) and sonorous crooned vocals high in the mix set to a simple retrograde drum machine beat that stays out of the way from the exotic Middle Eastern melody concocted.

At the lyric end, we're back in a familiar place, awake in the middle of the night and tormented by love, in distress that it may be taken away. Has The Damned set another milestone for themselves in 2001? For surely this is the furthest away from traditional instrumentation they've ever been, although I've got my ear cocked to "Turkey Song" as a possible contender for that crown.

Obscene
(Vanian/Sensible) 2:46

Arguably the album's most exciting and creative track, "Obscene" rocks an' roils upon the same beat as 'Til the End of Time," but now with raucous Pinch drums (including tympani) along with a single repeating and piercing piano note from Monty. What makes it work so oddly and freshly is the way the Phil Spector-ish chorus is set against the very English melody of the verse, the totality of the song sounding like the work of a mainstream vocals-and-uniforms band from the mid '60s converting to psych on their third album.

The lyric is an extension, essentially, of the songs about John Lennon and Michael Jackson, addressing how we love to hear about celebrities crashing in flames, punctuated by the dramatic yet quizzical "Obscene, the scene, the dream" chorus. The song's maturity far outweighs its mere 2:46 width and girth, making an impression, right down to its surprise beat jazz conclusion. Seriously, if history has deemed "Democracy?" as the enduring song from *Grave Disorder*, it is "Obscene" that most deserves another look.

W
(Pinch/Savage) 5:05

Here's a pretty thoughtful and extensive series of extrapolated musings on the election of George W. Bush as President, more reflective than we should expect from a British band, both humorous and caustic, but mostly sort of cheerily cynical like a Captain smirk.

It's all set to a soundtrack of heavy Britpop, which draws from mod, a shared influence of that mid '90s genre with The Damned, who inject a little extra garage and psych into the proceedings for good measure, the sum total winding up as an example of that vague sub-genre we might call "psychedelic Beatles." Captain spices the proceedings with some wah-wah and funk guitar, whilst the rhythm track is a mix of electronic hip-hop beats and Pinch doing rowdy Pinch, first heard at the extensive chorus, rich of texture, rich of tone and verbose. Once back to the verse, Pinch sticks around over the halting electronic beat.

There's also a long break section which finds Monty playing a simple keyboard solo utilising a sort of comedic carnival tone. Then we're back to a quiet "crouching" verse that pounces into another round of the (superior) chorus. This takes us to the end where we get a nice and oddly youthful gang vocal along with Captain doing a bunch of noisy, kind of uninspired and annoying soloing in the backwash—the evidence is mounting that Sensible, more often than not, ain't too hot with guitar solos.

Beauty of the Beast
(Burrow/Vanian) 4:44

Monty's second credit on *Grave Disorder* comes with this deliciously haunting "Sanctum Sanctorum"-like keyboard piece, Oxymoron combining church organ with grand piano and faux strings, creating a black velvet bed for Dave's vocal. We actually don't hear Vanian until nearly two minutes in, and he makes up for time with phrasing that is surging and uneasy, his vampiric voice high in the mix. Dave frames for us cinematically every Gothic horror movie trope and soon we find out why, when he name-checks fully six of the celluloid greats upon which he's based his entire public life, really, his "story of the Damned," as he says in the song, capital D intentioned.

At the close, after a macabre sawing at the hands of Monty's conjured string ensemble and a long and ascending synth line, there's a sort of implosion marked by crashed cymbals, after which, faintly, the green fairy of "Absinthe" returns, wailing in anguish off in the distance, the end, amen.

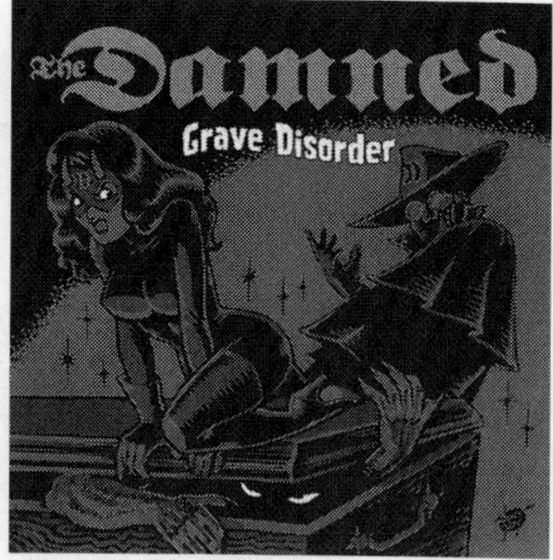

So, Who's Paranoid?

Seven years after *Grave Disorder*, a few changes are afoot. First, Patricia has left the band, due to pregnancy, giving birth to Emily—she never returns to the band. She is replaced by Stu West, a veteran of the punk scene since the '80s, most notably with English Dogs. West is also a big train enthusiast, so he gets along swimmingly with Sensible as the pair document and discuss all manner of rail travel as a sideline to throwing shapes as punks.

Second, the band is no longer on Nitro Records, a bit of a good riddance, given widespread dissatisfaction with Dexter Holland's stewardship of the imprint coming from the camps of Jughead's Revenge, TSOL, Guttermouth and Vandals, with the label getting sold off in 2013.

The band would wind up financing the record themselves and issuing it on their own label called The English Channel, after spending three weeks on the construction of it, at golden-era Jethro Tull drummer Barriemore Barlow's Doghouse Studios on the Thames. Captain says it's a wonder the record got made at all, given how much fun it was boating on the river, docking at various pubs and making use of the studio's swimming pool as well.

In interviews at the time, Captain was diplomatic, careful to point out that everybody in the band was writing. But truth be told, *So, Who's Paranoid?* is very much Captain's record, materially in the writing but also in the accumulated personality of the songs. As Dave told me, "What would spring to mind is the fact that I didn't write any songs on that album. Yeah, there's not much of my personality in that record. I sang all the songs, obviously, but I had absolutely no input on the writing for that *So, Who's Paranoid?* record." The credits filed for publishing purposes with BMI break this all down (these are also the credits used for our song entries) but officially, on the album, the band go with a simple group credit, save for the first track.

There's also a lot of Monty on the album, in the playing if not the penning. Laughs Dave on Oxymoron, "He's not playing a character; that is Monty—a nutcase. He's a wonderful person but he's very eccentric. I don't even know if he knows he's eccentric but he just is. The only difference with Monty is that onstage he changes into more florid clothing, perhaps. But other than that, he is that person all the time. He's a little bit paranoid and insecure, unfortunately, about the world, but then who isn't these days? A bit more than usual, I suppose. But he's driven musically in a different way; he's very much a percussive keyboard player as well and he's very good at improv. If you get him to improvise something, he's magnificent. But unfortunately you've got to catch it then because he might not repeat it."

As for the odd title, Captain says that it's inspired by the increase in surveillance culture in the UK, with security camera watching one's every move. He also wonders if the current war on terror will justify more and more Big Brother tactics at home and abroad, with the UK already looking remarkably dystopian.

The cover is silver-coated, creating a mirror, like Uriah Heep's *Look at Yourself*. Plain block lettering in black is crowded to the top and the bottom, leaving the middle to reflect the face of the purchaser, who is posed the titular question. In essence, the implication is that underneath the CCTV grid, if you're feeling paranoid, you bloody well should be. The CD itself is printed to look like a five-inch across eyeball.

Issued on November 17th 2008, the band's tenth album would be considerably less punk rock than both its predecessors, with Pinch less prominent in the mix than last time, and somewhat straightened-out. Indeed Pinch would imply that with Dave mentally checked out of the proceedings, the band is always going to suffer, that it takes a productive partnership between the two of them to make a Damned record really take flight.

All told, *So, Who's Paranoid?* represents a reflection of Captain's interest in that time in rock history when garage rock and psychedelia overlapped, and hence the organs, the fuzz guitars and even, intentional of the connection, tambourines.

On the complexion of the album, he's said that "life's too short" to be listening to noisy punk, and hence the preponderance of pop melody on the record—even the faster material is subtly, even succinctly arranged and then recorded with polish. It's an interesting chapter in the Damned catalogue, representing a logical bridge from the widely varied *Grave Disorder* to the uniformly not punk *Evil Spirits* album. In that respect, the persona presented is quite impressively a sort of reprise of the best instincts displayed on *The Black Album* and *Strawberries*.

Which, granted, is how Dave viewed *Grave Disorder*, even if that record feels like a bit of an awkward exaggeration of that idea. Here, there's something more noble and aristocratic at work, albeit with the thoughtful and almost regal songs enclosed undermined by the jarring and simple artwork, not to mention the difficult title and lack of booklet.

So Who's Paranoid? would see reissue on vinyl in 2010 with "Aim to Please" and "Forgotten Heroes" as bonus tracks and then in 2014 on vinyl and CD with an additional song called "Time" added to the mix, along with a smart liner essay from punk pro Alex Ogg.

****

A Nation Fit for Heroes
(Sensible/Newell) 3:57

Instantly, through the selection of "A Nation Fit for Heroes" as opener, The Damned let us know we're in a different place. The song is a co-write between Sensible and DIY legend Martin Newell, a sort of modern-day Roy Harper but with an XTC sensibility. Newell's most famed work is his 1993 album, *The Greatest Living Englishman*, recorded under his Christian name, although most of his records are made under the Cleaners from Venus banner. Additionally, Captain says he used an odd but simple tuning, inspired by a technique Newell frequented. Sensible calls Newell "one of our great unacknowledged poets."

Captain is behaved and jangly (a Newell trademark), thoughtful and structured, as the song ambles into view on a mid-paced groove, Monty bringing the vintage keys and Dave singing soberly. Partly a follow-up to "W," this is more about America in general, taking in commercialism and the country's obsession with fame (see "Obscene" like "W," also from the last record), admonishing the place atop a soundtrack that sounds like modern-era Stranglers. But really, the feel is nicely timeless, certainly bearing no hallmarks of 2008, more like 1968 mixed with the tidy and conservative guitar, bass and drums of post-punk from 1988. On a major label. From America. Or from The Stranglers.

"A Nation Fit for Heroes" was issued in 2010 as a limited and numbered 7" single on various coloured vinyl, by Devils Jukebox Records, backed with the non-LP "Time."

Under the Wheels
(Sensible/Pinch) 5:02

So here's the thing, even when The Damned do punk on this album, there's a discipline and succinctness, welling up from the solid timekeeping from Pinch, and the behaved recording thereof, to Stu's bass, which lacks carnal bite and definition (outside of the extemporaneous intro on this song), instead delivering what an old school bassist does, namely melody in the bass range. But it is Captain that is most indicative of this new scholarly style, who, atop a brisk near D-beat from Pinch, plays like a pensive rhythm guitarist, fairly clean of tone, picking his spots and artfully commenting.

The melody is a mix of the best of the British, from The Jam to Madness, The Cure and The Chameleons, with a velvet blanket of exotic Middle Eastern thrown on top. And it is for the most part carried by Dave and his dramatic vocal melody (voicing lyrics that are surreal yet colourful), with help from a pervasive, simple and driving Stu.

All told, there are only three parts, but all of them interesting: the above-described verses, performed essentially by Dave, Stu and Pinch, plus a poignant and lengthy pre-chorus that serves more like a chorus, and then the brief and ersatz chorus itself, at which time Pinch gets to pause the beat and perform some nice single-stroke snare rolls. It's definitely a strong track on the record (becoming a live favourite), and even though it goes for five minutes, it doesn't feel long.

Dr. Woofenstein (Sensible/Pinch) 5:54

It's nice when your drummer, as Captain says, silences those who grumble, "Where's Rat Scabies?" But it's also helpful when he writes substantive lyrics, here Pinch commenting politically about a White House warmonger like a Donald Rumsfeld or a Dick Cheney, or, as Captain says, Pinch's own cat, depending on if you ask him when he's been into the drink or not.

That's all fine, as is the gorgeous old British glam-meets-laid-back Stones feel to the music—half-time and resplendent like Roxy Music—along with Dave's low-of-register rendering of Pinch's wisdoms. But most exciting to Captain was the use of the Brighton Gay Men's Chorus, as conducted by Lorraine Bowen, who Sensible credits as musical director. The choir was recorded in a church around the corner from where Captain lived, with Sensible impressed with the results despite his dodgy computer skills, which were overcome by how good the room sounded.

More on the music, this is one of those songs that begins with a refrain of the chorus, two in fact, which then collapses into the moody and Gothic verse. Monty is featured playing very grand piano, the choir is featured extensively dominating what stands for the song's break section (it's just them and Monty and some classical-type cymbals), and Pinch gets to create a fairly energetic and almost stadium rock groove when all is said and done (of note, his tracks for this were recorded at Audio Design in hometown San Diego, engineered by Ben Moore).

Shallow Diamonds (Sensible) 3:34

Captain says, glowingly, that "Shallow Diamonds" is the closest the band ever got to The Monkees. It's certainly poppy and immediate and a song one would think destined to be a single, but it was never launched as such. Cheap Trick might be another comparative via that band's love of chaos years The Who, a tendency shared with The Damned.

The lyric is directly stated, about the illogic of diamonds being worth so much, the illusory quality of the shiny rock, the brainwashing of the symbolism, but also at the base of it, how much workers in Africa have to suffer to dig them up so that we in the West can rattle our jewellery. In fact the lyrics are a bit too self-evident, with the chorus refrain, "What's the big idea about diamonds?" sounding pedestrian from these talented wordsmiths. Still, there are literally a dozen tossed-off lines that are both amusing and insightful, favourite being "You can lose the plot over shallow diamonds," although "Make a businessman shaggable" is pretty good too, especially when you picture Sensible trying to carry on a conversation with "a businessman."

Still, the music is sturdy and memorable, and everybody gets to play pretty hard and punchy despite the pop precept of Sensible's composition. There's no telling, really, what is chorus and what is verse; we're expected to just go with the flow, punctuated spritely by Pinch, who sneaks in an erudite four-on-the-floor beat as part of the proceedings.

Kind of cool, and part of what is a forgotten time in TV history, but The Damned got to perform "Shallow Diamonds" on CBS' *The Late Late Show* with Craig Ferguson on Halloween night 2008, with "Neat Neat Neat" being aired the previous night. Gate Night, as we used to call it where I grew up in rural British Columbia, although apparently we weren't alone in this celebration of Scabies-like vandalism.

Since I Met You
(Burrow) 4:07

Here's an exquisite and rare case of Monty collaborating with Dave the way Roman did, with Oxymoron writing a classically-oriented pop song of dark deliciousness onto which Dave's voice gets added, making it a song for The Damned. As musical accompaniment, at the outset it's Monty playing simple piano chords along with Stu on bass and Pinch tapping cymbals, clearing the way for Dave to perform his live theatre. But then it's full set, with Captain kerranging in with stadium rock power chords, while Monty mimic's woodwinds and the like.

Oxymoron's lyrics are mischievous, loving but cynical and wary, and appropriate for a music nerd, framed around love songs as much as love itself. Count as impressed Captain, who appreciates the experience of the ups and downs of a lifetime of love won and then lost that must have prompted such musings. In particular, Sensible got a laugh out of the idea of the lyrics of songs meaning something new and sounding more real, "even the stupid ones."

Late in the sequence, Dave and Monty conspire vocally on the twist in the tale that has them reflecting that "It's a load of whitewash... or is it?" This leads into a grand guitar solo sector like Guns N' Roses, which gives way to a verse sung, again, with Monty ornately in on the arrangement, echoing Dave, before the song ends both choral and classical.

A Danger to Yourself
(Sensible) 4:04

With "A Danger to Yourself" we're back to the hard-hitting end of this erudite record, but still nowhere near chaos years punk. To be sure, Pinch is driving things briskly and actually quite violently, but Captain's writing keeps us in a somewhat academic or music nerd zone, everybody on point, production exacting, ear candy appointments (handclaps, backing vocals, multiple keys) reminding us that this is an upscale, mature version of The Damned. Monty gets the solo spotlight, jazzing on Hammond like Jon Lord, with Captain eventually joining in like the Man in Black (well, actually more like Wayne Kramer), while At the word end, Captain is up to his old tricks, making points rarely made. This time he's on about expensive adventure vacationing of all things, cognisant of the environmental damage that ensues, rescues at the expense of taxpayers, and in general, the idea of rich people's problems with regard to illusory forms of self-fulfilment. The song lurches to a halt with Dave, exasperated, shouting "You're bad for your health!"

Maid for Pleasure
(Sensible) 4:34

Change of pace here, with the band going for a punchy, geometric beat along with odd Cheap Trick-like chord changes. It's hard to tell if the protagonist of the tale is a real maid during the day and a dominatrix at night or even if the she is a he. But the penner of this bad pun (and possible metaphor for class struggle) explains that it's the story of a guy who visits a dominatrix dressed as a maid, Sensible citing "Maid for Pleasure" as his favourite lyric on the album.

Captain also reminds us that he's game to dress up from time to time, a tradition that famously goes back to the nurse's outfit on the back of the first album. He even says he made it onto a burlesque show one night, dressed, in fact, as a maid.

Just in case we didn't get enough from Dave's actually quite disinterested vocal, there's an extended musical break where the song is acted out. These guys know of which they speak, with Captain saying that The Damned tend to be visited backstage by their fair share of dominatrixes, sensible given that the female version of Dave's Goth rock image is not far off from the official female S&M look. Captain jokes that he's fine with the backstage visits, but not happy when they want to come onto the stage during performances, "riding crops flailing."

Perfect Sunday
(Sensible/Vanian) 4:42

Speaking of The Monkees, those cats had "Pleasant Valley Sunday" back in 1967, and now forty years later Sundays in the suburbs haven't changed—the initial verses of both songs got the kids forming bands while dad mows the lawn. The first of two tracks on the album recorded at Chapel Studios in Lincolnshire with Ewan Davies engineering, "Perfect Sunday" is a bit of a heavy metal song, crouched around a roots metal riff and the hint of a blues structure, albeit uptempo and raucous. But some of the record's most elaborate arrangements are here, on the break section and the later modified chorus, again Cheap Trick, maybe when George Martin showed up for the one album, *All Shook Up*, with "Stop This Game" immediately coming to mind.

Lyrically, this is Dave reflecting on his childhood in the '60s, how the family can see the daily routines of the weekend with rose-tinted glasses but Monday ain't so hot, with Vanian hinting of strife and hardship, enough of it to be plotting an escape. In this respect the song charts a through-line back to The Beatles and The Kinks, and later on, The Jam and XTC. The disconnect is that the music actually sounds quite American.

Nature's Dark Passion
(Burrow) 4:11

"Nature's Dark Passion" finds Monty writing an egregiously Gothic keyboard epic as a vehicle for Dave's voice, much like he did with *Grave Disorder*'s "Beauty of the Beast." Both songs feature lush church organ-type keyboard underpinnings with slow and deliberate grand piano accompaniment and both find Dave accentuating feverish nocturnal words in actorly waves of anguish.

Also amongst the layers of orchestral electronic keyboards (including Mellotron) are dramatic backup chorals, classical percussion (namely tympani and cymbals) as well as howling, deftly played saw and (less discernable) cello from Bela Emerson.

Despite complaints in record reviews about these kinds of "indulgences" directed toward Dave or the idea of Dave or the boss that is Dave, and as much as I love my *Machine Gun Etiquette* and *Music for Pleasure*, I absolutely appreciate one or two of these on any given Damned album. In fact I kinda wish all of *Phantasmagoria* sounded like this.

Little Miss Disaster
(Sensible/Carr) 4:23

This co-write between Captain and Louisa Carr goes back as far as demo sessions with previous drummer Spike in early 1999. In its final incarnation, it joins "Perfect Sunday" as the other of two tracks recorded at Chapel Studios where the mix for the album took place.

In fact it was recorded back in 2005 and issued in November that year as a single as a collaboration with Rob Reger, the creator of *Emily the Strange*, a mischievous looking little Goth girl cartoon character. Emily figures prominently in the artwork of the single, with the vinyl itself pressed in her red-and-black colour scheme. The single was numbered and limited and issued on the band's own Lively Arts label, backed with a live version of "Anti-Pope" from the December 4th show at the Manchester Academy, which is available as a DVD called *MGE25*. The band even called the spate of shows at the time of the single release in late '05 the Little Miss Disaster Tour. Besides the retro 7", there was also a CD single version.

Captain says the song was written about a woman he knows who shall remain un-named that had been living too fast but thankfully has pulled through and is now living happy and productive. But of course the lyric somewhat fits Reger's character, with the memorable chorus now sounding like her calling card.

The intro to the track represents some of the most exciting music on the album, the band rocking out briskly like heavy and sinister Hawkwind. After forty-four seconds of this the happy chords arrive (with an instrumental run at the chorus) and we're into what is essentially a *Grave Disorder*-appropriate pop punk song.

But the playing is so tight and the production so clinical, the effect is almost like The Tubes back at *Remote Control* and *The Completion Backward Principle*, in other words, studio session-level musos playing American new wave. Monty plays "commercial" keyboards, Captain plays "just what the song requires," Pinch sounds like a guy you can rely on at your next jingle session and Dave croons peacefully, coming across like someone you'd have over for tea and never mind the funeral parlour attire.

There's a nice break with some Mellotron pumps from Monty, and then Captain dashes off another guitar solo that adds nothing to the song (save for a bit of melody at the front of it), with the usual thin and bloodless tone put to his piercing axe. The song closes with an ornate backing vocal arrangement that further underscores the slickness of what has come before.

Just Hangin'
(Sensible) 3:58

Captain indulges in the time-honoured punk tradition of attacking the royals, with "Just Hangin'" taking aim at Prince Phillip, Prince Charles and most pointedly Princess Anne. On April 1st 2002 in Great Windsor Park, one of her dogs, a three-year-old English bull terrier named Dotty, bit two children. Captain fumes that the dog escaped getting put down, but he forgets that Princess Anne became the first royal in a hundred years to wind up with a criminal conviction, under the Dangerous Dogs Act, paying out £1,148 in fines and compensation.

Come chorus time, the implied sentiment toward hanging the royals is softened through use of the catchphrase "just hangin'," with its benign meaning, and also the double meaning of soap, with Captain calling the history of the royals "a lousy soap" (opera) but then by placing the word rope so close by, implying soap on a rope—now we've got two versions of hanging that don't involve a gallows.

As for the soundtrack to all this, it's squarely unsatisfying. Although there are many parts and chord configurations to plant one's flag, most of them are unremarkable and, crucially, further ruined by Dave's weirdly annoying vocal melody decisions. There's a long, unexpected psychedelic Doors-like break to get us away from the B-grade pop, but then it's back to more gamely bashed runs at the chorus of a song that is sniping and swiping of lyric, but just sort of browned-out at the music end.

Nothing
(Sensible/West) 3:41

Pinch lashes out with a frantic D-beat, followed by a dissonant Captain lick and then, oddly, the chords to "Street of Dreams," before we're thrown into a rote punk rocker vaguely along the lines of obscure non-LP track "Nasty." Stu gets a credit on this one, about how everything's gone to hell and nothing can fix it. Mixed into the fray are vague hints at conspiracy, of it all being run by the unseen hand of ancient "global" bloodlines, with their devil signs and bio-scans and wheels within wheels and all-seeing eyes on dollar bills.

Captain says that the song was put there to speed the album up a bit, as a scrap of red meat to the pit. But "Nothing" is a nothing burger put through this production grinder. Sensible's guitars and Pinch's drums are too thin (no snare, no bass, no nothing) and Stu's bass is too fat (and he sure ain't no Paul Gray). Nor is Dave pushing much air, essentially crooning at the chorus despite the accelerated BPMs. To be sure, at the verse he's getting a bit of a rise from us, but even with the increased vocal fry, there's a sense that his approach is designed to make it easy on his brain and his throat.

Dark Asteroid
(Sensible/Vanian/Burrow/West/Pinch) 14:02

Long like "Curtain Call" but more like "Prokofiev," "Dark Asteroid" is a Damned tribute to psychedelic-era Pink Floyd leader Syd Barrett, who had passed two years previous on July 6th 2006. The song is in two distinct parts. First there's a dreamy and loose psych song proper, clocking in at four minutes, with Dave singing in an unnatural sort of stoned high voice, occasionally out of tune, presumably to channel the spirit of Syd. The lyrics are also like something Syd would write (or the Dukes of Stratosphear), the apex image being that of a "technicolour whimsical gramophone."

Pinch provides a loping beat, upon which all manner of mostly Monty-generated madness is piled, although it's really Dave that hogs the spotlight with this sort of found teenage gear. Indeed when the album came out, who was singing this song was the main point of debate amongst Damned-watchers, with it soon being confirmed that it was Vanian. There are also some nice cosmic and slanting backing vocals, plus some faux horns, but there's something not fully realised about the song, like it's a parody of someone big like the Stones or the Beatles trying to muscle their way in to the psych space just to see if they can dominate there too.

But if you think nothing much happens during part one, part two is ten minutes of instrumental with no chord changes, like Krautrock or your most egregious free festival Hawkwind jam. Captain says the piece was accomplished in one take, fuelled perhaps by some "fairy cakes" Pinch had baked for the boys. There was the thought to edit it down but nobody could decide on where to make the cuts. Fortunately there was no point. After part one, the guys had consumed only about fifty minutes of space and a CD holds eighty, so there was room aplenty to just leave it as it is. Besides, the session was purportedly visited by the ghost of Syd, so best not to upset the roly-poly shadow figure.

Across the song's expanse, Sensible plays heavy and he also plays a lot of wah-wah, but it's Monty who really goes to town and gives us the bus tour of all of his gear, seeming spurred on by Pinch, who throws a few shapes dynamics-wise, even busting up the beat at one point. Bottom line on this one: a minority of fans love it to death but most are bored by it, and actually not even particularly happy with the song part. However the studio version is a bit of a gateway to live renditions, which, in their unexpected twists, give the chattering class new things to talk about.

Singles, B-sides, Bonus Tracks

Half Forgotten Memories
(Sensible) 6:02

How times have changed. Up into this era, when we step off the official album, we're looking at not particularly newsworthy bonus tracks rather than momentous comedic stand–alone singles and their even more ridiculous B-sides. "Half Forgotten Memories" is an admirable post-punk song like murky early-days The Cure, classic Chameleons or Echo and the Bunnymen. For the first minute-and-a-half, there are no drums, as Dave sings over a pensive and hypnotic music bed of regrets and old friends barely remembered. Soon Pinch joins in with arch-post-punk tribal toms for a little more of the same or at least similar, given how things aren't much more wakeful, with Captain clean of tone and Joy Division spare.

At the halfway point, Dave figures he's done talking for the day, leaving the rest of the band to jam on out, augmented by a few ghostly backing vocals, Captain doing his best Roman Jugg impression, really exploring this Manchester-moody mode of guitar playing, firing off some of his best licks of the (expanded) record.

Aim to Please
(Sensible) 2:43

Here's one that would have made a nice addition to the album, but then again, we already had an S&M track. Still, "Aim to Please" has so much going for it, other than the sassy pleasure and pain lyric. This is Pinch's best drumming of the era, with the man manhandling a fresh beat with a ton of energy and starting the whole thing with one of those neat inside-out time inversion tricks. Captain plays a riff like "T.V. Eye" from The Stooges, but with the panache of Wayne Kramer.

There's also a bit of freakbeat to the thing, as well as British blues boom to the old rock 'n' roll structure. And just to show who's boss, despite the song being only 2:43 long, there's a bunch of odd chord changes come chorus time and a fresh set of tyres stuck on at the end, for the "I'm morally bankrupt, overdrawn" coda to take us out happy and renewed, every nerve alive.

Time
(Sensible) 3:41

The non-LP "Time" finds the Damned doing purist, archival Naz Nomad-style '60s garage rock, but with one eye to the psych future and one looking back to surf and beat. Dave sings clenched and histrionic, sort of nerdy, in an approximation of what he does on "Dark Asteroid," while Captain fires off Stonesy licks a fair way back in the mix behind him, making up for it first with a loud fuzz guitar solo (with Pinch trying to steal the spotlight) and then more soloing later on that he shares with Monty making deft B3 moves. There are a couple breaks one barely notices, and then it's back to the verse/chorus combo, essentially one not distinguishable from the other. The song closes with a hepcat, "Hey man, what's the time?" followed by a ticking alarm clock and fade.

As mentioned, "Time" missed the cut for the 2010 reissue but showed up on the expanded *So, Who's Paranoid?* in 2014. However it was also used as the B-side to the 2010 single issue of "A Nation Fit for Heroes."

Evil Spirits

Has it really been ten years? Yes it has, and arguably seventeen since a Damned record was properly above radar, and then close to that again to find *Anything* of importance (that record at least finding silver certification in the UK). Surprisingly, The Damned crowd-funded their way to this swanky affair, through a successful campaign using *PledgeMusic*.

Evil Spirits, the band's 11th studio album, would be issued April 13th 2018, produced by David Bowie enabler Tony Visconti at hectic New York sessions that also featured classic-era bassist Paul Gray back in the fold.

Evil Spirits finds The Damned skittering across and skirmishing with a level of sophistication not heard since the notoriously glossy *Phantasmagoria* and *Anything* era but goosed by the jittery energy and '60s psych know-how of *The Black Album* and *Strawberries*. In other words, it's an evolution from *So, Who's Paranoid?* with the clear difference being that anything resembling hard-charging punk or even energetic pop punk is gone, which seems like a deliberate result of having Tony Visconti on board.

"He's a man who understands how to get the best out of a situation where things are mic'ed up correctly," explains Dave. "Which isn't always the way now; it's usually just straight into the desk. And also he's very good with melody and voices. He's probably the first producer I've worked with where I've actually really enjoyed all the vocal work. It sounds weird, but over the years I've suffered sometimes from recording my voice and it winding up not sounding the way I sound. I know that sounds odd, but the frequencies go out of it and it changes and it's not me. This record I feel is the best sounding we've had for a long time. In the past, sometimes, there's been a thing where the singer is the last thing you think of. It's all down to the rest of the stuff and then, 'Oh, let's have a listen to the vocals now' (laughs). I've been a bit low in the mix. I've got a baritone, there's quite a lot of mid in my voice, and if you pull that out, it can sound a bit odd. And when you're in the studio, you're often not aware that that's happening."

The Damned actually have never had a full-on production legend at the helm. But they picked Tony from his work on something very recent, David Bowie's *Blackstar* album. Again, maybe predictably, he's steered the band toward making a record that is of one sound, sort of a single mandated view of arrangement, really, for the first time since *Anything*, not that there's a Tony Visconti sound. Captain stresses that the record sounds the way it does because it was recorded like the first album was. Sounds like a reach, but his description of Tony specialising in "beautifully crafted old school production" is perfect against the results attained: *Evil Spirits* sounds timeless but correct.

"Tony brought all the skills of his production techniques that are the techniques we've embraced for a long time anyway," explains Vanian. "It brought us back into the part analogue, but also the modern and the old together. So you've got the ProTools editing but it's all analogue sounds. You've got valve amps, you've got a Neve desk. The only thing you didn't have is that it obviously wasn't recorded to quarter-inch tape (laughs). But it's a great mix."

"Again, I just felt that the sound I was hearing with Tony was exactly the sound I wanted to hear coming back," continues Dave. "There was nothing done to it. We used a beautiful old Neumann mic and it was a pleasure. Also he's brilliant at melody and working with the structures we had with the backing vocals. And he sang a lot of the backing vocals with me. So it was a good experience for me, personally, as a singer. It's different to have someone who's on the side of the vocalist as opposed to wanting to sonically work on drums or guitars. A lot of producers are possessed by getting the drums absolutely... I mean, you want them perfect, but that's all they're listening to. That's their main thing or whatever. So it's nice working with someone who works with singers, basically. That was the point."

Vocals aside, *Evil Spirits* just sounds great period. Not particularly fully correct or high fidelity, but organic despite the challenge of so many great sounds incorporated, including mostly quite clean Captain guitar tones, buzzy bass from Paul, tight and urgent (and way less busy) drums from Pinch, and an array of keyboard textures from Monty. Tony apparently had to just hang on tight for the ride and deal with a band of veterans who came in knowing what they wanted, but there's no way the record would have turned out this way without him.

"Everything was already done," explains Dave. "When we brought Tony in, he hadn't heard anything. Simply because we hadn't gotten anything to play him at that time. He didn't know that. I don't think, when he said yes (laughs), when we asked him if he would produce the new album. And of course it's, 'When do I get to hear something?' I don't think he heard anything until a couple of days before we actually went into the studio to record. But the arrangements of the songs, and the actual songs themselves, he didn't change at all. So I guess we got that right, which is good."

"But working in partnership with him to get the sounds sounding as beautiful and clear as he could and also the kinds of sounds we were after... it was a trip through memory lane with this album. Sonically, it's things we are influenced by, on our own records when we were young but also there's a bit of Joe Meek in there, a bit of Phil Spector, a bit of James Brown, in the sounds of certain instruments. And he said that too. He said, 'I know exactly what you're saying. And I also know how to get that sound.'"

But first the ideas have to be cooked up, mostly back home in England.

"I've got two places I work," explains Vanian, when I asked him about his modus operandi. "One is the study, which I'm sitting in now, which is basically a tallish, higher-ceiling purple room and it's full of books to the ceiling. If I look around, there's a fox head, there's a swordfish on the wall, a stuffed bat, a raven, an old valve wireless 1934 phone, a zeppelin. It's full of things I've collected on different trips throughout the years and it's a bit like a traditional Victorian gentleman's club library. So there's bits of art and paintings and too many books I haven't read yet. Lots of Victorian lamps with beading on them, glass-coloured lamps. No fireplace, unfortunately, because there's a huge bookshelf in front of the fireplace. I might add, it's also a bit in disarray at the moment. At my feet, I'm looking down, I've got a bunch of 78s from my father, which are the kind of music that I used to hear when I was very small, a mix of 1930s German tango music and rock 'n' roll and big band."

"So that's the study. The other place I work, which is where I actually do more of the music side of it, is a building at the bottom of the garden, beneath an oak tree, which is a 10' x 10' wooden shack, a Victorian Gothic building. Inside of it, it kind of resembles Frankenstein's laboratory, I suppose. There's a Theremin in there and lots of archaic, electrical appliances and switches that turn everything off and on. A little steampunk, perhaps. In fact, some parts of the album, vocals and various bits and bobs, had been done previously in that shed. I was using GarageBand, believe it or not, not even a pro set-up, and I managed to get quite a lot done that way—it's quite cool."

"I don't think anybody knows how Dave works," laughs Paul. "It's the unique enigma of Dave. He's got a writing shed, which I think is really cool, a very English thing to do, having a shed in the garden. And that's his writing retreat. Apart from the few minutes on stage when I'd joined them for a song or two when they'd come to town, I haven't really seen Dave since 1983 apart from a few reunion gigs. So I don't really know how he works, but I know that the songs he comes up with are fantastic—there are some great lyrics, great lyrics on *Evil Spirits*."

"I got approached fairly late in the process, because the bass player had left at some point," adds Paul, happy but somewhat bemused to be back in the fold. "I got a call from Captain in August, I think, late summer. 'Oh, you know, Paul, Stu has decided to leave. We haven't got a bass player, blah blah blah' as Captain does (laughs). 'Would you be up for it? cough cough.' I know you probably think, well what a bunch of wankers and all that, but it's one of those bands where you'd be daft to say no. So of course I jumped at it."

"But all the songs had been written. I didn't have a hand in writing any of the songs on *Evil Spirits*. They'd been demoed to some degree, and I got sent a bunch of the songs, some of which had a guide bass on. I think Captain played bass on one, and I think a guy who works with The Damned had some bass on another and some had no bass on them at all. So I did what I normally did and I ignored everything that was on there and just played the way I play and that's how it ended up on the album. "We never rehearsed. In true Damned style. We all got the visas through the day we were recording, flew out, went right to the studio in New York (Atomic Sound in Brooklyn), last minute stuff. Like I say, nobody had played the songs together so it was quite a bit of work. It was edgy; it put you on the spot. But I think the first day we had three backing tracks down and maybe even more than that."

"It helped that Tony was easy to work with and that we had a good rapport," reflects Paul. "We loved all that kind of T Rex stuff he did back in the day. We had a guy named Kevin Killen engineering as well, who did the engineering on the last few Bowie things, *Black Star* and stuff, so that was really cool. We had a really good team and stuff got knocked down really quickly—no messing about. It was like, 'Okay, cut the take, great, let's crack on.' The whole recording process was done in about ten days. That was really quick, because none of the band had played the songs together. I came in having heard them pretty much three or four days beforehand. Nothing was laboured with. Tony recorded us as we sounded, but he also had some great ideas for vocal parts and harmonies."

As for what Monty brings to The Damned, Paul says, "He brings a lot of red wine. Monty is completely out there. He will sit there in the studio, quiet as a mouse reading these intellectual books about how the brain works, and then come out with this absolutely crazed solo, the kind of trip where you think where the hell did that come from? From this guy who has said nothing for the last two hours. He reaches into his brain and comes out with these absolutely mad keyboard parts. He's an absolute genius keyboard player and everything that he does fits straight away—he slices through everything."

"It was pretty strange coming back, which was initially just to do the album, with Visconti," continues Gray. "I hadn't met Pinch before. I'd jumped up and did a couple of shows at Cardiff, but I'd never played with him before. So it was a total unknown whether we would hit it off rhythm section-wise and personality-wise. We could've hated each other's guts. But within five minutes it was clear that it was gonna work pretty well. And with Monty it was just like fitting back into an old glove, because I played with him years ago in Captain's band back in the '90s. The years had gone into this black hole and yet there was this almost smooth transition from back in the day, up until 2017. That's one of those rare things about The Damned, and one of the reasons that it works so well. Everybody is very different personality-wise, and unique, but musically, when we get together, it works. You can't make that happen. I'm blessed with having these pretty fantastic people to bounce ideas off of. *Evil Spirits* just worked a treat and was an immense amount of fun to do. It was quite a lot of pressure because we only had a maximum of two weeks to do everything. But it fell into place—as we all figured it probably would—and it's a corker."

With fully four singles issued from the record (albeit not with physical commitment), *Evil Spirits* would become The Damned's first album to get into the Top Ten on the official UK charts, reaching No.7. It would touch off a bit of a revival for the band, resulting in a substantial new compilation called *Black Is the Night* the following year, plus the surprise announcement of a reunion tour to come, featuring Dave Vanian and Captain Sensible creating chaos once again with Brian James and Rat Scabies.

****

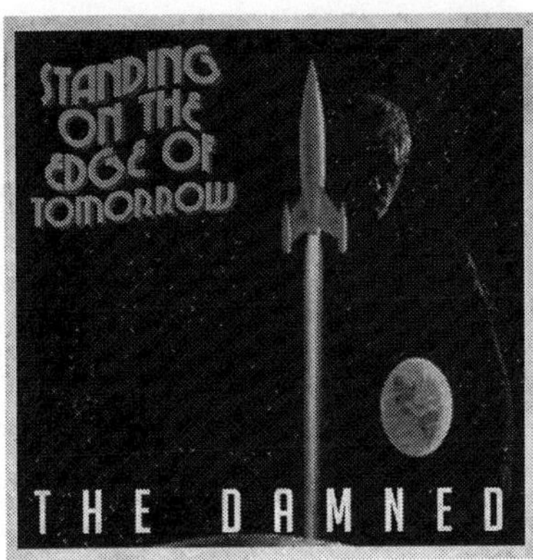

Standing on the Edge of Tomorrow (Vanian) 4:10

With "Standing on the Edge of Tomorrow," *Evil Spirits* instantly shows this new detailed face and grace of The Damned brought to the table through the collaboration with Tony Visconti. An echo-drenched surf 'n' psych guitar line opens the proceedings, joined by a hip-hop beat. Turns out that's a psych in itself, as the song blossoms in its sober '60s glory, with the beat retained but over-ruled by Pinch, creating a sort of boomerang percussive effect steady and tempered by Paul's busy but structured bass.

The song begins with a round of chorus, then verse and two pieces of pre-chorus before a quiet crouch back to the opening premise before we're back to the chorus. This elaborate pattern is played out again until a sophisticated modulation takes place and the width and breadth of the last full minute finds guest trumpeter Chris Coull trading lines with Captain, who plays spare and tasty licks like he's discovered his inner David Gilmour. A fade happens and we're left with a fairly long section of sort of phase-shifting jet sound.

At the lyric end, Dave told me that he was hesitant whether he should be repeating himself so much in a song, referring to the simple "standing on the edge of tomorrow" of the chorus, conceding that in the end, the guys had come up with "a perfect pop song." Dave frames the song as optimistic but reserved about the state of the world, urging us to wake up and fix the place before it's too late.

He also claims inspiration from Joe Meek's "Telstar," although it's been pointed out that the band's communal influence from Scott Walker has also once again reared its head. Not surprising, because like The Damned's celebrated cover of the Ryan brothers' "Eloise," we're in that same place, shared by Walker, that combines elegant and pastoral song craft with psych, bypassing the earlier garage era of psych addressed on so many other Damned songs.

Devil in Disguise (Pinch/Beers) 4:31

"Devil in Disguise" was written by Pinch and guitarist Pat Beers from San Diego band The Schizophonics—Englishman Pinch has been based in San Diego since around 2002. The drummer says that he wrote the song, inspired by The Saints' "This Perfect Day," similar to the way he composed "Look Left," which is coming up with a demo and running it through a talented guitarist. Hard to discern as such, the lyric Pinch came up with is making the point that an unseen hand, a hidden system, a puppetmaster is to blame for the state of the world, and that directing our ire toward the leaders that seem to call the shots is missing the target.

The arrangement of the song supports this idea that Visconti has dialled in a specified and certain melange of sounds for the guys, giving continuity and persona to the album internally and against the rest of the catalogue. It's even the same tempo and length as the first track, with the break in the same place, just past the three-minute mark. Pinch in fact says that by the time Captain and Dave added some "lovely" parts to it, it was so transformed from his original that he wasn't sure he even wanted the track on the album, relenting only because the record company people loved it so much.

Dave's vocal is oddly clenched on the song, telegraphing the aggression of the lyric. There's not much to the conservative chord sequence, but Paul adds some admirable complication, with Tony also utilising some vintage Monty Farfisa and two different and subtle tracks of Captain. Pinch finds a place to insert some Rat-inspired single-stroke rolls as well as some extremely fleeting double bass. There's a quiet bit that sounds like The Who during one of their reflective loitered jams. But other than that, we're once again in a strange record collector-worthy psych zone, as is usual with these guys, tending toward the grey end of the melodic scale.

We're So Nice
(Sensible) 4:09

There's a pop psych *Anything* vibe to this Captain track, with Pinch's one-and-three Motown beat conspiring with the whimsical XTC melody to make the song sound eminently British. The "don't we" chorus refrain, with Monty's pretty synth washes, is a highlight of the entire record, gorgeous of melody, with Pinch subversive like Rat underneath it.

Sensible's lyric is an indictment of Western involvement in Iraq, even if the curious "we're so nice" conceit is so intrinsically and acerbically Captain, in fact, making the lyric sound like a profile of The Damned itself circa the chaos years. But underscoring the military premise is the deft and barely detectable massaging in of political demonstration samples at one of the break sections. At the 3:05 mark, the effortlessly enjoyable "don't we" passage gets a smart backing choral arrangement before Captain takes us out—amidst handclaps and a pretty Rat-active Pinch—with some solo licks high up in the mix.

Look Left
(Pinch/Priestley) 4:43

High point of the record "Look Left" comes from secret weapon of the band at this point, Pinch, he of the lowly drummer position. Co-written with Jon

Priestley (also credited with pre-production), "Look Left" is described by Pinch as "a love song to the human race." The sentiment is quite close to that of the opening track mixed with that of "Devil in Disguise." Pinch wanted to make sure he didn't bury the message in an Oi!-ish and hardcore punk song, and boy did he succeed in that, crafting a textbook exercise in shifting and advancing and culminating melody, reminiscent of The Smiths at points, especially at the "freedom of the mind" twist in the tale. In fact Dave marvelled at the time how Pinch would listen to heavy punk all the time, yet come up with something as beautiful as this, likening it to a theatrical show tune, making Pinch a man after Dave's heart.

The song is further enhanced by a showcase section for Paul, plus one for Monty. Captain gets his say as well, through guitar, as does Dave, who is built (and dressed) for this kind of Damned excursion. The only complaint: the song could have done without the tacked-on intro piece, essentially a verse without full band participation.

Of the record's four singles, "Look Left" would feel most like a proper single, given the enormous plushness of the production video created for the song, the clip combining storyline and performance (at Koko, in Camden) artfully and enigmatically. Everybody is featured throwing shapes, but it is Monty and especially Paul whose contributions are most enhanced by close-up shots.

Evil Spirits
(Sensible) 3:54

Is *Evil Spirits* the most serious Damned album? Tracks like this almost Santana-esque jam band exploration would have us believe it's the most seriously crafted. In fact, Tony's clean and high-fidelity disposition of/for The Damned works a charm on this sober exercise, from Pinch (sounding like a sturdy session drummer) on up. Since *Machine Gun Etiquette*, The Damned have split hairs and crosses genres, at one specific corner of rock history combining psych with this and that. Well, on "Evil Spirits" we're pushed into an examination and understanding of a time when psych crossed over into jazz and fusion, post-blues boom, bring on the horn arrangements—of note, Dave's vocal melodies are pure blues rock, but befuddled by the music behind him.

We may as well bring up the MC5 of that band's last record *High Time*, with Sensible throwing at the cops a political lyric about the futility of supporting either of the two major parties (in his realm, Labour or Tory) against a hectic hepcat beat which frames a jazzy melody from a bad acid trip, again, with the dark minor chords of Santana serving as tension-building touchstone. Indeed, there's a full-on Latin jam, with Captain blunderbussing his way in with typical ear-piercing licks while everybody else struggles to keep things academic—or musically nerdy, which is the same thing.

Dave likens the vibe of "Evil Spirits" to The Who, which is of course valid as well, with Vanian reminding folks that The Damned have also featured some big noses in the band, winner of that contest being Roman Jugg!

Shadow Evocation
(Vanian/Burrow) 4:10

Yes, *Evil Spirits* is the most serious Damned album, with sober production tour de force "Shadow Evocation" further creating timeless new (yet rootsy and pedigreed) dark music from obscure psych underpinnings. Like the song before, there's a Latin vibe to this one, or at least Tex Mex or Route 66 road-songful. Indeed Dave's lyric has us cruising through the night in the backseat of an old convertible with huge tailfins, Vanian driving, speeding in a panic escaping what has turned his world pear-shaped in the day.

It's not the parts that impress on this one; it's the textures, with Tony once again overlaying an electronic or looped percussion part on top of a brisk and grooving Pinch. The melody is carried by Paul and Dave, with Captain laying back in the mix with simple rhythm and Monty plinking his way across the plains with grand piano. Punching the time card at the door of this time machine are Phil Spector-ish tympani sounds that quake like thunder.

Also heard in the hot winds are the soprano vocals of Visconti-produced singer-Kristeen Young, most clearly at the end when she does a little solo vocal vamp, replacing what was originally intended to be played on Theremin. Yet again, there's a break at the three-minute mark on a song that is four and change, and yet again, the close of an *Evil Spirits* Damned song ends with stormy sound effects.

Sonar Deceit
(Sensible) 4:12

Here's a faithful throwback to the Dozier-Holland-Dozier Motown sound, The Damned continuing their tour of '60s tropes with Visconti loving every minute of it—for a later more famed reference point, think Billy Joel's "Tell Her About It" or, oddly both from the same era, The Jam's "Town Called Malice" and David Bowie's cover of 1962 Leiber-Stoller classic "I Keep Forgettin'."

Sensible is the writer but it's Paul Gray and his aggressive bass that is by far most prominent in the framing, the pick-using Gray not rendered as nasty as Algy but still rendered with cut. Other nice touches include return visits from Kristeen Young on banshee effect vocals and Chris Coull on trumpet, some tambourine and sonar sounds.

Why sonar? Well, Captain's lyric is about his theory as to why whales and dolphins beach themselves, namely because submarines are playing their war games, sending out sonar blips into the waters and driving sea mammals insane with sounds that are deafening and terrifying to them. Like Pinch has done, Captain manages to deliver a heavy moral message sort of sugar-coated, atop a jaunty backbeat, even if the "Never question why" chorus to "Sonar Deceit" is one of the album's mournful and heart-rending best.

Procrastination
(Burrow/Sensible) 3:54

Adding further dimension to the album, "Procrastination" finds the band deeper into Stranglers mode than they'd every been before. Many times in the past we've heard J.J. Burnel geometric stun bass and Dave Greenfield Farfisa, but somehow "Procrastination" is the best example yet of The Damned locating that band's sense of goofball melody, perfect for Monty's song about goofing off. Captain has quipped that the humorous lyric has Monty admonishing himself, but also wonders if he's talking about The Damned in general, given that it's been ten years since the last album.

Even the chorus sounds like commercial Stranglers, with Dave singing up in a range we rarely hear from him while Pinch does a nifty march-and-flam beat in the background, all very English and XTC-like as well.

And at the lyric end, it really is an insightful and concentrated look at putting things off, with the best cracked joke coming at the smoothly melodic break, Oxymoron opining and pining about seeing the pyramids one day, but it's gotta be at the right time of the year.

Daily Liar
(Vanian/Sensible) 5:57

Procrastination and "Procrastination" over, The Damned are back to business, sculpting an ambitious six-minute retro-rocker, riffing like the Beatles over a brisk beat with a feel like "Sonar Deceit." Dave explained to me that he rarely writes political lyrics but was particularly proud of this one, wanting to get across the point that we're fed so much information from so-called official sources and stand-up press, but that we should use a better filter and take it all in with a healthy dose of scepticism.

He also admires the song's "nice, almost Monkees-style melody" despite the message, which lines up with what both Captain and Pinch had done on *Evil Spirits* songs earlier in the track sequence. He says you can dance around to it or instead sit down and ponder the words, with both exercises worth something. For his part, Captain likes the lyric because of its relevance with respect to kicking against the pricks like Trump who would call inconvenient reporting "fake news."

As for musical appointments, instantly we get shakers, congas and very English (and Kinks-like) clarion call trumpeting. There are also lush but not showy backing vocals, more Kristeen Young, plus a huge multi-part jam session that is various of chord sequence, getting darker or at least more blustery each time.

At this "Dark Asteroid"-like turn of events, first Captain solos with wild abandon, a style that Pinch has somewhat questioned, lamenting that Captain seems to play to his Dennis the Menace persona when he could be so much more lyrical and sublime as a guitar player, potentially cementing his legacy as one of rock's best.

Pinch himself gets in on the act, exercising his double bass drum skills while Paul gamely joins the jam, wedging in a bass solo opportunely, capitalising on the solidity of Pinch's quick but constant beat. Eventually we're into a "No, no, no" vamp from Dave with Paul way up the fret board and the whole thing sounding like a Motown rave-up, with Rob Tyner's and Wayne Kramer's twist on that tradition also chucked into the roiling pot.

The song ends with a sample from the BBC World Service informing us that "The human race seems to have lost its mojo," a recurring theme across the record.

I Don't Care
(Vanian) 3:16

A delicious way to end the record, "I Don't Care" finds Dave offering a spare and nihilistic lyric across two movements of a three-minute song with three movements. The first minute has Vanian crooning like he's done so many times before over a Gothic piano and assorted keys arrangement, torch ballad-like, including faux strings.

The second movement opens with a pomp and circus pants tympani roll and we're off to the races with a full band version of essentially the same chords and lyric. Captain is jangly, Pinch is intensely active and Chris Coull is back with clouds-parting trumpet. Also included are the most galactic background vocals on the record, saved for this last space jam.

Keeping up the "Stairway to Heaven" geometry (that song is eight minutes, with four two-minute parts), the last exact minute shifts to instrumental easy listening jazz, with Coull recorded playing two tracks of trumpet, one of them with bell in horn. The dramatic and unravelling wind-up chord becomes a gorgeous way to close not only the song but the album, serving as a complex, intellectually stimulating metaphor for *Evil Spirits* as a whole, specifically its emphasis on both production and music history.

Singles, B-sides, Bonus Tracks

Keep 'em Alive
(Sensible) 5:25

Unfortunately the multi-talented Andrew "Pinch" Pinching wound up leaving The Damned, playing his last gig with the boys on October 27th 2019 at the London Palladium. Captain hints that he and Dave were just too much for him to put up with, with Paul telling me that it was more about being based in San Diego and the travel time it took him to get together with the guys, not to mention his business interests in southern California. Further isolation due to the pandemic complicated matters as well.

But he was still part of the fold to record with the guys a clutch of follow-up tracks to *Evil Spirits*, constructed at Rockfield in Wales, over two sessions earlier in the 2019. *The Rockfield Files*, named as a bit of a pun on '70s US cop show *The Rockford Files*, would see issue on October 16th 2020, offering four new songs, one of which, "Black Is the Night," would also be included on the compilation of the same name from November 1st 2019.

Producing is Tom Dalgety, who has worked with a large range of critic's darlings, including Rammstein, Opeth, Ghost and Killing Joke. Paul told me that Rockfield is the band's "spiritual home," with The Damned having recorded two of its most acclaimed albums there, namely *The Black Album* and *Strawberries*. As Gray frames it, everybody loves the memories associated with the place, as well as its easygoing nature, the room sounds and the fact that all the equipment works. The front cover of the EP was shot there, depicting, as Captain describes it, Dave communing with one of the cows he would talk to every morning.

Opening track "Keep 'em Alive" is very much along the rural theme of the jacket, with Captain lamenting the loss of bees due to pesticides, and how crucial pollination is to the entire food chain. Spiders, flowers, crickets and sparrows are also mentioned, with the closing foreboding image being of a cork back in the bottle, the mixed message being that us fixing the climate is an impossibility, but that life will indeed "start anew" when Mother Nature fixes it against the wishes of those spraying the pesticides and otherwise running the economy. This is all made doubly clear by the classy video clip produced for the song, which makes deft use of drone technology, offering a bee's eye view of the damage man has done, and how as contrast, there's so much beauty in nature.

At the music end, "Keep 'em Alive" sounds like an *Evil Spirits* song, well-appointed, poppy, sparkling. It opens with a reverse fade and bird chirping, with Monty mimicking bees on synth (there's an image). Then we're into the percussive and hypnotic title refrain, followed by the verse, which is framed by a halting, complicated beat but with lots of flowery folk psych melody. The groovy pre-chorus provides rhythmic respite until we're back to the hard-hitting title sequence.

Captain says that just like the old days with the likes of "Curtain Call," the band was inspired to stretch out. Indicative of that is the solo guitar break just after the three-minute mark, which quickly gives way to a slow section upon which Monty solos on synth. Then we're back to the "Keep 'em alive" mantra but without drums, with Pinch gradually reintroducing himself before everybody is thundering away, really driving home the point of Captain's commendable but disturbing plea.

Manipulator
(Gray) 3:43

"Manipulator," Paul told me, is a "kind of punky song written on the bass." True on both counts, except recorded this cleanly, with Captain far off in the distance and more concerned with licks and texturizing than riffing, "Manipulator" squanders much of its punk potential, living and dying on a hill built by bass with a little Monty thrown into the mix.

In fact Monty is the most memorable thing about the song, dashing off a strange synth solo at the first break, followed quickly by Captain who offers a sort of new melody line instead of a solo, before an ascending bridge that takes us back to the chorus (which gets tiring fast). Late in the sequence the ascending set of chords is extrapolated upon and expanded, as the song collapse into a sort of contemplative, quiet jam at the end followed by a fade. On the word front, there are only a couple of brief verses, eight lines that nonetheless insightfully point out some of the characteristics of manipulative people. But the chorus says nothing, and then says as much over and over again, to boot, over a backing track that is not much different than the verse.

The Spider & the Fly
(Sensible/Gray) 3:51

Here's another track that proves that *Evil Spirits* was not completely a Tony Visconti trip. Not only are the sounds we get out of Tom Dalgety more or less the same, but the band seems content with this high-fidelity sound for everyone but Captain, who sounds bloodless of tone (save for the slight rise afforded a bit of wah-wah here on the pre-chorus) and way back in the mix as well... hell, as always.

It's no surprise that this one originates with Paul, because the song is carried by his effortlessly enjoyable parts and bold tone, with Monty also relegated to colour commentary, some of it with Mellotron. Paul told me that he'd had this one for a long time (the song in fact goes back to the '90s, when Paul was briefly in the band again) and he credits Captain for transforming it a fair bit. He also told me that Dave and his vocal decisions really changed the "nuance" of it, but that the darkness of the song ultimately made it perfect for the band, given its "Damned-traditional pop element."

By the way, Paul also makes clear that none of the EP songs were leftovers from the *Evil Spirits* sessions, either partially written or demoed or finished and left off the final product.

Speaking of darkness, "The Spider & the Fly" arguably represents the best lyric on the EP and certainly the most voluminous, with Gray using the idea of a fly caught in a web as a metaphor for sexual anticipation and seduction, not to mention both mental and physical possession. The entire song is sung from the point of view of the spider, whose thoughts and emotions are racing in anticipation of the bite that will end the fly's life. It's most definitely quite macabre, and as Captain points out, it's the second song on the EP about bugs.

Black is the Night
(Vanian) 4:39

The marquee track from the recent compilation serves as the last track on *The Rockfield Files*, offered here as an extended version, adding about thirty seconds. Outside of the fairly rote (but pretty and poetic) inky-black Gothic lyric, the song is quite ambitious and well-constructed.

Opening rhythmically on toms, next we relax into a pre-verse section upon which Captain plays clean surf guitar lines like Roman Jugg. The verse music is more grey than black, semi-tuneful but still in the realm of gothic. For what stands for the chorus, we move to an energetic psych beat where the snare is punched by Pinch on the one, two, three and the four. There are angelic backing vocal arrangements and tambourines and cleaner twangy guitar from Captain perfect for a spaghetti Western.

The most surprising piece of music however is the ultra-lush dream sequence about halfway through. Textures conspire to create a psychedelic collage that is oddly conventional and conservative of construct, classical, essentially. There's a unifying "Bolero"-like bass line, and around it, Pinch hitting cymbals like someone at the back of the orchestra and Monty playing both grand piano and synths from outer space. Adding to the tension are distant vocal mumbles, high-hats and sort of harp sounds.

Coming out of this dream state—typically phantasmagorical as soundtrack to many a Damned lyric—is an equally lush and pop-magical coda of new inviting music, first Dave singing "Carry my heart" and then "Black is the night." Gorgeous and groovy, over this closing sequence Captain does some of the tastiest soloing of his career, still disconcertingly down in the mix but accentuated appreciably through the clean tone and uncommonly bluesy playing. If this soothing concluding ensemble jam is the last thing we hear from The Damned, so be it—may black be the night.

All shots on these six pages by Martin Popoff, April 30th, 2017, at The Phoenix in Toronto, Canada.

Interviews with the Author

Gray, Paul. November 18 2017.
Gray, Paul. September 2 2020.
James, Brian. July 28 2015.
Scabies, Rat. 2009.
Scabies, Rat. July 29 2015.
Scabies, Rat. August 31 2020.
Sensible, Captain. October 16 2001.
Shaw, Alan Lee. June 28 2021.
Vanian, Dave. October 16 2001.
Vanian, Dave. April 3 2018.
Ward, Algy. May 17 2015.

ampeg
Rickenbacker

GRETSCH

Acknowledgements

First off, although all direct quotations in this book are from the author's own interviews, it would have been far less substantive without the smart scholarship previously conducted by Barry Hutchinson, who has penned *The Damned – The Chaos Years: An Unofficial Biography*, issued in 2017. The book is available from lulu.com. I'm glad you got my book, but to complete your library, really, now all you gotta do is get Barry's.

Second, I'd like to cite Carol Clerk as well. I've never seen her book, but because Barry has repeatedly listed her as a source, I figure some of the good things about The Damned that I've learned from Barry's book likely have originated with the earlier source. Her 1988 book is called *The Light at the End of the Tunnel: Official Biography*, and at press time it was out of print.

Third, after hooking up with awesome Damned aficionado Kevin Shepherd to provide a handful of colour drawings for his illustrated Damned lyrics project, I received from him a couple of press clippings anthologies. These are called *The History of the Damned Part One* and *Part Two*. Having those in hand saved me from going through these five heavy plastic blue tubs I have of press clippings from yer *Melody Maker*, *Sounds*, *NME* and *Record Mirror*. Not sure that's a good thing as I may have missed a few things, but I'm pretty sure these two booklets caught most of the good stuff.

Fourth, other than that, it's been a bunch of reading through scattered interviews with The Damned through the years, pretty much looking for one thing: comments on specific songs, or failing that, at least some concrete trivia concerning the construction of the album at hand. I must say that for all the interviews conducted across the decades, this exercise in tomfoolery didn't yield much, as conversation usually followed a pattern whereby after a couple of softball questions on the latest album, the interviewer would steer the conversation to the historical, which would then get hysterical. Entertaining to be sure, but not of much use given the very specific mandate of this book.

In any event, this survey took me through my own collected print archive. Because of Hutchinson's fine book and Shepherd's exhaustive early days press cull, this had me concentrating on the '80s, '90s and early 2000s—and mostly North American mags—as well as myriad Internet sources. In the end, there was enough to enhance my song-by-song analysis to the point where I didn't feel entirely alone in my Damned fanaticism. And for that, I'd like to thank all the journalists over the years that have had the good taste to express interest in talking with The Damned.

Finally, special thanks to Agustin Garcia de Paredes who applied his eagle eye to a copy edit of this book. Bonus: I think I've caused a new Damned fan.

About the Author

At approximately 7,900 (with over 7,000 appearing in his books), Martin has unofficially written more record reviews than anybody in the history of music writing across all genres. Additionally, Martin has penned approximately 115 books on hard rock, heavy metal, classic rock, punk and record collecting. He was Editor-In-Chief of the now retired *Brave Words* & *Bloody Knuckles*, Canada's foremost metal publication for fourteen years, and has also contributed to *Revolver, Guitar World, Goldmine, Record Collector*, bravewords.com, lollipop.com and hardradio.com, with many record label band bios and liner notes to his credit as well.

Additionally, Martin has been a regular contractor to Banger Films, having worked for two years as researcher on the award-winning documentary *Rush: Beyond the Lighted Stage*, on the writing and research team for the 11-episode Metal Evolution and on the ten-episode Rock Icons, both for VH1 Classic. Additionally, Martin is the writer of the original metal genre chart used in *Metal: A Headbanger's Journey* and throughout the Metal Evolution episodes. Martin currently resides in Toronto and can be reached through martinp@inforamp.net or www.martinpopoff.com.

Martin Popoff
A Complete Bibliography

2022: Feed My Frankenstein: Alice Cooper, the Solo Years, Easy Action: The Original Alice Cooper Band, Lively Arts: The Damned Deconstructed, Yes: A Visual Biography II: 1982 – 2022, Bowie @ 75, Dream Evil: Dio in the '80s, Judas Priest: A Visual Biography, UFO: A Visual Biography

2021: Hawkwind: A Visual Biography, Loud 'n' Proud: Fifty Years of Nazareth, Yes: A Visual Biography, Uriah Heep: A Visual Biography, Driven: Rush in the '90s and "In the End," Flaming Telepaths: Imaginos Expanded and Specified, Rebel Rouser: A Sweet User Manual

2020: The Fortune: On the Rocks with Angel, Van Halen: A Visual Biography, Limelight: Rush in the '80s, Thin Lizzy: A Visual Biography, Empire of the Clouds: Iron Maiden in the 2000s, Blue Öyster Cult: A Visual Biography, Anthem: Rush in the '70s, Denim and Leather: Saxon's First Ten Years, Black Funeral: Into the Coven with Mercyful Fate

2019: Satisfaction: 10 Albums That Changed My Life, Holy Smoke: Iron Maiden in the '90s, Sensitive to Light: The Rainbow Story, Where Eagles Dare: Iron Maiden in the '80s, Aces High: The Top 250 Heavy Metal Songs of the '80s, Judas Priest: Turbo 'til Now, Born Again! Black Sabbath in the Eighties and Nineties

2018: Riff Raff: The Top 250 Heavy Metal Songs of the '70s, Lettin' Go: UFO in the '80s and '90s, Queen: Album by Album, Unchained: A Van Halen User Manual, Iron Maiden: Album by Album, Sabotage! Black Sabbath in the Seventies, Welcome to My Nightmare: 50 Years of Alice Cooper, Judas Priest: Decade of Domination, Popoff Archive – 6: American Power Metal, Popoff Archive – 5: European Power Metal, The Clash: All the Albums, All the Songs

2017: Led Zeppelin: All the Albums, All the Songs, AC/DC: Album by Album, Lights Out: Surviving the '70s with UFO, Tornado of Souls: Thrash's Titanic Clash, Caught in a Mosh: The Golden Era of Thrash, Rush: Album by Album, Beer Drinkers and Hell Raisers: The Rise of Motörhead, Metal Collector: Gathered Tales from Headbangers, Hit the Lights: The Birth of Thrash, Popoff Archive – 4: Classic Rock, Popoff Archive – 3: Hair Metal

2016: Popoff Archive – 2: Progressive Rock, Popoff Archive – 1: Doom Metal, Rock the Nation: Montrose, Gamma and Ronnie Redefined, Punk Tees: The Punk Revolution in 125 T-Shirts, Metal Heart: Aiming High with Accept, Ramones at 40, Time and a Word: The Yes Story

2015: Kickstart My Heart: A Mötley Crüe Day-by-Day, This Means War: The Sunset Years of the NWOBHM, Wheels of Steel: The Explosive Early Years of the NWOBHM, Swords and Tequila: Riot's Classic First Decade, Who Invented Heavy Metal?, Sail Away: Whitesnake's Fantastic Voyage

2014: Live Magnetic Air: The Unlikely Saga of the Superlative Max Webster, Steal Away the Night: An Ozzy Osbourne Day-by-Day, The Big Book of Hair Metal, Sweating Bullets: The Deth and Rebirth of Megadeth, Smokin' Valves: A Headbanger's Guide to 900 NWOBHM Records

2013: The Art of Metal (co-edit with Malcolm Dome), 2 Minutes to Midnight: An Iron Maiden Day-by-Day, Metallica: The Complete Illustrated History, Rush: The Illustrated History, Ye Olde Metal: 1979, Scorpions: Top of the Bill - updated and reissued as Wind of Change: The Scorpions Story in 2016

2012: Epic Ted Nugent, Fade To Black: Hard Rock Cover Art of the Vinyl Age, It's Getting Dangerous: Thin Lizzy 81-12, We Will Be Strong: Thin Lizzy 76-81, Fighting My Way Back: Thin Lizzy 69-76, The Deep Purple Royal Family: Chain of Events '80 – '11, The Deep Purple Royal Family: Chain of Events Through '79 - reissued as The Deep Purple Family Year by Year books

2011: Black Sabbath FAQ, The Collector's Guide to Heavy Metal: Volume 4: The '00s (co-authored with David Perri)

2010: Goldmine Standard Catalog of American Records 1948 – 1991, 7th Edition

2009: Goldmine Record Album Price Guide, 6th Edition, Goldmine 45 RPM Price Guide, 7th Edition, A Castle Full of Rascals: Deep Purple '83 – '09, Worlds Away: Voivod and the Art of Michel Langevin, Ye Olde Metal: 1978

2008: Gettin' Tighter: Deep Purple '68 – '76, All Access: The Art of the Backstage Pass, Ye Olde Metal: 1977, Ye Olde Metal: 1976

2007: Judas Priest: Heavy Metal Painkillers, Ye Olde Metal: 1973 to 1975, The Collector's Guide to Heavy Metal: Volume 3: The Nineties, Ye Olde Metal: 1968 to 1972

2006: Run for Cover: The Art of Derek Riggs, Black Sabbath: Doom Let Loose, Dio: Light Beyond the Black

2005: The Collector's Guide to Heavy Metal: Volume 2: The Eighties, Rainbow: English Castle Magic, UFO: Shoot Out the Lights, The New Wave of British Heavy Metal Singles

2004: Blue Öyster Cult: Secrets Revealed! – update and reissue 2009); updated and reissued as Agents of Fortune: The Blue Öyster Cult Story 2016, Contents Under Pressure: 30 Years of Rush at Home & Away, The Top 500 Heavy Metal Albums of All Time

2003: The Collector's Guide to Heavy Metal: Volume 1: The Seventies, The Top 500 Heavy Metal Songs of All Time

2001: Southern Rock Review

2000: Heavy Metal: 20th Century Rock and Roll, The Goldmine Price Guide to Heavy Metal Records

1997: The Collector's Guide to Heavy Metal

1993: Riff Kills Man! 25 Years of Recorded Hard Rock & Heavy Metal

See martinpopoff.com for complete details and ordering information.